41 Ways
to
Lick The IRS
With A Postage Stamp

SIMPLE LETTERS CAN SAVE BIG BUCKS!

by Daniel J. Pilla

WINNING Publications
St. Paul, Minnesota

WINNING Publications
506 Kenny Road, Suite 120
St. Paul, Minnesota 55101

First Edition, October, 1990.

Printed in the United States of America

Library of Congress Catalog Card Number: 90-71404

ISBN: 0-9617124-8-1

Notice from the Author and Publisher

This book is designed to provide the author's findings and opinions based on research, analysis and experience with the subject matter covered. This information is not provided for purposes of rendering legal, accounting or other professional advice. It is intended purely for educational purposes.

The author and publisher disclaim any responsibility for any liability or loss incurred as a consequence of the use and application, either directly or indirectly, of any information presented herein.

Because the United States currently functions under an evolutionary legal system, the reader bears the burden of assuring that the principles of law stated in this work are current and binding at the time of any intended use or application. Caution: The law in this country is subject to change arbitrarily and without notice.

To Jeanne...

"Who can find a virtuous woman?
Her price is far above rubies.

"The heart of her husband doth safely trust in her,
so that he shall have no need of spoil.

"She will do him good and not evil
all the days of her life."

—Proverbs 31:10-12

Contents

Introduction

In the beginning, God created the heavens and the earth. He then created the beasts of the field, the birds of the air and the fish of the sea. Then he created man—and that's when all the trouble began. You see, man created governments, and governments established leaders who required financing. In order to finance the leaders of these governments, the idea was spawned that people, on whose behalf the leaders were *supposed* to act, would incur the costs of government. In order to carry this plan to the people, *taxes* were created and *tax collectors* were hired to ensure that each citizen bore his respective burden.

Since that time—the dawn of recorded history, thousands of years before the birth of Christ—governments and their people have been locked in, at best, a game of cat-and-mouse, and at worst, mortal combat, over the questions of the right, authority and limitations of the former to the latter. As civilizations became more sophisticated, tax collection tactics followed suit. With the increase in the collector's savvy, came the concomitant desire of the citizen to *avoid* the collector's reach.

As we moved into the era of modern civilization, we find that the game has not changed. Only the implements of the game and players have changed. The United States, while boasting a fundamental difference in its form and manner of government from those of the rest of the world, both modern and ancient, has had its own version of "tax tag." It began in earnest in 1913, when the 16th Amendment to the United States Constitution went into effect. That amendment was most significant because prior to that time, this country was not financed by an income tax. Other taxes, including duties and imposts, were levied to support the functions of government. Thus, until 1913, the American people were largely omitted from the game of "tax tag" enjoyed by the citizens of so many other nations.

But not to worry. The level of competence of the players of this game, both on the side of the people and of the government, has grown by leaps and bounds. In fact, in recent decades, it has well surpassed that of any other nation. The bold steps achieved by the United States government in this game can be imputed to its tax collection arm, the Internal Revenue Service. The IRS has grown to become the most respected—and feared—tax collection agency on earth. Surely the power and authority, the sheer reach of the agency, even in our Constitutional Republic, makes the IRS one of the, if not *the*, most powerful police force in the world.

That is where I enter the game. I am a tax litigation consultant. I work with individuals, attorneys and accountants in the specialized areas of tax audit defense, IRS problems resolution and IRS abuse prevention and cure. Believe me when I say, there are not very many of us out there. There are precious few who have made it their day-to-day business to take on the IRS on behalf of the American citizen. Even fewer are those who, like me, have written extensively in an effort to equip the *average citizen* (not highly polished lawyers and accountants) to handle and solve routine tax audit and IRS abuse problems.

In my 14-year tenure as a consultant dealing with both simple and complex tax problems, I have publicly asked some hard questions of an agency which has come to be the most feared agency of our massive and often intrusive federal government. How, I would like to know, has this agency been able to persuade Congress to provide more money, more manpower and more equipment to the IRS, than to any other federal law enforcement agency, including the F.B.I. and the D.E.A.? Why has Congress written, and the federal courts upheld, statutes and regulations which hand the agency more power, investigative and enforcement authority, and legal latitude than any other law enforcement agency in this country? Most importantly, why is the IRS able to treat otherwise law-abiding citizens as if they were criminals, forcing the citizen to prove himself innocent?

Some of these questions are rhetorical in that I believe I know the answers. They were asked for the sole purpose of stimulating thought on the part of the public. For too long, the public has taken these troubling issues at face value, failing or refusing to look behind the headlines into the goings on developing before their eyes. In the past decade, and most particularly, the past five years, much has occurred which will profoundly affect the average American in future years. So much, in fact, that it has come to pass that we all—each and every American citizen with responsibilities under the federal tax laws—must be prepared to confront the IRS at some juncture regarding a financial dispute of either small or great import. Your level of preparedness will adjudge whether you will be required to part with your money or retain it for your family.

For many years, as long as I can remember, the IRS has kept the American people terrorized with fear. The belief that the IRS can and will "put you in jail" for the slightest infringement, or worse, will destroy you financially, has left the public suffering from a kind of "battle fatigue"; a condition which prevents them from standing up to the IRS. The public would, by and large, simply pay whatever additional dollars the agency demands, under the notion that such an act will end the problem.

The fact of the matter is that most Americans, while they can and should look forward to an audit, will never experience the ultimate wrath of the agency. Rather, the vast majority of Americans will see the IRS to be as some critics call a bungling, overworked, underpaid army of uncaring and somewhat incompetent bureaucrats. This army, replete with soldiers of this description, will make mistakes—lots of mistakes—and will be reluctant to correct those mistakes. Such an army will send bills which make no sense, reply to citizen inquiries with letters that are unresponsive, provide wholly incorrect information in answer to citizens' questions, and otherwise, bump along through one muddled mess after another, much like the fumbling Inspector Clouseau.

Despite what the IRS would have you believe, the vast majority of Americans will *never* be truly destroyed by the IRS. Yet most will experience the hopeless *frustration* that accompanies one's attempts to manage what appears to be a mindless machine.

Trust me when I say that this frustration, and the eventual cost that follows the effort, can be avoided almost *every* time. What does it take? I said it already—preparedness. And an understanding of the basic ways in which this machine works and how you can make it run—or not run—to your advantage. The solutions to most IRS problems, if confronted correctly and *early* are simple, painless and fast-acting. It is only when simple problems are not handled quickly and properly that they become major, sometimes life-threatening encounters.

This book is all about everyday IRS problems. It is about simple problems. It is about the kind of problems which, more than anything else, lead to confusion and bafflement, and cause one to ask, "Who on earth is in charge over there, anyway?" Of course, by solving such problems early on, it is assured that you will *save money*. By ignoring the problems or not addressing them correctly, not only will that *cost* you money, but you increase the likelihood that the minor inconvenience and hindrance will grow to hideous proportions, threatening, perhaps, your very life.

Therefore, be prepared!

Daniel J. Pilla
St. Paul, Minnesota

*"If I have set it down it is because
that which is clearly known hath less terror
than that which is but hinted at and guessed."*

—Sir Arthur Conan Doyle
The Hound of the Baskervilles

— CHAPTER 1 —

The Future of Tax Collection

Perhaps the most loved colloquialism spoken in our society is, "Nothing is certain but death and taxes." While I agree with the former, the truth is, the subject of taxes is a highly *uncertain*, shifting concern. We can be confident that our fearless leaders in government, both federal and state, are monotonously predictable in their efforts to gain unfettered access to our wallets, but we never know from whence they will attack next.

Year after year, Congressional session after session, we are forced to brace ourselves for the next procession of "tax simplification" proposals to come down the pike. The legislative hysteria with which our elected officials approach the matter of taxes renders it the single most unstable area of our federal law. The truth be told, taxes are as far from certain as east is from west.

Changes in the federal tax laws occur with such regularity, the result is that very few tax professionals—and almost no individuals—are able to keep pace. In the inaugural issue of *Pilla Talks Taxes*,[1] (April, 1988), I called for a "Moratorium on Tax 'Reform'." The reason: "The tax laws can never be simple or fair if they are constantly changing... Constant changes do nothing to simplify matters, they lead only to more and deeper confusion over what is and is not proper and legal.***"

The article to which I refer was written on the heels of the effective date of the most sweeping tax changes in decades. The Tax Reform Act of 1986 is *still* causing tremors in the nation, and our discussion in April of 1988 examined the confusion it created. I drew from a study conducted by *Money Magazine*, March, 1988, in which 50 tax professionals were quizzed regarding the bottom line effects of the Tax Reform Act of 1986. The study asked the 50 professionals to determine the tax liability of a hypothetical family under a given set of financial circumstances. The results of the study were that *not one* of the 50 tax professionals arrived at the same bottom line figure as any of the other 49. In fact, the range of tax liability was from $7,200 to over $11,300!

Since then, *Money* has made the CPA quiz an annual affair. The results have been posted three times now. In all three annual tests, the results were *identical*. *Not one single* professional reached the same conclusion as any other! Imagine, three years running and some of the nation's top tax eggheads cannot agree on the implications of the federal law for the average family. God help us!

My sentiment—hardly debatable—is that tax reform, while regularly touted by Congress as *intended* to simplify and reduce one's compliance burden, in fact does the *opposite*. Taxes take more of our money every year while compliance costs, in terms of time, money, effort and frustration, increase. This has led me to pose the question, "What is 'Tax Reform' anyway?"

A retrospective of "tax reform" in the decade of the 1980s is shocking. It reveals that *each and every year* since 1980, we have seen *at least one* and sometimes more than one tax measure enacted by Congress. Permit me to list *just a few* of the more significant edicts with which we have been forced to deal over the past decade:

Popular Name / Date	Enactment
Crude Oil Windfall Profit Tax Act of 1980	4-2-80
Multiemployer Pension Plan Amendments Act of 1980	9-26-80
Installment Sales Revision Act of 1980	10-19-80
Miscellaneous Revenue Act of 1980	12-28-80
Economic Recovery Tax Act of 1981	8-13-81
Omnibus Budget Reconciliation Act of 1981	8-13-81
Tax Equity ad Fiscal Responsibility Act of 1982	9-3-82
Subchapter S Revision Act of 1982	10-19-82
Miscellaneous Revenue Act of 1982	10-25-82
Social Security Amendments of 1983	4-20-83
Interest and Dividend Tax Compliance Act of 1983	8-5-83

Now I ask you, "Have you done your patriotic duty as a taxpaying American and read and kept abreast of *each and every one* of these tax acts over the past 10 years? Is it any wonder that the citizens of this country are confused about the tax laws; that tax professionals find it difficult to keep pace with the changes; and that the IRS itself scores horribly when it comes to providing *accurate* answers to citizens' questions about the tax laws? If there were any question before you read this, there should be no longer! We have been buried in a blizzard of bills that has pounded us year after year. Will there be no end?

One would have thought that after the sweeping reform we witnessed in 1986, Congress would have settled back to observe whether the changes realized the desired and intended effect. Yet, while the ink was still wet on Public Law 99-514 (the 1986 Act), Congress began drafting Public Law 100-203 (the 1987 Act) and passed the latter into law just *14 months* after the former was enacted. Even as I write, Congress has begun the process of again altering the laws which in some cases, were amended by the sweeping Act of 1986. Honestly, let us catch our breath!

Congress' infatuation with changing the rules of the tax game is not a new or recent phenomenon. On the contrary, it dates to the inception of modern income taxation in 1913. For example, in 1913, the rate of tax was only one (1) percent on the first $20,000 of income. The average citizen paid just $79.01 in federal income taxes. By 1923, a mere 10 years after the idea of a personal income tax was imposed, the rate had climbed to four (4) percent, a 300 percent rate increase.

By 1945, America was out of World War II, but the tremendous tax hikes placed into effect to fund the war remained. The too-high rate for idividuals in 1945 was 11.10 percent, but the *average* rate for all taxpayers, including corporations, was 14 percent. That represents an increase of 350 percent over the 1923 rate. More importantly, individual citizens paid, on the average, $343 in taxes in 1945, compared to $86.21 in 1923. That increase is a 398 percent hike in the individual burden. The question now is, where are we headed? What will the decade of the 1990s hold for us? Can we trust the prolixic babble of our Washington representatives to the effect that they will truly simplify the tax laws? I find it fascinating to ponder the statements made by Congressional leaders year after year on the subject of simplification. The most recent declarations and announcements regarding simplification were made by Representative Dan Rostenkowski, Chairman of the powerful House Committee on Ways and Means. This is, of course, the committee of Congress in which all bills with respect to taxes are introduced or written.

On February 7, 1990, Rostenkowski announced the "initiation of a major tax simplification study." In connection with the study, he invited the public and certain government officials to submit their simplification proposals to the Committee on Ways and Means for its analysis. Rostenkowski's opening remarks, released in May of 1990,[2] are, in my opinion, a sterling example of prolixic babble. Rostenkowski's remarks read, in part, thusly:

"These are the *first steps* in an ongoing effort to simplify the tax laws. After enactment of the Tax Reform Act of 1986, I expressed my personal interst in simplifying the existing tax system. If the policies reflected in the Internal Revenue Code can be achieved with simpler rules, I would strongly urge the Congress to pursue such simplification.

"Although efforts to simplify discrete sections of the Tax Code do not create headlines, I remain convinced that the Committee on Ways and Means and the Congress have a responsibility to pursue meaningful tax simplification, both to ease the compliance burdens facing many taxpayers, and to maintain the viability of our voluntary system of taxation.

"The current complexity of the Tax Code has evolved over decades. It is not reasonable to expect that it can be cured overnight or in a single session of Congress. Tax simplification is an ongoing process, an ongoing commitment of all those concerned about the integrity of the Federal tax system. Nevertheless, I am encouraged by the important steps taken in the first session of this Congress to simplify and make more rational the corporate alternative minimum tax, tax-exempt bond rebate rules, and civil penalty provisions. These efforts demonstrated that meaningful simplification can be accomplished in discrete sections of the Tax Code without sacrificing underlying policy objectives or violating current revenue constraints.

"It is my hope that the proposals submitted in response to my invitation might serve as a catalyst for additional tax simplification." (Emphasis added.)

I find it nothing short of astonishing that Rostenkowski would refer to his most recent act of calling for a hearing and the submission of simplification proposals as "the first steps" in an ongoing process. What he is telling us is that all of the previous efforts of Congress to simplify the Code have been, as I have stated many times, pure nonsense, if not outright fraud. Please review the earlier list of tax legislation which stormed out of Congress in the decade of the 1980s. Remember, this list is just a *fragment* of the legislation which spewed forth from the Hill. In almost every case, we—the public—were told that such measures would "simplify the Tax Code and ease the compliance burden." Yet, after amendment upon amendment was shoved down our collective throats, we find Rostkenkowski, one of the leading political figures responsible for this smorgasbord of law, declaring that is *just now* beginning! Pardon me while I cringe!

More troubling to me is the Congressman's statement that, "After enactment of the Tax Reform Act of 1986, I expressed my personal interest in simplifying the existing tax system." Wait just a moment! Rostenkowski and his congressional brethren, as well as the Reagan administration, demanded the sweeping changes enacted in 1986 in order to *simplify* the Tax Code. Why was the tax system not simplified by the changes to over 2,000 provisions of the Tax Code in 1986? Why, for three filing seasons now, have we, the IRS and the tax professionals struggled to understand and operate under the newly "simplified" system if simplification was to begin *after* the 1986 Act was ratified? Call me crazy, but I feel as though we have been conned! What I honestly do not understand—to this day—is why the reasonably intelligent body of citizens known as the United States taxpayers continue to buy this line *year after year*.

The introduction of the new evidence just examined, causes me to remain resolute in my observation that there is no such animal as "tax simplification." Much like the mythical unicorn, which was believed for centuries to possess magical powers against the deadly effects of poison, there seems to be magical powers in the "tax simplification" animal. The powers are two-fold. First, to any politician who spreads the potent tax simplification dust will flow the benefits of a constituency lulled into deducing that such politician will indeed make every effort to lighten the financial and reporting load. Second, and more substantially, such politician will reap the long-term benefits of creating the illusion of competence and concern, by being re-elected! This logic no doubt contributes to the incumbent re-election rate for the Congress and Senate of the United States which is in *excess* of 98 percent! Whoever said there is no such thing as magic?

Yes, indeed it appears that the only thing certain about the future of tax collection is that the rules of the game will change, again and again. But not for the purpose that is generally passed off to the public. Rather, as we have examined, the purpose is to ultimately, if not covertly, *increase* the financial burden on the taxpaying public. The increase in the financial burden almost always translates to the increased need, real or perceived, to strengthen the resources of the tax collector, in this case, the Internal Revenue Service. This, too, is borne out by the statistics. At a time when the IRS is whining that its manpower, budget and resources are at an all-time low, examination of the evidence proves the opposite to be the case.

For example, IRS' annual reports for the three fiscal years from 1986 to 1988 indicate that its manpower levels increased from 102,206 employees in 1986, to 123,198 employees at the close of 1988. That is an *increase* of 17 percent in just three years. At the same time, the IRS' budget has risen from $3.8 billion in 1986 to $5.09 billion in 1989. That is an *increase* of 24 percent in the same three-year period. Currently, however, the IRS' budget is set at $6.135 billion. That represents an increase from 1986 of *62 percent* in just five years.

So it appears that the only winners in the "tax simplification" game are, (a) the politicians who are habitually re-elected after spewing the magical dust, and (b) the Internal Revenue Service as an agency, which has its budget, manpower, resources and legal authority fortified year after year. Who are the losers? You had better know the answer to that question by now.

The real impact of tax simplification, apart from the obvious fact that taxes are always *increased,* is the reality that the law becomes more and more confusing, as if to stir the pot. This is true *whether or not* any legitimate, measurable steps have been taken to comply with the law. This is so for the simple reason that we expend a great deal in educating ourselves regarding the *current* status of the law. When the status quo is altered, however simple or complex it may have been, we are thrown into a tizzy by the need to be re-educated. When this event transpires year after year, there can be no such thing as simplification.

A confusing law is one which cannot be complied with. Consequently, it is a law which can be abused, twisted and misrepresented by those who are in a position of authority with respect to the law. The first line of authority here is, of course, the Internal Revenue Service. And I believe the IRS prefers this condition. It prefers this condition because when the citizen is confused, the IRS is able to extract more money in less time with less effort than if the citizen understands the law.

So, too, does the IRS prefer a condition where the citizen is terrified of the agency. This is so because a citizen who is terrified of the agency will not resist when it attempts to extract more money in less time with less effort. A citizen who is terrified of the agency, and who is ignorant of his rights with regard to tax procedure, will merely write a check as opposed to attempting any realistic effort to battle the injustice.

To the extent that the condition of terror exists, the IRS has either caused it, or allowed it to persist. It causes the terror by carefully and premeditatedly publicizing, or allowing to be publicized, celebrated cases of enforced tax collection efforts or major criminal prosecutions. Those most notable in the recent past are the cases of Leona Helmsley, who was criminally prosecuted on numerous counts of tax evasion in New York, and Redd Foxx, whose Las Vegas home was raided by the IRS in the spring of 1990. What we did not see in the media was that the IRS was forced to return to Foxx much of the property taken from him during that raid because the IRS violated the law in the process.

Publicity is just one way the IRS stays "in front" of the average taxpayer. In 1984, the IRS issued its *Strategic Plan*[3] which was exposed by me in my first book, *The Naked Truth*.[4] The IRS Plan is, among other things, a plan to audit every taxpayer for every year. This claim was made in *The Naked Truth*, and events which we shall examine later, buttress this claim.

The Plan was broad in its approach to the future of tax collection from the viewpoint of the IRS. A major goal of the plan, as pointed out in *The Naked Truth*, was for the IRS to implement programs which would "enhance the public's awareness of the seriousness of tax cheating and the importance of compliance with the tax system."

Have you wondered why the IRS has turned to television commercials in recent filing seasons in an effort to communicate the notion that tax problems are caused by *citizens* who file their returns at the last moment? And, have you wondered why the affairs of the Leona Helmsleys and the Red Foxxs of the world receive such broad media coverage? The answer lies within the pages of the Plan which states:

"There is a definite need to recognize the Public Affairs function as a proactive link to the public, both within the Service and the outside. Given that the IRS touches more lives than any other agency in the Federal Government, i.e, the 94 (now 107) million taxpayers in this country, it is important that Public Affairs do more to assist in improving voluntary compliance. We have not yet explored how effective it might be to channel Public Affairs resources to highlight actions not currently publicized and activities which are underway or planned in compliance programs.

"The media has a direct and dramatic impact on public attitudes and behavior. Using an outside firm to recommend an IRS communications effort to impact positively on compliance has not been previously attenpted. It could prove to be a beneficial, relatively low-cost effort." IRS Plan, pages 55-56.

Since the issuance of the Plan and the call to use increased media coverage of "compliance programs," we have seen the media deluged with not only the studio-produced commercials regarding early filing, but a wider, broader range of spectacular coverage—show trials—of IRS enforcement action. Without question, this is a direct result of the IRS' perception that the media is a strong and powerful tool in keeping the American public convinced that the IRS cannot be beaten, and therefore, should not be challenged. I pointed out this eventuality in *The Naked Truth* in 1986.

Another important aspect of the *Strategic Plan* has come to pass since the publication of *The Naked Truth*. In that book, I decried the significance of a major, overall IRS proposal designed to "create and maintain a sense of presence" in the lives of all Americans. In 1986, I found it particularly troubling that the IRS, a tax collection agency, would find it critical to so impose itself upon citizens that the result is, wherever we go, in whatever we do, we are constantly thinking and wondering about the IRS. Stated another way, the IRS has taken the concept of "Big Brotherism" to its ultimate conclusion. If successful, it will achieve what no other government police force has ever been able to do. That being the ability to truly control the thoughts and actions of its citizens. In this case, through the threat of selective enforcement of the tax laws.

How was this awesome goal achieved? Simple. While other police forces around the world and throughout history concentrated on the threat of physical punishment and denial, the IRS would use something perhaps even more serious, the threat of an *audit* and the threat that the agency's incredible computers would somehow "track you down" and take your money. In 1986, after I examined the *Strategic Plan*, I wrote that as part of the effort to achieve the goal of "creating and maintaining a sense of presence," the IRS would use computer-generated contacts—notices and bills sent through the mail—as a weapon. In fact, page 61 of the *Plan* describes as one "Initiative" in this area, to "Expand our computer-generated contact programs to increase presence."

The *Plan* sought, as I explained, to increase computer-generated contacts with citizens, for the purpose of collecting more money with less effort. While one might, under normal circumstances, appreciate the bureaucratic effort to become more efficient, it was clear that increased efficiency was purchased at the price of accuracy in the agency's billing practices. At page 62 of the *Plan*, we find:

> "Adequate data on the marginal yield of the Information Returns Program (IRP) and other contact programs is limited until imple-mentation of the IRP Management Information System. Therefore, it is *difficult to reach conclusions* about how productive computer contact programs are, compared to traditional enforcement programs. However, since the Service cannot realistically expect to receive large increases in operations staffing to enhance traditional enforcement programs, expanding our relatively low-cost computer-generated contact capabilities is the logical approach." (Emphasis added.)

I believe this paragraph of the *Plan* is the key to the charges I levied against the IRS regarding the accuracy of its computer-generated contacts initiated after the issuance of the *Plan*. First, it is plain from the language of the document that IRS advisory and planning personnel were *unsure* of the effectiveness of computer-generated contact programs which were in operation at the time the *Plan* was written. At that time, the IRS was in the infancy stages of a program known as the Information Returns Program. This pro-gram is referred to in the language quoted above. That program was specifically designed to, via computer, match the information returns—such as 1099's and W-2's—submitted by the citizens, with 1040 Forms filed for the same person. The effort was designed to uncover tax return "non-filers" and those who underreported income.

The program functions thusly: A person earns W-2 wages in 1985 in the amount of $20,000. The employer files a Form W-2 with the IRS, which bears the social security number of the employee. But the employee fails to file a Form 1040 for 1985. The IRS' computer, responding to a specially designed program, will "locate" all Forms W-2, by social security number. The computer will then attempt to "match" the social security numbers shown on the W-2 with the *same* social security number on a Form 1040.. If the computer is unable to locate a Form 1040, it has discovered a "non-filer." If it does locate the Form 1040, it will then determine whether the income shown on the W-2 is reported on the 1040. If not, the computer has unearthed an "underreporter." The appropriate notices and demands are mailed to the citizen by the computer.

In 1984, when the *Plan* was released, the IRS was *unsure* of just how effective IRP had been. Yet, despite the fact that the system was unproven, the IRS chose to expand it solely to "increase presence" merely because it saw this system as a "low-cost" way of expanding its "contact capabilities."

When *The Naked Truth* was written in 1986, I knew then that a great number of the computer notices received by citizens around the country were bogus. As a matter of fact, *The Naked Truth* refers to many computer-generated notices as "arbitrary notices," in that they made statements and demands, especially for the payment of taxes, which had no basis in fact. Yet, my experience also revealed that people by the thousands were paying these bills. It was not until much later that I learned the true extent to which the IRS, through its "low-cost," questionably effective computer-generated contact program, bilked the public for billions of dollars.

The Naked Truth was released in October of 1986. Immediately upon its release, I began a radio tour which took me, via the airwaves, border to border and coast to coast. I challenged the IRS and exposed its *Plan* on virtually every major radio talk show in the United States. My chief accusation was that the *Plan* called for the systematic audit of every American taxpayer, and that one principle way this would be accomplished was through the use of computer-generated notices demanding payment of, in many cases, an arbitrary amount of taxes and penalties based upon non-existent errors. This, the "arbitrary notice," was at the very heart of the *Plan*, and the major means the IRS would use to "increase presence" through computer-generated contacts.

By April of 1987, just six months after *The Naked Truth* was released by WINNING Publications, and after the nationwide blitz of radio talk shows on the subject of bogus IRS computerized notices and demands, the United States General Accounting Office began a study of the IRS correspondence process. The study was done to "determine whether the Adjustments/Correspondence Branches (of the Service Centers) are corresponding with taxpayers accurately and clearly and are complying with established administrative procedures."[5]

The GAO's findings were released in July of 1988. Based upon its study, the GAO concluded:

"***Our review of correspondence and related cases at three service centers indicated that the IRS' letters, the adjustment discussed in the letters, and/or the action taken by IRS in response to the taxpayer's inquiry was often incorrect, unresponsive, incomplete, or unclear. Such responses sometimes resulted in the assessment of incorrect tax and penalties. Equally serious, however, are the potential confusion and frustration on the part of taxpayers and the extra time and expense IRS and taxpayers incur in processing additional correspondence needed to resolve the issue." GAO Report, page 14.

More specifically, the GAO found that *48 percent* of all IRS' actions or letters regarding account activities were "incorrect, unresponsive, unclear or incomplete." In Exhibit 1-1, I have reproduced the table which appears on page 14 of the GAO report. The table indicates the specific problems identified with IRS correspondence, and the percentage of letters which fall into a particular category. It is shocking to see that in *68 percent* of the cases studied, the IRS *failed* to comply with procedures designed to foster good taxpayer relations. And why not? Why would the IRS be concerned *at all* with fostering good taxpayer relations, when the sole purpose of the increased computer-generated contacts was to "create and maintain a sense of presence"?

It seems clear that the IRS was never interested in good taxpayer relations, nor was it interested in accuracy in its billing practices. Rather, the language of the *Plan* indicates that the IRS was merely out to collect more money, at the *expense* of fairness and accuracy.

And collect the money it did! According to the IRS' *Highlights* for 1989, the IRS' 1989 letter-writing crusade netted it $2.55 billion in increased taxes, interest and penalties. Yet if we believe the findings

EXHIBIT 1-1

Type of problem	Percent[a]
A/C Branch's action or letter was incorrect, unresponsive, unclear, or incomplete	48[b]
Critical problems involving incorrect adjustments and incorrect or unresponsive letters	31[c]
Noncritical problems involving unclear or incomplete letters and incomplete A/C Branch action	16[c]
A/C Branch did not comply with procedures designed to foster good taxpayer relations	68
Correspondence contained typing, spelling, or grammatical errors	22

[a]These percentages add to more than 100 because some cases were included in more than one category.

[b]This number differs from the total of the critical and noncritical problems due to rounding.

[c]If a case involved both critical and noncritical problems, it was counted only as a critical-problem case to avoid double counting.

Table 2.1: GAO-Identified Problems With
Adjustments/Correspondence Branch
Cases

of the General Accounting Office that *one-half* of all notices mailed by the IRS were wrong, about $1.29 billion in taxes, interest and penalties were collected in 1989 alone which *never* should have been collected. In 1988, the IRS collected $2.83 billion from its mail order efforts, half of which is $1.41 billion.

The 1988 GAO study, at page 23, showed that incorrect adjustments were made in favor of the IRS to the tune of, on the average, $581 per notice. Remembering that the *Plan* projected that the program of increased computer-generated contacts was to take effect 12 months after the *Plan* was issued, we can surmise that the IRS has been collecting, on the average, about $1.35 billion in unjustified tax, interest and penalty assessments for over five years! That amounts to $6.75 billion stolen from the American public.

The real horror in this billing nightmare is not so much the amount of erroneous tax, interest and penalties demanded by the IRS. Rather, the trouble develops when one sets out to correct an obvious problem. The GAO study reported a poll of 406 members of the Tax Division of the American Institute of Certified Public Accountants. The poll was conducted by *USA Today*. The results showed that:

"...(1) 75 percent of the respondents felt that IRS was least efficient in handling inquiries, (2) 83 percent of the respondents noticed unusual delays by IRS in answering clients' correspondence, and (3) 75 percent said they had unusual difficulties getting IRS to correct problems." GAO Report, page 9.

Bear in mind, the respondents to the *USA Today* poll were *trained tax professionals*, supposedly with the inside skinny on how to handle the typical IRS problem. Yet as shown, an overwhelming majority of the seasoned pros experienced frustration and delays in attempting to resolve clients' problems created by erroneous IRS billing notices. Unless you have been on the receiving end of IRS correspondence and have yourself attempted to correct an error, you can only imagine the frustration and puzzlement the *average* Joe feels over the seemingly deliberate attempt by the IRS to obstruct his efforts to resolve the trouble.

The GAO Report acknowledged this factor as significant, and attributed the failure of IRS to provide responsive answers and decisive action to the increased workload of IRS Service Centers. After all, if the IRS is not adequately responding to initial citizen inquiries and requests concerning account action, it can expect to receive second, third and even fourth letters of inquiry because "taxpayers are understandably persistent about having adjustments made to their accounts." The GAO observed:

"In addition to the unnecessary cost associated with processing repeat correspondence and incorrect adjustments, inappropriate letters can frustrate taxpayers, as indicated by the tone of some taxpayer correspondence we reviewed. For example, one taxpayer wrote:

'I have either written, or telephoned on this issue in the past to try and resolve the problem, but all I seem to get is the run around'."

GAO Report, page 23.

As a follow up to the 1988 study, the GAO released a second report in March of 1990. Its conclusion was not encouraging. The GAO found that a program or system to more efficiently manage the problem, "has not yet been designed.". Obviously, the IRS has not made this a matter of top priority and I can only imagine why. After all, why fix a "problem" producing an additional $1.35 billion in revenue each year?

The difficulty of resolving the problems created by the erroneous billing notices is compounded by the prevailing attitude suggesting that nothing can be done to correct the situation. Those who write the IRS with demands are frustrated by correspondence which is unresponsive, misleading, or, in some cases, totally nonexistent. Others who phone have the pleasure of speaking with IRS employees who either do not know or do not care to provide specific answers to questions, or suggestions of how one can receive specific answers to questions. Callers are usually told, "You owe the tax, you must pay,"—period.

To the incompetency or deliberate duplicity of the IRS, add the reports generated by the media on the subject. For years we have been told over and over that the IRS does not know what it is doing. We have come to accept this as a fact. We tend to fall back upon it when confronted with erroneous notices and mindless IRS responses. Others in the media tell us point blank that there is nothing which can be done. In his recent book, *A Law Unto Itself, Power, Politics and the IRS,*[6] investigative reporter David Burnham discusses the IRS' notices and demands for payment. Referring to the notices which I have called "arbitrary notices," those which are generated as a result of computer exams of the mathematical accuracy of one's return, Burnham declared that:

> "***From the point of view of the agency, one of the interesting points about the accuracy tests and clerical tests is that the taxpayer does not have any right to appeal any correction." *A Law Unto Itself,* page 51.

Given the amount of research Burnham obviously did on his extensive volume concerning the history, power and political disposition of the IRS, I find it to be a glaring oversight at best, and negligence at worst, to make such a statement as that indicating that one has no right to challenge the IRS' determination of increased liability through a computerized check of the return. This is the very kind of ignorance I have been battling for 14 years. This is the kind of misinformation I have endeavored to eradicate through the writing of now my fourth book dealing with the rights of citizens and the *limitations* on the power of the IRS. Through all of my efforts, we continue to find a popular journalist who declares, with seemingly irrefutable evidence, that the IRS is "unbeatable." And with that message of hopelessness it follows that, "There is no point in fighting."

In *The Naked Truth,* I exposed the IRS' computerized notices, which have been the subject of this discussion. Not only was I the first to publically declare that a significant percentage of the notices were bogus, a fact later confirmed by the GAO Report, but more importantly, I was the first to publically demonstrate, in simple, easy to understand language, that the arbitrary notices *could in fact be neutralized*, with the burden then placed on the IRS to demonstrate the verity of its computations! Why were Burnham and others like him not paying attention? After all, I appeared on every major radio show in the country, including the powerful WRC which broadcasts to Burnham's present hometown of Washington, D.C.

In keeping with the theme of "creating and maintaining presence," increased computer generated contact is just one way the IRS envisions accomplishing the goal of staying in your face. This is not accomplished any better than when an IRS agent is knocking on your door. To this end, the IRS has consistently requested of Congress increases in its manpower. Naturally, Congress has been more than happy to comply with these requests. For example, the IRS' Collection Division, the arm of the agency which is solely responsible to collect delinquent tax accounts through the efforts of revenue officers, has seen a 14 percent growth rate in the period from 1987 to 1989. Still, the IRS is hollering for more.

The president's budget proposals for fiscal year 1991 call for an increase in the IRS' revenue officer staff of 1,356 positions. In as

EXHIBIT 1-2

Uncollected Dollars vs. Collection Staff

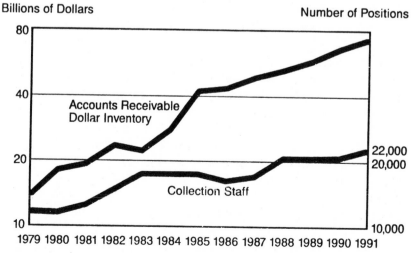

much as this has been approved, the number of revenue officers employed by the IRS will jump to 9,594. That is a 16 percent increase in collection staff personnel in just one year. It cannot be expected to end there. Recent hearings conducted before a House subcommittee on oversight, Committee on Ways and Means, questioned the rise in the IRS' accounts receivable (taxes owed but not paid in full) during the 1980s and inquired as to ways in which the increased could be stemmed. In testimony before the committee, Robert M. Tobias, president of the National Treasury Employees Union, presented his own plan to the committee for solving the IRS' accounts receivable inventory problem. Can you imagine what solution the chief union official for the Internal Revenue Service proposed as the only answer to the apparent problem? He can tell you in his own words:

"The solution we suggest is that the IRS needs more resources. The resources are needed over an extended period of time.*** With an increase of *5,000 positions* over the next five years from fiscal year 1991 to 1993, we could collect $6.1 billion." (Emphasis added); Testimony of Tobias before Submittee on Oversight, Committee on Ways and Means, February 20, 1990, page 214.

Perhaps I am entirely too cynical, but it seems that the only possible solution which could be expected from the president of the IRS' union is to call for an increase in its personnel. What Tobias is saying throughout his testimony, is that with an increase in personnel, the problem of uncollected taxes can be brought under control. But Tobias' own facts seem to contradict his conclusion. In his testimony, he points to the fact that accounts receivable have grown steadily from 1979 to the present. He also points out, however, that the IRS' collection staff has grown steadily during the same period. In fact, as shown by Tobias' chart presented to the committee, the IRS' collection staff has grown by 200 percent during the same period. See Exhibit 1-2.

If Tobias is correct and the solution to the problem indeed lies with increasing the IRS' staff, why haven't the regular and substantial staff increases realized over the past 10 years been of any effect? Certainly, if Tobias' logic is sound, an increase in the IRS' staff *should* result in a decrease in the IRS' accounts receivable. But clearly, from Tobias' own evidence, such has not occurred. Why not?

There are two answers. The first is provided by IRS Commissioner Fred T. Goldberg in his testimony to the same committee. Goldberg cautions the committee to "beware of first impressions." He goes on to point out that the problem is not as great as it may appear to be. His statement reads, in part:

"***Much of the increase in our inventory during the 1980s was caused by economic growth, law and accounting changes, and increased IRS enforcement activities. Our accounts receivable generally reflect liabilities arising over a six year period. Between 1984 and 1989 we collected over five *trillion* dollars in revenue. Our current inventory is less than two percent of that amount, and we will ultimately collect most of what is due. During the mid-1980s we projected growth in our accounts receivable inventory through the end of the decade. Due in part to various management initiatives, our inventory is $10 to $15 billion *less* than we had projected." (Emphasis in original); Testimony of Goldberg, February 20, 1990, page 19.

Thus, from Goldberg's lips, we see that the IRS' accounts receivable problem is not nearly as out-of-control as Tobias and others seem to think.

Secondly, and more significantly, a recent General Accounting Office study has shown that IRS' estimates of enforcement revenues obtained by adding staff personnel are consistently *off the mark*. The GAO found:

"Policymakers have generally thought the annual revenue impact of IRS' enforcement programs was about $50 billion. IRS cited a number of that magnitude in testifying before Congress, and the Office of Management and Budget used those numbers in its budget analysis. In fact, however, IRS does not know how much revenue its enforcement programs actually generate.***" GAO/GGD-90-85, page 4.

The GAO has documented that for years, the IRS has been misleading Congress on its ability to collect revenue based upon the resources handed it. Still, the IRS continues, year-after-year, to impose upon Congress for staff and other increases, and Congress seems willing to accommodate the agency. At the present time, however, the GAO has made it clear that Congress and the Administration need "reliable information" on the IRS' ability to deliver based upon its promises. As noted by the GAO:

"***This information has become even more critical in recent years as decisionmakers have deliberated the prospects of increasing tax revenues by expanding the size of the IRS' enforcement staff." GAO Report, page 21.

Between Goldberg and the GAO, we have the real story on the IRS' accounts receivable program and reasons why increases in staff do not seem to help.

1. The accounts receivable are not nearly as bad as many argue. Indeed, much of the problem, as identified by Goldberg, is due to tax law and accounting method *changes*, and not tax cheaters who need to be actively pursued by revenue officers.

2. The IRS has simply not been accurate in its testimony to Congress regarding the potential impact that increased collection staff will have. As the GAO noted in its lengthy report, the numbers anticipated by the IRS and those actually achieved reflect "unexplained variances" of up to 50 percent.

3. In light of the results of the GAO's study on the correctness of millions of IRS bills and notices sent to taxpayers each year, we must ask, "How much of the IRS' accounts receivable problem is created by the issuance of incorrect billing notices?" As we examined earlier, the GAO found that 50 percent of IRS' demands for payment are without foundation. Certainly the IRS should be expected to dedicate at least a portion of its newly acquired funds and manpower to alleviate this problem. Rather than attempting to *collect* the taxes created by the inappropriate assessments, it should *abate* those assessments. Without a doubt, a substantial portion of the accounts receivable would be reduced through such action. Based on this fact it appears as though the IRS is *not* concerned with efficiency in tax collection.

Given these facts, Tobias' solution to the problem is, in itself, a problem! Still, the requests for increased personnel and equipment continue, and the Administration and Congress seem content to play along. Of the $6.135 billion handed the agency for fiscal year 1991, $3.310 billion is earmarked for "Tax Law Enforcment."

The last point to make regarding the future of income tax collection is also the most ominous. The IRS' 1984 Plan called for the eventual elimination of the paper income tax return. A system of electronic filing would be ushered in with the new decade, and the new century. The advances in the IRS' information systems and the legislative elimination of deductions would make it possible for the IRS to know all there is to know about your finances to the end that it could compute your tax liability for you, without your ever having to file a return.

When these remarks were first made in 1986 in *The Naked Truth*, many scoffed at the idea of the IRS preparing your return for you, and others marveled at the prospect of never having to file another tax return. Let us address each expression in turn.

With regard to the paperless return system, since the issuance of the Plan, the IRS steadily increased its computer capabilities. Despite the major strides the IRS made in the mid-1980s in revamping its computer systems, including the creation of 21 Automated Collection Sites and the installation of optical scanning equipment capable of reading the handwriting on numerous tax forms, it continues to update and expand its electronic capabilities. This year alone, Congress handed the IRS $242.88 million for "tax systems modernization."

Add to this the fact that each and every year, Congress eliminates more and more deductions, while at the same time, increases the information reporting burden on all citizens. Since 1984, legislation has been passed requiring the reporting of virtually every transaction between citizens and businesses. Moreover, the IRS has mandated that these hundreds of millions of transactions be reported in machine-readable format. That is to say, in many cases, you must submit to the IRS the information required in a format which is compatible with its computers. Because of the huge volume of information returns presented to the IRS, *it* cannot be expected to do the work necessary to incorporate that data into its computers. No sir! You must bear the cost and do the work or risk being penalized for your failure.

The purpose of full-spectrum information and transaction reporting is simple. With this kind of information, the IRS can use its computers to track your financial life and compare its findings to that which you reported on your tax return. As deductions are eliminated from the law slowly but steadily, the IRS becomes more and more capable of preparing your return for you, without the need of doing so yourself.

If you think this is that far off, consider that in 1988, the IRS introduced to the public on a "trial basis," the idea of electronic filing. While you still had to prepare the return yourself, selected sites around the United States could file the return with the IRS electronically. That is to say, it was transmitted via computer directly to the agency. The "sales" pitch was that it would speed your refund by weeks, with the assurance that there would be no greater likelihood that your return would be audited.

By 1989, the electronic filing program was offered nationwide to any citizen who wished it. Nationally, the IRS reported that 4.2

million returns were filed electronically, compared to just 1.2 million in 1988. As stated by the IRS in its monthly newsletter to the tax profession, "The results show great promise for the future success and expansion of the program. Our focus is now on the future." (*Tax Topics*, June, 1990, published by IRS.)

With that we now turn our attention to the proponents of the electronic filing system, and the paperless tax return. To those who argue that we should permit the IRS to gather all needed information electronically, and we should permit the agency to compute our liability based upon that data, I would ask a simple question: if the IRS is wrong over one-third of the time in answers it provides to the public, how can we possibly expect that it will compute our taxes properly through the paperless return system? Moreover, if we have IRS abuse now, how much more so will the abuse be present under a system in which you have *no say* in the manner in which your return is prepared? At least now, you have the right to do it yourself, or employ a professional, and you have the ability to, at least in some degree, plan your affairs in such a manner as to have a beneficial impact on your tax burden. Under any paperless return system, surely you can kiss those benefits goodbye!

But there is another aspect to this which must be examined. Many people lose sight of the fact that we *presently* function under a paperless return program at the *federal level*. Each and every year, about 35 percent of all federal revenue is collected through a paperless return system. Each and every year, a significant amount of your wages is taxed under this system. However, you do not file a tax return with respect to this tax; you do not claim any deductions with respect to this tax; you never claim a refund; the IRS never sends you notices and demands for payment of this tax; and perhaps you do not even recognize that this tax *increases each and every year*. Worse, at half the rate of tax, you pay as much or more of this tax each year than you do income taxes. Have you guessed the tax to which I am referring? It is the social security tax.

The social security tax is taken from your wages each and every pay period. You do not file a return at the end of the year, you have no control over the amount taken, you are not entitled to any deductions, you did not receive a refund, but the tax rate is increased year after year. The social security system is a study in a paperless return system. The social security tax represents the ultimate abdication of control by you over your tax affairs. In every respect, the IRS and Congress alone dictate your future, and you have no recourse.

Is this what the future holds for the income tax system? I believe that this is exactly what the IRS has in mind, and may well be on the mind of Congress. Only time will tell as to the latter, but as to the former, we have fully identified the agency's goal.

In the meantime, the IRS bumbles along, committing errors and statute violations of both large and small proportion. At the same time, it has made it abundantly clear that it is headed your way, through one of its enforcement programs or another. What follows will equip you to deal with most any eventuality.

Notes To Chapter 1

1. WINNING Publications, monthly, $97/year.

2. See Committee on Ways and Means, U.S. House of Representatives, *Written Proposals on Tax Simplification,* May 25, 1990, WMCP; 101-27.

3. IRS Document No. 6941, issued May 9, 1984.

4. WINNING Publications, 1986, $9.95.

5. GAO Report, GGD-88-101. *Tax Administration, IRS' Service Centers Need to Improve Handling of Taxpayer Correspondence,* July 1988, page 11.

6. Random House, 1990.

— CHAPTER 2 —

How To Fight Back
With A Postage Stamp

The IRS is certainly the most powerful police force in the United States, if not the world. And it's growing. Recently, the House of Representatives passed H.R. 5241, the *Treasury, Postal Service and General Government Appropriations Bill* for fiscal year 1991. This bill provides funding to the Internal Revenue Service in the amount of $6.135 *billion*, $3.56 billion of which is earmarked for law enforcement.

Despite the sheer size of the agency and its formidable budget, the vast majority of Americans will never see its true might wielded. I have repeatedly declared, and through Chapter One of this book, endeavored to prove, that the agency's expressed goal of auditing every citizen every year will not—indeed, *cannot*—involve a face-to-face audit of each citizen. The size and financial wherewithal of the agency notwithstanding, it cannot achieve such a goal. However, as revealed in the *Plan* and subsequent developments in the IRS' technology, it can *and does* conduct computer audits of tens of millions of tax returns every year. It is as a result of these computer audits that the lion's share of Americans will be dragged through the quagmire of frustration, and usually over just a few hundred dollars.

While it is true that the vast majority of American citizens will not face the unbridled wrath of the IRS, it is equally true that *most*, if not *all*, will undergo an audit of their return. As explained, the audits of which I speak will not be of the face-to-face variety. Rather, such an examination will involve the IRS' computers and your tax return. When the IRS publically declares, as it did in early January of 1990, that fewer than one percent of all tax returns filed for tax year 1989— approximately 110 million—would undergo an audit, it is misleading citizens at best.

As a matter of fact, *all tax returns filed* undergo a computerized examination. Now, be not deceived. The mere fact that you have not been summoned to face a tax examiner with your shoe box full of receipts and cancelled checks is no indication that you have slipped through the IRS' safety net known as the "examination process." The examination of income tax returns is done ostensibly to determine and ensure the correctness of the document. *Any* effort on the part of the IRS to ascertain the correctness of a return is, in point of fact, an audit.

The primary computerized examinations to which all returns are subjected cover three areas. The first is referred to as the Information Returns Program. This computer program searches the IRS' files for all information returns, such as forms 1099 or W-2, bearing your social security number. The computer then compares those information returns with your income tax return to ensure that all income reported on the information returns is reflected in the tax return. When a failure to report is detected, a notice and demand is mailed to the citizen.

The second area covers errors, either mathematical or mechanical, which may exist in the return. The computer analyzes the return to ensure that all mathematical computations shown in the return are accurate, and to determine whether any mechanical or procedural failures exist. Such a failure could include a situation where a Schedule C is attached to the return, but the citizen inadvertently neglected to transfer the profit shown on the Schedule C to the face of the 1040 to enable the correct income tax to be computed. When such a failure is detected, a notice and demand is mailed to the citizen.

The third area of computerized examination performed on *every return* is a statistical analysis of your tax return as it compares to other returns of persons with the same income and who are in the same profession. The program is known as the Discriminate Function System (DIF). The purpose of the DIF program is to, through the use of the sophisticated computer program, identify tax returns which bear a *potential* for change based on predetermined statistical data.

The predetermined data are the averages which have been determined in the past through Taxpayer Compliance Measurement Program (TCMP) audits. These audits are grueling line-item examinations of each and every entry on a return. From the data gathered through the TCMP audits, the averages and "scores" used to administer the DIF program are established. When your return is run through the DIF program, it is examined for consistency with other returns for persons in the same income and professional category as you. If the computer detects any difference in your return in excess of predetermined variances, your return will be selected for a face-to-face examination.

When the agency runs your tax return through any of its computer programs for the sole purpose of detecting possible unreported income, errors or omissions in the preparation process, or mechanical shortcomings with your filing, you have been *audited*.

If you think this is insignificant, consider this: In 1987 the IRS issued a total of 2,705,000 notices to citizens to the effect that their tax returns were incorrectly prepared or failed to report all income received during the year. These bills demanded payment of an additional $1.223 *billion* in increased taxes and penalties! In 1988, just one year later, the number of such notices mailed by the IRS had jumped to 3,905,000. That is an increase of 70 *percent* in just one year.[1]

Now, for those of you thinking, "But I file the short form. This cannot possibly apply to me," let me respond. In 1988, approximately 20 million citizens with "total positive income"[2] of *less than* $10,000 filed Form 1040A, Individual Income Tax Return, short form. Of these, about 91,350 were *examined* by the IRS and amazingly, *86.5 percent* were found lacking. As a result, the IRS billed the *short form* filers for increased taxes and penalties at the rate of $4,105 per short form audited! In 1989, the number of short forms audited more than doubled to 208,722! Because the amount of $4,105 per audit may seem incredible, I am including a copy of the IRS' Chart 7, from its 1988 *Higlights*. See the arrow on Chart 7.

Of these totals, examinations conducted by the Service Centers through their Corrections and Information Returns Program are a smaller segment. These examinations encompassed 38,943 returns, and accounted for $158 million in added taxes and penalties. That averages to $4,057.21 in additional taxes and penalties per return examined!

TABLE 7

Table 7. – Returns filed, examination coverage and results (1988)

Individuals, total	Returns filed CY 1987	Revenue agents	Tax auditors	Service centers	Total	Percent coverage
			Returns examined			
Individuals, total	**183,251,000**	**252,801**	**532,324**	**175,982**	**1,960,807**	**1.83**
1040A, TPI[1] under $10,000	20,198,000	10,224	42,183	38,943	91,350	0.45
Non 1040A, TPI under $10,000	10,050,000	8,269	21,272	6,091	35,632	0.35
TPI $10,000 under $25,000, simple	21,599,000	24,497	86,406	20,725	131,628	0.61
TPI $10,000 under $25,000, complex	10,044,000	32,243	69,875	23,311	125,429	1.25
TPI $25,000 under $50,000	24,951,000	80,198	186,144	36,328	302,670	1.21
TPI $50,000 and over	10,177,000	106,266	86,125	44,089	236,480	2.32
Schedule C-TGR[2] under $25,000	1,931,000	14,943	12,361	772	28,076	1.45
Schedule C-TGR $25,000 under $100,000	2,156,000	28,135	15,669	1,928	45,732	2.12
Schedule C-TGR $100,000 and over	1,216,000	39,288	8,801	2,970	51,059	4.20
Schedule F-TGR under $25,000	244,000	901	920	83	1,904	0.78
Schedule F-TGR $25,000 under $100,000	443,000	2,570	1,497	157	4,224	0.95
Schedule F-TGR $100,000 and over	242,000	5,267	1,071	285	6,623	2.74

	Recommended additional tax and penalties (in millions)				Average tax and penalty per return			No-change percent	
	Revenue agents	Tax auditors	Service centers	Total	Revenue agents	Tax auditors	Service centers	Revenue agent	Tax auditor
Individuals, total	**3,446**	**1,166**	**737**	**5,343**	**9,750**	**2,190**	**4,195**	**14**	**14**
1040A, TPI[1] under $10,000	163	54	158	375	15,934	1,277	4,052	13	14
Non 1040A, TPI under $10,000	48	22	4	74	5,778	1,025	705	19	20
TPI $10,000 under $25,000, simple	48	87	11	146	1,958	1,007	54	15	12
TPI $10,000 under $25,000, complex	65	68	15	147	2,006	977	622	16	12
TPI $25,000 under $50,000	207	272	58	537	2,585	1,459	1,609	16	13
TPI $50,000 and over	1,782	455	436	2,673	16,770	5,277	9,890	12	18
Schedule C-TGR[2] under $25,000	55	26	1	83	3,693	2,135	1,678	11	11
Schedule C-TGR $25,000 under $100,000	156	63	9	228	5,553	3,989	4,753	10	11
Schedule C-TGR $100,000 and over	844	112	41	996	21,479	12,683	13,724	12	16
Schedule F-TGR under $25,000	2	1	0	3	2,725	669	763	22	26
Schedule F-TGR $25,000 under $100,000	7	1	0	9	2,828	926	1,829	16	22
Schedule F-TGR $100,000 and over	62	6	3	72	11,810	5,649	12,173	14	21

Now tell me, which of you short form filers ever believed that the IRS would hit you for over $4,000 in taxes and penalties, particularly when the form you filed claimed a total of just $10,000 or less income? Wouldn't you agree that short form filers are indeed in a "high risk" category when it comes to the potential for receiving notices and demands for payment?

Earlier I stated that despite the IRS' size, power and reach, most citizens will not feel its full wrath. However, what we have shown through the above analysis is that clearly all citizens, including those filing short forms declaring very little gross income, run the risk of falling victim to an IRS computerized audit, a fate which the IRS has in store for every American. Moreover, these computerized audits are no small matter. The IRS' own internal documents demonstrate that the computerized audit is a highly lucrative undertaking for the agency, netting hundreds of millions in increased taxes and penalties each and every year. Perhaps more importantly than the amounts realized through this collection technique is the fact that this program, as anticipated in the *Plan*, is relatively low-cost, involving in most cases, a simple notice and demand to the citizen, which is, in most cases, promptly paid *regardless* of its accuracy.

And it is the accuracy of these notices upon which we focus here. We know from the July, 1988, General Accounting Office study mentioned in Chapter One, that the IRS' computerized notices and demands have been found to be in error 48 percent of the time. In 1988, 3.9 million such notices were mailed, and in 1989 3.76 million were issued. With an error rate of 48 percent, a good case is made that in 1988 and 1989 the IRS collected some $1.88 billion in additional taxes and penalties which was *not* due and owing.

But, then, what of a cure? Must we, in the face of the IRS' overwhelming array of computers and persons to operate them and a demonstrated unsurpassed capacity for failing to correct—or even acknowledge—problems, merely relent and pay these demands regardless of their correctness? The answer is as simple as the problem. If you receive an incorrect bill from the phone company, or the department store, or any other business in the private sector, you refuse to pay it! Instead, you inform the sender that his notice is in error, you politely but firmly demand that his records be corrected and the dunning notices be terminated.

When the IRS sends a dunning notice which you know to be in error, or which fails to explain the reasoning behind the increase in taxes and penalties such as to enable you to come to an intelligent decision regarding its correctness, your course of action to remedy the problem *should be no different.* A letter must be written informing the IRS, politely but firmly, that the action taken by the agency is in error. You must demand it be corrected immediately. "What?" you say, "Tell the *IRS* that I am not going to pay the tax? You must be crazy! Don't you know that they will seize everything I own, or worse, *put me in jail* if I don't pay?!"

Not only is this *not true,* but this prevailing attitude concerning the presumed likely result of less than full and immediate payment is the principal reason that the IRS mail order tax collection campaign has been so successful. In reality, the IRS' rights to collect the tax may be *as limited* as are the phone company's, the department store's or those of any other private sector business. But this is true *only* if you, the aggrieved citizen, act promptly and correctly when initially faced with an incorrect or potentially incorrect collection notice.

If It's So Easy, Why Do So Many Pay?

The IRS has gone to great lengths to persuade the public that running afoul of the agency's wishes will sound the financial death knell for any citizen so foolish. As plainly expressed in the *Plan,* the IRS must ensure that its "presence" is known and felt throughout society in order that its pronouncements never be questioned on anything close to a wholesale level. If such were to ever transpire, it is acknowledged that the IRS *lacks* the capacity in every respect to deal with widespread dissension.

Let me be careful to point out here that I am not now, and never have encouraged any lawless conduct on the part of the citizens of this country. As a matter of fact, in the Introduction to my last book, *The Taxpayers' Ultimate Defense Manual,*[3] I explain the need for citizens to "break the cycle of lawlessness" created by the IRS when it acts in disregard of citizens' rights. I explain that the IRS can never be brought under control if the citizens of this country answer in kind the lawless acts of the IRS. Therefore, nothing in this work, nor in any of my writings, is to be construed as encouragement to either break the law or deliberately disrupt the system.

On the other hand, we must understand that the IRS is certainly not correct in every case. Under these circumstances, we as citizens have rights, and we are entitled to exercise those rights to ensure that we are not taken advantage of by the IRS, or worse, financially destroyed by the agency.

When we are talking about the IRS' computerized notices and demands, and the computerized audits which precede them, the rights of the citizen are simple and they are important. Beyond that, if properly and timely exercised, these rights are inexpensive and highly effective. A postage stamp is often the difference between successfully fending off an improper IRS attack, and falling victim to its beguilement.

Why, then, do so many people simply pay? We have already identified one reason. The IRS has the public duped into accepting the fallacious proposition that if one's pockets are not turned out upon demand, the agency's only and assured reaction will be to loose the dogs on the recalcitrant bum. A second, and equally dispositive reason, is that the IRS is more than lax when it comes to explaining the rights of the citizen and how they may be employed in a given situation. As will be explained in detail later in this chapter, one in receipt of an incorrect IRS correction notice enjoys the *absolute right* to object to payment of the bill, and demand that the IRS abate—or cancel—the tax. When this request is made properly and timely, the IRS has no choice but to act in compliance with the citizen's wishes. The law creating this right is carved into the Internal Revenue Code[4] and affords the IRS no exceptions or excuses for failure to honor the plea.

Yet, the correction notices themselves breathe not a *single word* of the right to demand an abatement of the tax when the notice is in error. When a correction notice is mailed, the IRS generally includes a copy of Publication 586A, *The Collection Process (Income Tax Accounts)*. This publication purports to be a statement of "the rights and duties as a taxpayer owing a bill for taxes." The publication explains, on page one, that:

> "Each tax return filed with the Internal Revenue Service is checked for mathematical accuracy and to see if appropriate payment has been made. If all the tax has not been paid, we will send you a bill (including tax, interest and penalties), which is a *notice* of tax due and *demand* for payment. In most cases you are given 10 days[5] from the date of the notice of tax due before we may take enforced collection action.***" IRS Publication 586A (Rev. 7/89) (Emphasis in original.)

Clearly, the language of Publication 586A *addresses* the potential receipt of a correction notice, but it is wholly deficient in explaining a citizen's rights regarding a correction notice. The publication is silent on your rights to demand an abatement of tax claimed in a correction notice. Continuing on page one of the publication, under the heading, *Payment Procedure*, we find the following subsection:

> **"Tax Bill Contains Error.** If you believe your bill contains an error, you should immediately reply in writing to the office which sent the bill. You should send copies of any records with your reply which would help in correcting the error. *If we determine* you are correct, we will adjust your account after you pay any tax, interest and penalty still due." Ibid, page 1. (Emphasis mine.)

This language gives the clear impression that the decision to "adjust" your account is solely within the discretion of the IRS, that you have no right to obtain the adjustment on your demand. I find it woefully negligent on the part of the IRS to claim that the agency must "determine" that you are correct before it will adjust your account when the subject is mathematical corrections. As I mentioned earlier, and as we shall examine later, the IRS is under a unilateral *obligation* to wholly cancel any tax determined through mathematical correction procedures when you *demand* an abatement. This obligation exists and is operative *regardless* of the IRS' view on the matter (which, by the way, is entirely predictable).

If Publication 586A is indeed a "statement of your rights" as a taxpayer, why has it failed to address your right to demand an abatement of taxes created through a mathematical correction notice? Is this important and critical failure deliberate? This we do not know, but certainly it contributes in great measure to the reason why so many citizens merely pay these taxes rather than prosecute an effective objection.

I have unearthed discussion of the correction notice and the right of abatement elsewhere in IRS literature. For example, IRS Publication 1, *Your Rights as a Taxpayer*, was prepared in response to the passage of the Taxpayers' Bill of Rights Act by Congress in 1988.[6] I have written concerning Publication 1 in the *Taxpayers' Ultimate Defense Manual*, and have previously criticized its treatment of the correction notice, both in print and through the medium of radio.

I believe Publication 1, in spite of its hypnotic title, does not clearly and fully address your rights when faced with an inaccurate correction notice. The Publication, in fairness, at least makes an *effort* to describe your rights (unlike Publication 586A), but falls short of the mark. For example, the document explains that "you have the right to ask for a formal notice" providing an opportunity to contest mathematical correction notices, but is entirely *silent* on the citizen's requirement to request an "abatement" of the tax in writing.

Not long ago, I found myself in a radio debate with an employee of the IRS on this very subject. I was a guest on a popular major market radio talk show and an employee of the agency phoned in to speak with me. He challenged my declaration that the IRS fails to inform the public of its right to abate taxes created by correction notices. The IRS representative declared that Publication 1 does explain that one in disagreement with the correction notice may write for a formal notice and an opportunity to appeal the decision. His contention was that Publication 1 was entirely responsive to the issue.

I responded by asking, "Do you have Publication 1 in front of you?" He answered, "Yes."

I said, "Please look at page three under the heading, 'Fair Collection of Tax'."

That section reads, in relevant part:

"If we tell you that you owe tax because of a math or clerical error on your return, you have the right to ask us to send you a formal notice (a 'notice of deficiency') so that you can dispute the tax, as discussed earlier. You do not have to pay the additional tax at the same time that you ask us for the formal notice, if you ask for it within 60 days of the time we tell you of the error." IRS Publication 1, page 3.

After reading the paragraph, he stated, "There it is. It tells you to respond within 60 days (the required time period) and explains that you do not have to pay the tax if you do so."

"Wait a minute," I cautioned. "Where in the document does it explain that the citizen must request an 'abatement' of the tax before the formal notice will be issued? Nowhere does it state that, and the request for abatement is *specifically* required by law."

"You are playing word games," he accused. "You are inserting your own words to confuse the issue."

I responded boldly, saying, "They are not *my* words! I did not write the law. Congress wrote the law, and Congress, *not me*, used the term 'abatement' in the law. Congress, *not me*, declared that a citizen must specifically request an 'abatement.' Furthermore, I *did not* write Publication 1, and I am *not* responsible for omitting the term 'abatement' from that document. *Your agency* wrote Publication 1, and *your agency* is responsible for omitting the term. That makes your Publication 1 incomplete and misleading. There is no other conclusion which can be drawn!"

It is interesting, given the staggering volume of regulations written by the IRS to interpret and implement the thousands of provisions of the tax code, that *not one* regulation exists to interpret or implement the legal provision allowing for the abatement of taxes created by correction notices. Still, the language of the statute is plain, and that language provides that a "request for abatement" must be made in writing before the tax will be cancelled. I submit to you the question whether I am playing "word games" or whether the IRS has indeed published a document, or documents, purporting to be concise statements of your rights, but, which in fact, are unclear, incomplete and misleading.

Regardless of your verdict, two facts are irrefutable. First, the vast majority of the public—with many tax accountants included—have no clue that the right of abatement exists with respect to correction notices. Second, we *are not* learning of this right from the IRS.

What To Expect From The "Beast"

At the dawn of the computer age, critics prophesied of the day when the massive, all-knowing "beast-like" computer in charge of the department store or the phone company would spit out an errant bill for a million dollars. Shocked, the poor bloke in receipt of the outrageous demand would immediately pick up the phone and plead for understanding and assistance in correcting the obvious mistake. The nightmare of which we were foretold in the computer dark ages was, that because everything was controlled by the computer itself, there would be no way to correct the problem. "I am sorry, sir," would be the response, "the computer will not allow us to correct the situation. You'll just have to pay the bill."

Now we are up to our knees in the computer age. Our offices have computers. Our homes have computers. Our cars have computers. Heck, even my computer has a computer! And, now that we have mastered the computer and its many uses, I am happy to report that the paranoid prophets of doom who attempted to close the door on the computer age, were, *absolutely correct!* The computer is in control of society, and yes, the computer does indeed make mistakes; and when it does, no, you cannot fix them! Or so it seems, at least with the IRS' computer.

In the past 10 years, the IRS' computer systems have undergone massive changes in hardware and software applications. Perhaps the most significant hardware "improvement" was in the installation of Optical Scanning Equipment, or computers which actually "read" handwritten tax forms, then transfer the data to memory banks. The tax forms themselves are referred to as Optical Character Recognition (OCR) forms. This fancy bit of automation wholly eliminates the need to manually key punch the data into the system.

The IRS currently has equipment which will read certain simple tax forms, such as 1040EZ, information returns, Forms 1099 and W-2, as well as a broad range of document transmittal cover forms. With nearly *one billion* information returns filed (that is *four* sheets of paper for every man, woman and child in the United States) each and every year,[8] you can only imagine the amount of time and effort saved through the OCR forms process. In addition, in 1988, about 93 percent of all information returns filed, about 845 million documents, were submitted to the IRS by the private sector on magnetic media.[9] That is to say, we are doing the IRS' data processing work for it, providing the information in a machine-readable format which the IRS need only "plug in" to be "up and running."

Where I am heading with this is, with the massive influx of paper and machine-readable media containing the details of your private life, the IRS is able to operate its Information Returns Program much to its satisfaction. As already explained, this program enables the IRS to match information returns to tax returns in an effort to ensure the accuracy of the latter. As stated by former IRS Commissioner Lawrence B. Gibbs:

"When return information does not agree with filed information documents, taxpayers are asked to explain the discrepancy. IRS sent about 3.9 million notices (in 1988) reflecting discrepancies to taxpayers. In addition to the above matching program, the Collection function sent out about three million notices to taxpayers for failure to file a tax return based upon information returns filed." 1988 IRS *Highlights*, page 11.

The notices born of the computer as a result of this system-wide matching program are the subject of this chapter. At this juncture, we will focus on the various correction notices which the computer regurgitates from time to time.

Neutralizing The Computer

Under ordinary circumstances, the IRS has absolutely no authority to alter a tax return and increase one's tax liability without your consent. When the IRS detects an error in a tax return, it may lawfully correct the error and if additional taxes are due as a result, it may bill the citizen. It is with these bills, or correction notices, that we are so concerned because, as shown earlier, the IRS is mistaken so often in the actions it pursues.

Under authority of law,[11] the IRS may correct a return and issue a bill for additional taxes only when:

1. An error in addition, subtraction, multiplication or division has occurred;

2. An incorrect use of any table provided by the IRS with respect to any tax form has occurred;

3. An entry on a return of an item which is inconsistent with another entry of the same or related item has occurred;

4. An omission of an item which is required to be shown on the return to substantiate any entry on the return has occurred; or

5. An entry on the return for a deduction or credit in an amount which exceeds the statutory limit for such item has occurred. This can include a specific monetary amount or a percentage, ratio or fraction.

When a correction is made under this provision of law, the IRS is mandated to issue a notice which "shall set forth the error alleged and an explanation thereof."[12] This is where the IRS' failure seems to be the greatest. So often, the IRS' notices issued under the correction program fail to state the alleged error and provide no explanation. This adds to the public's confusion and greatly contributes to the large rate at which these notices are paid. In addition, the IRS has in many cases gone beyond the statute's authority, asserting corrections in cases other than those described above.

In either event, we have rights to appeal these notices. Even though the IRS is allowed by law to *assess* a tax created by correcting an erroneous return, the citizen has the *final* say in the matter. The law declares:

"...a taxpayer may file with the Secretary within 60 days after notice is sent under paragraph (1) (the correction notice) a *request for abatement* of any assessment specified on such notice, and upon receipt of such request, the Secretary *shall abate the assessment.* Any assessment of the tax with respect to which an abatement is made under this paragraph *shall be subject to the deficiency procedures prescribed by this chapter.*" Code §6213(b)(2)(A); emphasis added.

Hence, we see that when the citizen's *written* request for *abatement* is made within 60 days of the date of the notice, the IRS is compelled to abate—or cancel—the tax without delay. The agency has no alternative. Furthermore, should the IRS be persuaded that the tax assessment is correct, it may not reassess the liability without providing the citizen with a formal notice and an opportunity to be heard—the deficiency procedures. Thus, your right of appeal is fully protected despite the IRS' bold and callous demands for payment of the tax assessed. In the above provision of the tax law we find the ultimate vindication of my indictment of the IRS' "official explanations" as distributed to the public through its written publications.

The specific correction notices which one might expect from the IRS, together with an example of a successful response, follows.

1. The Mathematical Correction:

I use the phrase "Mathematical Correction" in a broad sense here. For purposes of this discussion, we can assume that the mathematical correction is any correction made to a return as a result of the IRS detecting one of the five errors previously listed. As you review that list, you will observe that in reality, an error in addition, subtraction, multiplication and division is just one of five errors which the IRS is permitted to correct. Whenever a Mathematical Correction—a notice which falls into any one of these five areas—is received, it can be abated by following some very simple procedures. An example is apropos.

Dave operated a small printing business. His business was unincorporated so he operated as a proprietorship. He attached a Schedule C, statement of Profit or Loss from the Operation of a Business, to his annual tax submission. After filing his 1986 income tax return, Dave received a curious notice from the Service Center. The notice was clearly marked, "Correction Notice—Amount Due

IRS," and showed that an additional $84.25 was due the agency. Under the heading, "Correction Explanation," the IRS provided the reason Dave's return was "corrected." Please see Exhibit 2-1, Dave's Correction Notice.

In the space provided on the notice for an explanation, we find the following statement:

"An error was made in the income section of your return when the amount of your capital gain (or loss) was transferred from Schedule D."

"Hum...This seems simple enough," thought Dave. "I'll just look at my return to see what they're talking about."

After examining his return, Dave discovered that it was not so simple. You see, Dave *did not* file a Schedule D with his tax return. As a self-employed person, he filed a Schedule C, but because he had no income from capital gains, he did not submit a Schedule D with his return. Moreover, the income shown on the Schedule C, Business Income statement, was indeed "transferred" from the Schedule to the 1040 in order that the correct tax could be computed. In just a very few minutes, Dave realized that the IRS' correction notice was in error, as half of them are. With a postage stamp, he set out to abate the $84.25 bill issued by the IRS.

Earlier, I described your right to demand an abatement of the IRS' correction notice when it is either erroneous or incomprehensible. While Dave's correction notice was understandable enough, it was off the mark. Using the right of abatement provided by statute, Dave wrote a letter demanding an abatement. It is critical to note here, as pointed out above, that the demand for abatement must be made *in writing,* and within *60 days* of the date shown on the top of the IRS' notice. Should you fail to meet this deadline, the IRS earns the right to collect the tax with all the enforced collection tools available to it.

Dave's letter demanding abatement was simple as each such letter should be. The only critical attribute of such a communication is that it plainly states that you are in disagreement with the IRS' "correction" and that you desire, (a) the tax be abated in full, and (b) the IRS mail a notice of deficiency ensuring the right of appeal if the agency believes the correction to be accurate and justified. From Dave's letter demanding abatement, I have adapted an example of a letter which will serve admirably when one is in receipt of a correction notice involving *any* of the five types of corrections permitted by statute. Please closely review Exhibit 2-2, Letter Demanding Abatement/Correction Notice.

EXHIBIT 2-1

870803

Department of the Treasury
Internal Revenue Service
ANDOVER, MA 05501

If you have any questions, refer to this information:

Date of This Notice: AUG. 3, 1987
Social Security Number:
Document Locator Number:
Form 1040   Tax Year Ended: DEC. 31, 1986

Call: 291-1422   MNPLS.-ST. PAUL
or   800-424-1040   OTHER MN

Write: Chief, Taxpayer Assistance Section
Internal Revenue Service Center

ANDOVER, MA 05501

If you write, be sure to attach the bottom part of this notice. Please include your telephone number and the best time for us to call in case we need more information.

Correction Notice —
Amount Due IRS
As a result of an error we corrected on your tax return, you owe IRS $ 84.25 . If you believe this amount is not correct, please see the back of this notice. Make your check or money order payable to the Internal Revenue Service. Please write your social security number on your payment and mail it with the bottom part of this notice. An envelope is enclosed for your convenience.

Allow for enough mailing time to be sure that we receive your payment by   AUG. 13, 1987

Thank you for your cooperation.

Correction Explanation	Tax Statement	
AN ERROR WAS MADE IN THE INCOME SECTION OF YOUR RETURN WHEN THE AMOUNT OF YOUR CAPITAL GAIN (OR LOSS) WAS TRANSFERRED FROM SCHEDULE D.	Total Tax on Return ..... $	3,701.00
	Corrected Balance of Tax on Return ...... $	3,783.00
	Tax Withheld	3,560.00-
	*Estimated Tax Payments .	.00
	Other Credits	.00
	Other Payments	141.00-
	Total Payments and Credits	3,701.00-
	UNDERPAID TAX..........	82.00
	**Penalty	.00
	**Interest	2.25
	Amount You Owe .... $	84.25
	Subtract Payments We Haven't Included	
	Pay Adjusted Amount Due .... $	

* **Estimated Tax Filers —** Please check to see if you should file an amended declaration of estimated tax because your tax was refigured.
See Codes   09   on the back for an explanation of penalty and interest charges.

If you have any questions, you may call or write us — see the information in the upper right corner of this notice. To make sure that IRS employees give courteous responses and correct information to taxpayers, a second employee sometimes listens in on telephone calls.
Keep this part for your records.   FORM 4084 (REV. 8-86)

EXHIBIT 2-2

William E. Citizen
Address
City, State, Zip

Date

Internal Revenue Service
Service Center
Address
City, State, Zip

RE: Your Notice of (date -- copy enclosed)
     Tax Year _____
     SSN: 000-00-0000

Dear Sir:

Reference is made to your letter of (date), which states that my
return for (year) has been changed by you due to an error. I have
enclosed a copy of your letter for review.

Please be advised that I disagree with your statement that I owe
additional taxes. This is notice to you under the provisions of Code
§6213(b)(2)(A) that you are to immediately abate the tax assessment
reflected in your notice (copy attached). You will please note that I
have made this demand for abatement within the 60-day period
prescribed by law. Therefore, the IRS has no alternative but to abate
the assessment.

If the Internal Revenue Service insists that this assessment is
legitimate and proper under the circumstances, I demand that the IRS
mail a notice of deficiency to me as required by §6213(b)(2)(A) in
order that I may exercise my right to petition the Tax Court.

I will look forward to your notice that the tax demanded has been
abated pursuant to law.

Thank you very much,

William E. Citizen

encl. Tax Due Notice of (date)

Failure to follow these simple procedures will, in some cases, prove financially fatal. While on the radio in Atlanta about one year ago, I spoke with a distressed lady who informed me that she had received a correction notice regarding a tax return she filed. At first she was amazed that the IRS would pay any attention to her return whatsoever because it was a *short form*. As we have learned, however, short forms are a fruitful area indeed for the IRS when it comes to computerized audits and collection practices. It was most unfortunate that she was a victim of both IRS aggression and her own ignorance.

The woman, unmarried, had three young children and was literally living from paycheck to paycheck. *Any* unanticipated expense in her life often spelled trouble, so when the IRS' notice demanding over $350 arrived on the scene, she stood to be devastated. The notice, substantially in the form of that shown in Exhibit 2-1, declared that an addition error in her return resulted in an underpayment of tax. Kindly, the IRS declared that it corrected the oversight and, consequently, desired payment.

In a panic, she brought the notice to her tax preparer who reviewed the return. After carefully retracing his preparation steps, he declared that there was no error on the return. After all, how much can go wrong with a short form? Despite the preparer's commitment to stand behind the return, he had no clue as to how to properly rein in the IRS' collection machine. Rather than demand the abatement in writing as shown above, he made phone calls to the Taxpayers' Assistance staff. We know without further exploration that this office is woefully deficient in the quality of advice it gives citizens, and can easily anticipate that the preparer received no valid direction from them.

Additionally, the preparer wrote letters to the Service Center *questioning* the increase in taxes, but in none of his letters did he demand abatement. With the passage of time, the IRS issued a second notice, this one more firm in its demand for payment. By now, the 60 days were long gone. No longer did she enjoy any right of abatement. Furthermore, because no demand was made within the allotted time period, the IRS possessed the right of enforced collection of the tax through liens and levies. Because of a long period of silence after writing a letter of inquiry regarding the bill, the preparer and his unfortunate client were under the impression that the IRS was "looking into" the matter and would respond.

Respond it did, but in a manner which jolted the young lady and

her hired tax professional out of their quixotic conditions. The IRS
levied the lady's checking account. It took all the money it originally
demanded, plus accrued interest. The blow was devastating. Several
checks she recently wrote for such amenities as groceries and utility
bills, bounced. She was forced to borrow money from friends and
family to make the checks good.

The events described by the forlorn lady were, sadly, entirely
predictable. As discussed earlier in this chapter: for whatever
reason, the vast majority of the public, including many professional
tax preparers, are ignorant of the procedure for demanding
abatements. Without a plainly written letter demanding abatement
mailed within the 60-day period, the tax is collectable and will be
pursued by the agency. Make no mistake about it!

2. The Arbitrary Notice:

I have talked long and loud relative to what I call the "arbitrary
notice." The arbitrary notice is a mutant form of the mathematical
correction notice. There is an important difference, however, and
that difference is obvious when one compares the arbitrary notice to
a correction notice. Please see Exhibit 2-3, Arbitrary Notice;
compare with Exhibit 2-1, Correction Notice.

As shown in Exhibit 2-3, the arbitrary notice raises claims
regarding a "correction to your account" but wholly fails to describe
what "correction" was made and why the tax was increased. If this
notice is intended by the IRS to constitute a mathematical
correction, it fails to "set forth the error alleged and an explanation
thereof" as required by law. Moreover, as with nearly every
correction notice issued by the agency, it fails to describe any right of
abatement or process of appeal enjoyed by the citizen.

Beyond this failure, it is important to note that if the notice is *not*
intended by the IRS to constitute a mathematical correction notice
of the character described above, it is entirely unlawful! I say this
because the statute permits the IRS to correct the account of a
citizen only when one of the five mathematical—or preparation—
type errors is made in a return. The agency has no authority to assess
and collect taxes outside the deficiency procedures when other
failures, such as the failure to report all income, or even the failure to
file a return, is at issue.

Because Exhibit 2-3 does not specify the nature of the change

EXHIBIT 2-3

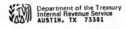 Department of the Treasury
Internal Revenue Service
AUSTIN, TX 73301

Date of this notice: JULY 4, 1988
Taxpayer Identifying Number
Form: 1040A   Tax Period: DEC. 31, 1983

For assistance you may
call us at:

291-1422 MNPLS.-ST. PAUL
800-424-1040   OTHER MN

Or you may write to us at
the address shown at the
left. If you write, be
sure to attach the bottom
part of this notice.

STATEMENT OF CHANGE TO YOUR ACCOUNT

WE CHANGED YOUR TAX RETURN TO CORRECT YOUR ACCOUNT INFORMATION.

STATEMENT OF ACCOUNT

ACCOUNT BALANCE BEFORE THIS CHANGE	NONE
INCREASE IN TAX BECAUSE OF THIS CHANGE	$7,620.00
CREDIT ADDED -- TAX WITHHELD	5,478.00CR
FILING LATE PENALTY ADDED - SEE CODE 01 ON ENCLOSED NOTICE	535.50
ESTIMATED TAX PENALTY ADDED - SEE CODE 02 ON ENCLOSED NOTICE	55.00
NEGLIGENCE PENALTY ADDED - SEE CODE 06 ON ENCLOSED NOTICE	967.75
INTEREST CHARGED - SEE ENCLOSED NOTICE - CODE 09	1,451.66
AMOUNT YOU NOW OWE	$5,151.91

YOU MAY AVOID ADDITIONAL INTEREST AND PENALTIES IF YOU PAY THE AMOUNT YOU OWE
BY JULY 14, 1988. PLEASE MAKE YOUR CHECK OR MONEY ORDER PAYABLE TO THE INTERNAL REVENUE
SERVICE. WRITE YOUR SOCIAL SECURITY NUMBER ON YOUR PAYMENT AND RETURN IT WITH THE BOTTOM
PART OF THIS NOTICE. AN ENVELOPE IS ENCLOSED FOR YOUR CONVENIENCE. THANK YOU FOR YOUR
COOPERATION.

To make sure that IRS employees give courteous responses and correct information to taxpayers, a second IRS employee sometimes listens in on
telephone calls.   Overdxy 6 Form 8488 (Rev. 11-87)
Keep this part for your records

Return this part to us with your check or inquiry

Your telephone number	Best time to call	
( ) —		
34,159	33,159	0

AMOUNT YOU OWE...................$5,151.91
LESS PAYMENTS NOT INCLUDED. $————
PAY ADJUSTED AMOUNT........ $————

515447855 KB 0000 30 0 8312 670 00000515191

INTERNAL REVENUE SERVICE
AUSTIN, TX 73301

22

d825   01,02,06,09   18254-561-64034-8

made to the account, we are unclear as to whether there was a mathematical correction or if the IRS found some other area of the return wanting. In all events, a timely and pointed response to the letter must be made to avoid the potentially disastrous ramifications. As you can see from Exhibit 2-3, the IRS has billed the poor soul for $5,151.91 in additional taxes.

Here is a prime example of the manner in which we use the letter of abatement to accomplish two goals in the face of the IRS' shortcomings. First and most important, a timely response to the notice will result in an abatement. This is critical, given the amount demanded in the example. Secondly, an abatement of tax will lead, if the IRS is so disposed, to the issuance of a notice of deficiency. The notice of deficiency is the document which must clearly and plainly itemize all changes and computations leading to the increase in taxes.

With a notice of deficiency in hand, one is easily able to determine whether the IRS' actions are proper and justified, or simply another in a series of maneuvers designed to separate you from your money. In the event of the former, my recommendation is to pay the tax. In the event of the latter, however, I would encourage you to exercise the important right incident to the notice of deficiency, that being the right to appeal the IRS' determination, seeking a review of its actions before you are required to part with a dime of your money.

The arbitrary notice shown in Exhibit 2-3 was sent to Rod from the IRS Service Center in Austin, Texas. Because of the failure to describe the reasons for the change, Rod was unable to determine whether the IRS lost his return, never received his return, disallowed deductions on his return, or simply took a wild stab at collecting over $5,000.

Because of the failure, Rod quickly demanded abatement of the tax assessment. In his demand, he pointed out that the agency failed to acquaint him with the reasons why his tax was increased, in violation of statute. Furthermore, Rod plainly demanded that a notice of deficiency be issued in order that the right of appeal be exercised. Please see Exhibit 2-4 as an example of this response.

Rod's response to this arbitrary notice was highly productive. Not only did the IRS cease billing him for the amount alleged, but never did mail a notice of deficiency. From this failure we can accurately glean that the IRS' notice *never was correct*. By forcing it to choose between abatement and a notice of deficiency, it was forced to look long and hard at the accuracy of its own claim. Having done so it

EXHIBIT 2-4

William E. Citizen
Address
City, State, Zip

Date

Internal Revenue Service
Regional Service Center
Address
City, State, Zip

RE: Your Notice of (Date -- copy enclosed)
     Tax Year _____
     SSN:

Dear Sir:

Reference is made to your letter of (date), concerning tax year
_____. A copy of the notice is enclosed for your reference. The
form states that "We changed your tax return to correct your account
information." The form goes on to show "Amount you now owe." It
demands payment of $_____.

The notice you sent does not provide any details whatsoever of the
reason why the IRS changed my account, and why it has demanded payment
of additional taxes.

Please be advised that I disagree with your statement of my account
balance. This is notice to you under the provisions of IRS Code
§6213(b) that you are to immediately abate the tax liability which is
created by your notice. Under the terms of that statute, the IRS has
no alternative, but to abate the assessment. Before any collection
action is taken, I demand that a notice of deficiency be mailed to me
in accordance with Code §6213(a) in order that I may exercise my right
of appeal. In any event, the tax must be abated.

Under the law, I have 60 days in which to protest the assessment you
have made. My protest is timely. Therefore, there is no legal reason
why the tax cannot be abated immediately.

I will look forward to your notice to the effect that the tax has been
abated.

Sincerely,

William E. Citizen

encl.

abandoned its claim entirely.

3. Notice of Unreported Income:

Within the past several years, a major evolutionary process has enabled the IRS to move closer and closer to achieving its goal of auditing every citizen for every year with the eventual *elimination* of the paper tax return and the installation of a completely electronic filing system. The process to which I refer is the steady flow of federal legislation which requires persons to report to the government all the details of their financial dealings with one another. With each passing year, we find a fresh round of Congressional mandates requiring that we file information returns with the IRS encompassing everything from interest paid by banks to the sale of real estate.

So pervasive is the flood of financial data to the IRS that the IRS currently receives and processes about *one billion* information returns each year. With this information, the IRS' massive computers cross-check tax returns to be sure that all income received by a person during the year is reported on his tax return.

When the "all-seeing" eye of the computer detects the presence of an information return which is unaccounted for by the citizen in his tax return, the computer generates a statement explaining the omission. The notice computes the additional taxes, with interest and penalties, and demands immediate payment. The notice very much resembles the Correction Notice, but is plain in its allegation that the additional tax, interest and penalties are computed on the basis of "unreported income" rather than an error, real or perceived, in the return's math computations or preparation procedures.

Recently, I worked with a man who received such a statement from the IRS regarding tax year 1987. The IRS alleged in the notice that it had evidence in the form of a 1099 that the man received dividend income of about $8,000 from a company in Vancouver, Washington. The notice pointed out that the $8,000 in dividend income was not reported on his return. It went on to compute the additional tax the man owed (including penalties and interest) based upon the unreported income. Lastly, the notice demanded payment of the total liability.

The IRS' computations of unpaid tax, based upon $8,000 in dividend income, were correct. The only problem, however, was

EXHIBIT 2-5

William E. Citizen
Address
City, State, Zip

Date

Internal Revenue Service
Regional Service Center
Address
City, State, Zip

RE: Your Notice of (Date -- copy enclosed)
      Tax Year _____
      SSN:

Dear Sir:

Reference is made to your letter of (date), concerning tax year
_____. A copy of the notice is enclosed for your reference. The
notice states that I under-reported my income by $_____. The
notice states that the IRS recomputed my tax liability based upon the
inclusion of the alleged unreported income.

YOU WILL PLEASE TAKE NOTICE, that I object to your having recomputed
my income tax liability for the year _____. Please take notice,
that I did not receive the amount of $_____ which you allege to be
dividend income from the _____ company. I did not then, and
do not now have anything whatsoever to do with the _____
company.

The tax return that I filed for the year _____ fully and
accurately reported all my income from all sources. I did not omit
any income and your claim that I under-reported dividends received
during that year is inaccurate. I did not receive any additional
income during the year _____.

This is notice to you under the provisions of IRS Code §6213(b) that
you are to immediately abate the tax liability which is created by
your notice. Under the terms of that statute, the IRS has no
alternative, but to abate the assessment. Before any collection
action is taken, I demand that a notice of deficiency be mailed to me
in accordance with Code §6213(a) in order that I may exercise my right
of appeal. In any event, the tax must be abated.

Under the law, I have 60 days in which to protest the assessment you
have made. My protest is timely. Therefore, there is no legal reason
why the tax cannot be abated immediately.

Under penalty of perjury, I declare that the facts stated in this
letter are true and correct in all respects.

Sincerely,

William E. Citizen
encl. -- Copy of IRS notice

that the man *never received* any dividend income from the company in Vancouver, and moreover, *never before heard* of the company in Vancouver. Still, the IRS demanded payment of the additional taxes.

In response to the demand, he sent a letter demanding abatement, similar in substance to Demand for Abatement shown in Exhibit 2-2. There is an important distinction, however. You will notice from Exhibit 2-5 that he specifically addressed the question of the so-called unreported income. The *specific statement* is made that no income was ever received from the company in question, and that as a matter of fact, all income received from all sources was accurately reported in the return. Lastly, he declared under penalty of perjury, that the facts contained in the letter were true and correct. In conclusion, he demanded, under the authority of Code §6213(b), an abatement of the liability.

A Standard Cover Form

The various IRS Service Centers throughout the United States receive and process millions of pieces of mail each and every month. Even under the best of circumstances, mailing a letter to the Internal Revenue Service can be much like placing a note in a bottle, and then dropping it into the Atlantic. In recent years, I have had experience with citizen notices and demands which have not received their rightful attention. That is not to say one's request is necessarily denied; rather, I am more concerned about those which are not *acted* upon by the agency.

Even assuming the IRS is not deliberately ignoring requests for abatement, and assuming each and every Service Center employee is able to *read,* requests for abatement such as these, as well as other communications to the agency, are often either misplaced, misclassified, or otherwise overlooked. To remedy this situation, it is my suggestion that one employ the use of a cover form to communicate plainly and quickly the fact that a *Claim* is being made which requires attention and processing by the agency. The cover form suggested is IRS Form 843, *Claim.* Please see Exhibit 2-6.

The Form 843 is typically used to make claims for refund from the IRS, but certain tax regulations also recommend the use of the form in making requests for abatement.[13] By completing the Form 843

EXHIBIT 2-6

DEMAND FOR ABATEMENT UNDER CODE SEC. 6213(b)

Form **843** (Rev. December 1987) Department of the Treasury Internal Revenue Service	**Claim** ▶ See Instructions on back.	OMB No. 1545-0024 Expires 9/30/90

If your claim is for an overpayment of income taxes, do NOT use this form. (See Instructions.)

(Use this form ONLY if your claim involves one of the taxes shown on line 8 or a refund or abatement of interest or penalties.)

Name of taxpayer or purchaser of stamps	Telephone number (optional) ( )
Number and street	
City, town, or post office, state, and ZIP code	

Please type or print

Fill in applicable items—Use attachments if necessary

1 Your social security number	2 Spouse's social security number	3 Employer identification number

4 Name and address shown on return if different from above

5 Period—prepare separate form for each tax period From , 19 , to , 19	6 Amount to be refunded or abated $

7 Dates of payment

8 Type of tax or penalty
☐ Employment   ☐ Estate   ☐ Excise   ☐ Gift   ☐ Stamp   ☐ Penalty IRC section ▶

9 Kind of return filed
☐ 706   ☐ 709   ☐ 720 IRS No. (s) ▶ _____   ☐ 940   ☐ 941   ☐ 990-PF   ☐ 2290   ☐ 4720
☐ Other (specify) ▶

10 If this claim involves refund of excise taxes on gasoline or special fuels, please indicate your tax year for income tax purposes.

11 Explain why you believe this claim should be allowed and show computation of tax refund or abatement of interest or penalty.

See attached letter explaining facts and demanding abatement.

Under penalties of perjury, I declare that I have examined this claim, including accompanying schedules and statements, and to the best of my knowledge and belief it is true, correct, and complete.	Director's Stamp (Date received)
Signature (Title, if applicable) Date	
Signature Date	

For Internal Revenue Service Use Only
☐ Refund of taxes illegally, erroneously, or excessively collected
☐ Refund of amount paid for stamps unused, or used in error or excess
☐ Abatement of tax assessed (not applicable to estate or gift taxes)

For Paperwork Reduction Act Notice, see Instructions on back.   Form **843** (Rev. 12-87) and attaching it to your written demand for abatement, the form acts as a cover letter immediately communicating to agency personnel the fact that you are making a claim against the agency. As a result, the claim, with the attached written demand, will be forwarded to the appropriate section responsible for processing the claim within the Service Center. Without the 843 as a cover form, you risk having your demand for abatement misrouted, or not processed at all.

Completing Form 843 and preparing it for submission with your demand for abatement is a simple matter. Begin by adding a line to the form in the top margin, above the word, "Claim." The line should read, "Demand for Abatement of Tax pursuant to Code §6213(b)." Next, provide the information sought in lines one through nine (line 10 is irrelevant and can be ignored). Line 11 is the space where the explanation justifying your requested action is provided. In this space, the words, "See Attached Letter" should be typed. Of course, you should be careful to attach a copy of your letter demanding abatement, written in accordance with one of the examples provided here.

Lastly, the Form 843 should be signed and dated.

How To Mail The Demand

Having prepared the Form 843 to function as a cover form, and having attached your written demand for abatement, the next step is to mail the demand. While this may seem childishly simple, believe it or not, many tragedies visited by the IRS upon the public can be directly traced to errors made by citizens in transmitting documents to the agency. Bear in mind, as stated earlier, that literally millions of pieces of mail are received by the various Service Centers each month. In most cases, there is simply nothing to evidence the fact that your *particular* letter was received by the agency. If your letter, which may have contained, for example, your income tax return, is mislaid by the IRS, how will you overcome the agency's claim that you failed to file the return?

The solution to the problem is to mail *each and every* letter to the IRS via certified mail, return receipt requested. This procedure is a function of the Post Office. For a small fee, the Post Office requires the recipient of a mail piece to *sign* for the letter. The signature verification card is then returned to the sender for possible future use. In all cases when the issue of receipt is in question, the production by the citizen of a signed Post Office return receipt card ends the dispute.

The Form 843 and letter of demand must be mailed to the Service Center which issued the notice to you in the first place. Be careful to make a photocopy of your response before sending it, and be equally careful to mail your response within the applicable time frame via certified mail, return receipt requested. Your postal receipts, including the certification card, should be attached to your copy of the demand. In this manner, a complete record of the transaction is made and kept *at your end.*

Little Problems—Little Solutions

The underlying message of this discourse is simple: You must *be prepared* to handle a computerized notice. I have gone to great lengths in Chapter One to demonstrate that the IRS' stated goal of auditing every citizen for every year, and eliminating the paper tax return, is fast becoming a reality. With every passing day, the potential for you to be on the receiving end of such a notice as discussed here becomes greater and greater. But when you are prepared, the problems created by the IRS' demands can remain "little problems." However, when you are unprepared and are taken by surprise with a notice, the little problem will quickly become a very large, ugly, costly and, perhaps, a personally devastating problem. We take comfort in knowing that virtually every IRS problem will begin with an IRS notice. Those discussed in this chapter are easily managed when you understand your rights.

Notes To Chapter 2

1. IRS Highlights, 1988, Table 10A.

2. This is an IRS created classification of tax returns for examination purposes. The term is defined by the Internal Revenue Manual as the sum of all positive income items on the return, such as wages, dividends, interest, rents, etc., with losses and other negative or deduction items treated as zero. Internal Revenue Manual 40 (10) 0, Handbook for the Conversion of Examination Classes from Adjusted Gross Income (AGI) to Total Positive Income (TPI).

3. WINNING Publications, 1989, $39.95.

4. See Code §6213(b).

5. This too is erroneous, since the law provides 30 days in which to pay a tax due before enforced collection action may be taken. See Code §6331.

6. For a full discussion of this Act, please see my Special Report on the Taxpayers' Bill of Rights Act, WINNING Publications, 1989.

7. See Code §6213(b)(2)(A).

8. See IRS 1988 *Highlights,* page 11.

9. Ibid.

10. Ibid.

11. Code §6213(g)(2).

12. Code §6213(b)(1).

13. See Code §6404 and regulation thereunder.

— CHAPTER 3 —

How To Create
Your Own Court
Be Your Own Judge

IRS problems range widely in their degree of complexity. Often, the problem itself seems quite simple, though a solution appears to be out-of-reach. Let me explain.

I was on the phone some time ago with a woman who was notified by the IRS that a form critical to her small business corporation was not filed. The woman questioned the attorney who created the corporation. He explained that because it was a tax form, the accountant would have been required to file the form. Upon confronting the accountant, she was told that the form "may have been filed," but he could not definitely recall.

In this suspended state the woman teetered, wondering whether the IRS was correct and the form was not filed, or whether the sleepy accountant actually did his job and merely neglected to keep an accurate record. Even with a definite affirmative answer from the accountant, how was she ever to persuade the IRS that the form was indeed filed? Given that it would be—at best—"her word against theirs," surely the IRS would reject her statements and conclude that the form was not filed, thus attributing any and all applicable penalties to the transaction. A solution to this very simple problem escaped both the woman, her attorney *and* the forgetful accountant. However, I had an idea! This chapter is a full presentation of that idea.

End The Dispute—Now!

The "my-word-against-yours" dilemma has steered many a person from the halls of justice. This is particularly true when one of the potential legal combatants is the government. "When it's your word against theirs, just who do *you* think the judge will believe?" Naturally, the tendency is to cave in, accepting the agency's demand or position without a fight on the assumption that it will reject your word over its claims. Fortunately, the "my-word-against-yours" is *not* a no-win scenario when the IRS is involved. Believe it or not, when the dilemma arises in a dispute with the IRS, the odds of prevailing are *decidedly* in your favor, *if* you use the proper tools.

For years, attorneys have used a very simple document to establish factual issues which arise in the "my-word-against-yours" dilemma. That document is known as an "affidavit." An affidavit is nothing more than a statement which sets forth, in writing, claims of fact—your word—which, when verified by a notary public, become "testimony." Affidavits are of vital importance in the "my-word-against-yours" contest. They are particularly important when the dispute is with the IRS because the IRS rarely, *if ever,* has any evidence with which to dispute or refute the sworn statement.

When an affidavit is written properly, signed and notarized, then presented to the IRS as proof of the verity of "your word," it must be treated as testimony just as though offered to a judge in a court of law. More incredibly, that testimony must be *accepted* and *acted* upon by the IRS *as truth* in the absence of controverting evidence. To put this into perspective, let us hark back to the lady whose vigilant accountant could not remember whether he filed a critical corporate tax form. The IRS claimed the form was not filed, thus depriving the lady of the favorable tax treatment she would otherwise have enjoyed. Rather than *suggesting* to the agency that "perhaps" the form was filed, or, that "we must have submitted the document," an affidavit declaring affirmatively that the form was *indeed* filed would have forced the IRS to accept the pronouncement as gospel.

You may be asking, "Why on earth would the IRS just accept my word when they know a form was not filed?

First of all, you must understand that the IRS does not "know" that you failed to file a given form. IRS employees are merely able to determine that the form does not "appear," from the computer records, to have been filed. Do you understand this difference? It is important. Let me elaborate. No person within the IRS can testify truthfully (nor will one lie in this regard) that he shadowed you all year and has personal knowledge of the fact that you did not file a given form with the IRS.

IRS notices from the Service Center regarding your failures to act *are not* based upon the personal knowledge of any person or persons working for the agency. The notices are based upon computer searches of the accounts and files. A document which was *mailed* to the IRS, but never *arrived* at the Service Center, or which arrived but was *lost* by a dutiful employee, will *not* appear on the computer record. That, however, does *not* mean that you failed in your duty to file the form. It is through the use of the affidavit that you present testimony to the IRS, testimony which would be valid in a court of law, to establish that you met your duty to file. This will dissuade any punitive action on the part of the agency.

Now you must ask, "But I *do* file my tax returns, and I *do* pay my taxes. Why would I ever have to worry that the IRS might suggest I didn't?" The answer is simple. As I have already explained, the approximately 110 million tax returns filed for 1989 (not even to mention the nearly 1 billion information returns) were mailed to just *seven* regional Service Centers throughout the United States. Employees at each Service Center perform the labor-intensive task of sorting the returns and documents, then preparing them for data processing. While the IRS has made great strides in data processing, the mail must still be opened and handled before the computers take over. Within this aspect of the production, great potential for error exists.

In an article appearing in the April, 1990, issue of *Money* magazine, it was reported that in the Manhattan district office alone, the fourth largest in the country, some *two million documents,* including Forms 1040 and W-2, were *lost* by the agency just in 1988. An Atlanta radio audience was once told by a local Service Center employee that a processing error rate exists of up to 10 percent of returns filed. With 110 million returns filed in 1990, we can expect that *10 million* citizens will be contacted in connection with alleged failures for which they are not responsible.

When IRS personnel lose documents, documents which the computers are programmed to retrieve, review and analyze, the *computer's* response is to kick out notices, demands and other correspondence of an adversarial ilk. True, some of the notices will take the form of those we have discussed in Chapter Two, but as likely, lost returns and other required forms will take the form of demands to file what you have already filed. Too, the IRS demands for filing action, even penalty assessments, may be based on forms which are entirely lost. It is plausible that the IRS has either inadvertently overlooked certain filings, or, never received them due to Post Office mishandling. In any event, you must be prepared to respond to the claim that you have failed to meet your legal duties. When an affidavit is part of your arsenal, the "my-word-against-yours" is not only a valid defense, it is one which is entirely winnable.

Proving You Filed A Form—The Basics

The axiom, "an ounce of prevention is worth a pound of cure" is never more true than when dealing with the IRS. If certain steps are taken prior to the filing of a form, *any form* which the law requires, you can avoid entirely the "my-word-against-yours" dilemma. Later in this chapter, I will illustrate how some very basic and extremely simple and inexpensive safety measures saved Paul hundreds of dollars. More importantly, in demonstrating that he filed a particular document the IRS claimed was unfiled, Paul did not have to succumb to the "my-word-against-yours" dilemma. Rather, the evidence he created and saved well in advance pulled him through, together with a carefully written affidavit we shall examine presently.

Many citizens take for granted the valuable service performed by the Post Office. Without a doubt, the Post Office performs a truly incredible task. Despite the fact that the Post Office is the subject of every late-night comedian's jibes and jokes, it cannot be gainsaid that it performs a Herculean task quite admirably. Still, you are naive if you think the Post Office delivers every solitary piece of mail to its intended destination on time and without interruption or misdirection. In the event you suffer any delusions, let me help you now; *it does not happen!*

Therefore, *you* must take some steps to ensure that your interests are protected once your package is placed into the helpful hands of your local postal carrier. These, my friends, are the basics.

FIRST: Never mail a letter to the IRS, including the transmission of tax forms, notices, responses, payment devices, etc., without keeping an *exact* photocopy of the letter or filing. Do not give me the excuse that no copy machine is handy. There is a copy machine on every corner, including at the Post Office, where you will have to travel to post the letter anyway. Believe me when I say that the "my-word-against-yours" defense is much more plausible when you have a copy of the disputed filing in your hands.

SECOND: Never, and I mean, *never* (did I say "never"?) mail any letter to the IRS, *especially* your income tax return and related documents without using *certified mail, return receipt requested.* The service is provided by the Post Office for a modest fee. When certified mail is used, the recipient of the letter *must sign* a card verifying that he has in fact received the mailing. That card is returned to the sender—you—for retention in your file and use at a later date, if necessary. Now don't you dare tell me that it is too expensive or too inconvenient to mail a letter via certified mail. In the first place, if you purchased coffee or cigarettes yesterday, you *can* afford the cost of certified mail. In the second place, you would travel to the local video store in a heartbeat to snap up Hollywood's latest smash, so you darn sure better be willing to spend an equal amount of time and gasoline protecting your financial future.

If I sound harsh and abrupt on this issue, it is only because I intend it that way. It seems I receive nothing but static when I declare that certified mail is the *only* way to communicate with the IRS. "Do I have to go to all that trouble?" one talk show caller asked me. "I don't think I have time for all that," he said.

If that is the case, your options are simple. As Minnesota businessman and author Harvey Mackay states in his book, *Swim With The Sharks Without Being Eaten Alive,* "There are no such things as problems—only expenses." That principle, applied to our topic, translates this way. "If you do not wish any difficulty with the IRS, just pay every dime demanded, when demanded, whether or not owed." What could be simpler? Unfortunately, the IRS' capacity to *demand* money far exceeds the average person's capacity to *pay.* And therein lies the problem.

The THIRD basic rule of thumb is to carefully file *both* the return receipt card (the "green card") *and* the postage receipt (the "white slip") with your copy of the letter or form filed. Both postage receipts, the green card and the white slip, are critical. The green card we already know bears the signature of the recipient and date of receipt of the letter. The white slip shows the *date of mailing,* and this is important in the case of tax returns, which must be postmarked by midnight on April 15th. If you do not use certified mail, you have absolutely no record whatsoever of the postmark date. That can be trouble and will surely intensify the "my-word-against-yours" debate.

Finally, friends, it is a good idea to *actually* mail the document—on time—which you claim was mailed. It is somewhat difficult to offer a "truthful" statement which is not in fact truthful.

Using An Affidavit To Prove You Filed

Prior to examining true-life situations in which an affidavit was successfullly utilized to defeat IRS claims, let us further explore the elements of an affidavit. Certainly it would be impossible to anticipate each and every claim that the IRS will or could levy against a citizen with respect to his filing obligations. After all, it is rumored that somewhere between two to three *thousand* tax forms exist, and as I reported in *How Anyone Can Negotiate With The IRS—And WIN!*, Chapter Four, you as an individual filer, are responsible for 112 of them. Add to that the 140 miscellaneous forms, such as Form W-4, and you see that the field is substantial.

For this reason, it will be beneficial to study the elements which comprise the affidavit with an eye toward providing a skeleton around which your facts and circumstances can be built. This will enable you to adapt my guides and examples to your specific facts and circumstances, a step critical to success.

Please examine Exhibit 3-1. It shows nine separate areas of an affidavit into which you will insert your specific facts. Let us address them in turn:

1. Area 1 consists of your name, address, SSN, and date of the affidavit.

2. Area 2 is a reference to the specific demand made by the IRS. You should note its date and attach a copy of the notice to the affidavit. The copy should be clearly marked, "Copy". I use a yellow highlighter and write in large letters.

3. Area 3 is the opening line of the affidavit, declaring that you have been sworn to tell the truth and what follows is therefore "testimony."

4. Area 4 begins the body of the affidavit wherein all relevant facts and circumstances will be set forth. Initially, it is a good idea to provide background information such as the year in question, the

EXHIBIT 3-1

Affidavit Skeleton

1. Name
   Address
   City, State, Zip
   SSN:
   Date of Affidavit

2. RE: IRS Notice Dated _____ (copy attached)

3. STATE OF _____)
) ss
   COUNTY OF _____)
)

   I, (your name), being first duly sworn on oath, depose and state:

4. Background facts regarding the IRS' notice, including:
   a. Date of receipt;
   b. Specific demand made;
   c. Tax year at issue.

5. **Specific** claims and facts to the contrary, including:
   a. Date your form was mailed, manner in which mailed and address to
   to which mailed;
   b. Copies of return receipt documents attached (if available);
   c. Copy of form in question attached, from your retained file copy
   (if available).

6. **Specific** investigative steps taken to prove filing, including:
   a. Conversations with T/P Assistance personnel;
   b. IMF documents, attach copies (if available).

7. **Ultimate** conclusion drawn from all facts:
   a. You did in fact file document or pay tax;
   b. IRS' claim to the contrary to be cancelled;
   c. All penalties and interest to be cancelled.

8. _____
   Your Signature
   Your full name typed below

9. Subscribed and Sworn to before me, a Notary Public, in and for the
   County of_____ State of_____ .

   _____
   Notary Public
   My Commission Expires: _____

type of claim made by the IRS, and the date you received its notice and demand. This data is set forth in area 4 in simple paragraphs.

5. Area 5 is where you will, in short, specific paragraphs, set forth *particular* facts to contradict the IRS' claim. For example, if its claim is that your tax return was not filed in a timely manner, you will declare with *specificity* the date on which the return was posted to the mails. Copies of your retained copies should be attached, including any copies of the postal green card and white slip if your filing was sent via certified mail.

6. Area 6 is used to provide information regarding any investigative steps you may have taken into the matter. For example, it is not uncommon for persons in this situation to phone IRS Taxpayer Assistance personnel and inquire regarding the matter. Sometimes conversations with these personnel can be telling in one way or another, and when set forth in an affidavit, become probative. Also, if you have obtained a copy of your Individual Master File (IMF) record through the Freedom of Information Act, that may provide additional helpful information with which to defeat the IRS' claim. This is particularly true when the IRS claims that taxes were not paid. A cancelled check will bear a Document Locator Number (DLN) which often ties back to the master file. Through the DLN, the payment of funds can be traced to a particular tax year. Any IMF photocopies should be attached to the affidavit.

7. Area 7 is important and must not be overlooked. It should set forth the *ultimate conclusion* to be drawn from the facts set forth throughout the affidavit. As an example, you should declare that you *in fact* filed a return or paid all taxes due, contrary to the IRS' claim. You should also declare that IRS' claims to the contrary, together with interest and penalties, should be cancelled or abated.

8. Area 8 is the space for your signature, which should be affixed to the affidavit in the *presence* of an authorized notary public in and for your county.

9. Area 9 is known as the "jurat," or official verification by the notary that the statements within the affidavit are your statements and are made by you under oath. With the signature of the notary on the affidavit, with the official notary stamp, your statements become sworn testimony entitled to the same respect as though made to a judge or jury in a court of law.

Through the vehicle of the affidavit, you have, for all practical purposes, carried to the IRS the powerful impact of sworn courtroom testimony. The following case examples demonstrate how others have used the affidavit to carry the day in similar disputes with the IRS.

1. The Form 1040

The 110 million individual filers of Form 1040, the vast majority of whom ignore good counsel and do not mail their tax forms via certified mail, face two potential problems. The first is that the form will not arrive at the IRS Service Center on time, or *at all*. The next problem is that after the form does arrive at its destination, it may become lost in a labyrinthine system of manual sorting and automated processing.

As reported in Chapter Two of this work, the IRS' 1988 Annual Report, *Highlights,* bragged that the agency's information return matching program was responsible for sending "3 million notices to taxpayers for failure to file a tax return based upon information returns filed." In light of the General Accounting Office's 1988 study regarding the accuracy of the IRS Service Center notices and demands, a good case can be made that as many as 1.5 *million* of those notices were mailed in error. That is to say, as many as 1.5 *million* citizens were erroneously informed by the IRS that they failed to file a tax return, when as a matter of fact, their return was filed in a proper and timely manner. Certainly, if you were one of the potential 1.5 million victims, the receipt of such a notice could be chilling.

Jack was one of those citizens who did receive an incorrect notice of failure to file a tax return. Jack's troubles with the IRS go back a number of years, and mercifully, we do not have to divulge all his problems in this discourse. It is relevant to state, however, that for the years 1986, 1987 and 1988, Jack did not file income tax returns with the IRS. At the same time, Jack had a collection problem with the IRS for other years in which he filed but was unable to pay the tax. Like many persons, Jack perceived that he was caught in a trap and could not file subsequent returns for fear that he would make his problem worse.

I first met Jack in the summer of 1989. Naturally, the first order of business was to cure his delinquency with regard to 1986 through 1988. I recommended that Jack have returns for each year prepared and submitted to the IRS. When the returns were completed, they were mailed via certified mail, return receipt requested, to the IRS'

Kansas City Service Center. Jack retained copies of his three tardy returns and was careful to preserve the white slip and the green card when it was returned to him several days later.

In the meantime, negotiations with the IRS were underway with regard to the collection matter. One requirement the IRS will always insist upon, when collection negotiations are proceeding, is that the citizen be and remain "current" with the IRS. That is to say, all returns must be filed and current year's income taxes, or estimates, must be paid. Several months after Jack filed his returns for 1986 through 1988, the IRS laid an unbelievable accusation at his feet. The collection officer monitoring the case declared that Jack failed to file his 1988 return. All negotiations would stall and Jack's wages would be levied if the oversight were not immediately corrected.

The first order of business was to draft an affidavit establishing that the return for 1988 was indeed filed. Because Jack filed three returns at once by mailing them in the same envelope, this would have to be set forth in the affidavit. We were careful to point out that the returns were mailed via certified mail, and we attached copies of both postal documents, and a copy of the 1988 return, to the affidavit. Please see Exhibit 3-2, Affidavit of Jack, for an example of what Jack submitted to the IRS.

Other than the bald claim that Jack did not file a return for 1988, the IRS was unable to present any evidence whatsoever to contradict Jack's affidavit. My speculation is that when his envelope containing three separate tax returns hit the Service Center, a processor noticed two returns, but overlooked the third. Consequently, it was never processed and the IRS' computer records indicated that it was not filed.

When presented with our affidavit, the IRS conceded that Jack's return was in fact filed as he claimed. More importantly, it did so *without* any further dispute. The presence of the affidavit, with its precise clarity and affirmative declarations, was sufficient to wholly disarm the IRS' contrary assertion.

A note for clarification: Jack's problem grew out of a pending collection matter. However, most situations involving lost returns are created by a Service Center notice to the citizen. These latter situations are even more simple to resolve than was Jack's. Jack had a revenue officer assigned to his collection account for prior years. In the case of notice from the Service Center, there typically *is no* open collection account. Thus, only Service Center personnel and *not* local collection officials will review your affidavit.

EXHIBIT 3-2   AFFIDAVIT OF JACK _____

STATE OF ____ . ___)
) ss
COUNTY OF _____)

1. My name is Jack _____. My address is _____. My Social Security Number is _____.

2. In February of 1990, Revenue Officer _____ made the claim that my federal income tax return for the year 1988 was not filed. This statement is in error.

3. As a matter of fact, my return was filed on November 3, 1989. The return was filed together with returns for 1986 and 1987. An envelope containing the three returns was mailed via certified mail, return receipt requested, to the IRS Service Center in Kansas City, MO. Attached to this affidavit as Exhibit A is a true and correct copy of the receipt for certified mail, item No. P 058 674 123, dated at (City, State) on November 3, 1989. Also in Exhibit A is the Post Office Domestic Return Receipt for Item No. P 058 674 123, bearing the "received" stamp of the IRS at 2306 Bannister Road, Kansas City, MO. (the address of the IRS Service Center).

4. All three returns were mailed to the IRS in the same envelope on November 3, 1989, with first class and certified mail postage pre-paid.

5. From this evidence it is shown that the IRS received my return for 1988 on November 6, 1989.

6. Attached to this affidavit is a true and correct copy of my retained copy of the original 1988 income tax return filed with the IRS on November 3, 1989. The original was mailed to the Service Center as indicated above.

7. The IRS' claim that I failed to file an income tax return for 1988 is incorrect. The return, as shown, was filed by mailing the same via certified mail to the IRS' Service Center in Kansas City. Based upon these facts, the claim of failure to file a 1988 made by the IRS should be set aside as invalid.

_____ Subscribed and sworn to before me
this _____ day of February, 1990.

Jack _____

Notary Public: _____
My Commission Expires: _____

There is a second situation in which an affidavit akin to Jack's is beneficial. That situation occurs when the IRS claims that your return was filed late. The rule of law is that a return is considered timely when filed when it is *postmarked* by midnight on April 15th. When tax returns are received by the IRS *after* April 15th, return processors are supposed to review the mailing envelope to determine whether it is postmarked accordingly. If not, they will date-stamp the return on the day it is received. It is not uncommon for return handlers to fail in their duty to review postmarks, thus errantly date-stamping tax returns in a manner which indicates they were filed late. When this occurs, a notice will be mailed to the citizen demanding the late filing penalty, as well as interest.

Into any of the scenarios discussed here, we can mix an ingredient known as "Post Office spice." That is to say, the Post Office is responsible for the tardiness or failure of the return to reach the IRS.

In any event, an affidavit as shown in Exhibit 3-2 will end the dispute. Obviously, when the facts and circumstances are different than those discussed in Jack's affidavit, you will be responsible to adapt your statement to your own facts. For example, when responding to the claim that you filed your return in a timely manner, you must be careful to note that timely filing means mailing *prior* to midnight on April 15th. These facts must be clearly set forth. Jack's affidavit provides a good example of how this is done, but is not intended to be a "form letter" used by you for any eventuality. Such may be said of every affidavit in this chapter.

2. The Form 4868

The Form 4668, well-known by many a procrastinator, is the Application for an Automatic Extension of Time in which to File Form 1040. The form is used to obtain a four-month extension of time in which to file Form 1040. The extension document is used, not for the purpose of winning additional time in which to *pay* taxes, but covers only the *obligation to file* a return. The extension of time to pay taxes is covered later in this chapter.

Paul is the biggest procrastinator I know. In fact, I spoke of Paul in my book, *How Anyone Can Negotiate With The IRS—And WIN!* There I told the story of how Paul stalled the audit of his 1985 income tax return for over a year, until he was good and ready to proceed with the matter. Paul also has an inexplicable propensity to attract IRS notices—like flies to the company picnic. In October of

1988, Paul's "gift" manifested itself in the form of a notice from the IRS assessing a "late filing penalty" in the amount of $116.52, including interest. The penalty was assessed due to Paul's apparent failure to timely file his 1987 federal income tax return. We shot back an affidavit. Please see Exhibit 3-3.

Prior to April 15, 1988, Paul submitted a Form 4868 to the IRS. That form provided an automatic extension of time, until August 15, in which to file the tax return. Paul's return was filed on August 9, 1988. Therefore, the return was filed in a timely manner. Paul's affidavit, as is seen in Exhibit 3-3, was careful to point out that Paul submitted Form 4868 to the IRS (a copy was attached) and also explained the reasons why Paul needed additional time to file. As it happened, Paul did not mail his Form 4868 via certified mail, so postal receipts were unavailable. Nevertheless, he firmly declared in his affidavit that the extension was filed *prior* to April 15, and his return was filed *prior* to August 15, the extension deadline.

Paul's affidavit was dated November 14, 1988, just a few weeks after he received notice of the penalty assessment. By January of 1989, two months later, the IRS notified Paul that the penalty was abated "for reasons shown" in his affidavit. No further attempts were made to collect subsequent to the abatement. Paul's one page affidavit saved him $116.52. Not a bad return on investment, considering the cost of mailing the letter was less than three dollars!

3. The Form 1127

Form 1127 is a great mystery. Nobody in the IRS, and precious few on the outside, seems to realize that the form even exists, much less understands its use. Frankly, it is vitally important that people understand what it is and how to use it. I have made an effort to explain this in *How Anyone Can Negotiate*. Consider this common situation:

The Form 4868 discussed above permits an extension of time in which to *file* your return. However, the extension granted through the Form 4868 *does not* provide additional time to *pay* the tax. All taxes due on your Form 1040 must be paid on or before April 15, lest compound interest and failure to pay penalties be added to the bill. The problem, however, is that most people seeking an extension do not need additional time to file. They need additional time to pay. But the IRS and private sector tax professionals alike are notorious

EXHIBIT 3-3

Paul M. _____
Address
City, State, Zip

Date: November 14, 1988
SSN:

Internal Revenue Service
Regional Service Center
Andover, MA 05501

STATE OF _____)
) ss
COUNTY OF _____)

AFFIDAVIT

Reference is made to your Request for Payment, dated _____ (copy
attached to this affidavit). The notice demands payment of $116.52 in
penalty and interest for "late filing" my 1987 federal income tax
return.

For the reasons stated in this affidavit, the penalty is inappropriate
and is due to be abated. These are the facts:

On April 14th, 1988, I filed with the IRS a properly signed and
executed Form 4868, Application for Automatic Extension of Time in
Which to File Individual Income Tax Return. A true and correct copy
of the Application is attached to this affidavit. The reason for
filing the application was because certain records of my income were
not yet available to me from which I could prepare and submit a
correct federal income tax return. Without the records, it would have
been impossible for me to submit a truthful and accurate federal
income tax return.

By filing Form 4868, the IRS extended the period in which I could file
a timely federal income tax return to and including August 15, 1988.
I submitted the return by mailing it on August 9, 1988. Thus, the
return was filed before the extended period of time had expired. My
reason for filing the application was to comply with my legal
requirements to submit a tax return which is both timely, truthful and
accurate in all respects. By filing the return prior to August 15,
1988, which I did do, I complied with the timeliness aspects of my
obligations.

Based upon these facts, it is clear that I did not file my return late
as alleged by the IRS in its attached notice. Therefore, the penalty
is entirely inappropriate and is due to be abated in full.

_____
Paul M. _____

Subscribed and sworn to before me
this 14th day of November, 1988.

Notary Public: _____
My Commission Expires: _____

for explaining that there is no way to obtain an extension of time to pay. "If you don't have the money," they counsel, "you must file anyway."

On the morning of April 15, 1989, I was in a Dallas hotel room. I was there to do a national radio broadcast. That morning I happened to turn on the television while preparing for the day, when I caught a portion of NBC's *Today* show. Jane Pauley's guest that morning was Acting IRS Commissioner Michael J. Murphy. In response to Ms. Pauley's direct question regarding the ability to obtain an extension of time to pay, Commissioner Murphy flatly declared that no such right exists. Rather, he stated, all taxes must be paid by April 15 and there was "nothing" one could do to extend that time.

This statement, made by the nation's chief tax collector at the time, to a nationwide television audience, was flatly false and misleading. Moreover, I have great difficulty believing that the nation's chief tax collector was unaware of the existence of a basic right created by the mystery form, Form 1127. The form is entitled, *Application for Extension of Time for Payment of Tax.* When submitted prior to April 15, it can win the applicant an additional *six months* in which to pay his taxes, without additional penalties! Later that very afternoon, you can believe that I made much of Commissioner Murphy's false declaration to the public. Fortunately, I too, had a nationwide audience.

However, within weeks of that radio show and my national declarations regarding Form 1127 and the right to obtain an extension of time to pay, the phones at WINNING Publications rang off the hook with persons who were told by the "experts" in the IRS' Taxpayer Assistance office, that, contrary to my pronouncements, no Form 1127 existed. Finally, as I often do when bored, I phoned a Taxpayer Assistance office myself with the question. This was the conversation:

"Can I get an extension of time to pay my taxes?"

"NO."

"What about Form 1127? Can't I file Form 1127?"

Answer: There is no such form.

"Can I speak with a manager please?"

Answer: Sure. (On hold for 20 minutes—manager finally picks up phone.)

"Can I get an extension of time to pay my taxes?"

Answer: NO.

"What about Form 1127? Can't I file Form 1127?"

Answer: There is no such form.

(Is there an echo in here?)

Just for grins, I decided to lodge a formal request through IRS channels for a copy of Form 1127. The request went to the IRS' Forms Distribution Center, located at 2402 East Empire, Bloomington, IL 61799.[1] Within a few weeks, the familiar brown envelope appeared at my door. With great anticipation, I tore open the package to find my long awaited treasure. Yes, friends, the non-existent Form 1127 found its way to my loving hands via the IRS' own Forms Distribution Center; and yes, I did save the IRS' own cover letter, Form 8483, with its computer codes, my name and address, and even a mention of the reclusive Form 1127. To my overwhelming joy, however, I was provided with not *one* copy of Form 1127, but *six copies* of the non-existent application!

The Form 1127 transmitted to me by the agency was the latest version, revised in October of 1988, *six months prior* to Commissioner Murphy's declaration to a national audience that no such right existed. Any remaining doubting Thomas need only consult page 178 of *How Anyone Can Negotiate*. That book, released in October of 1988, contains a copy of Form 1127 for all to see—and use! Also, see the last chapter of this book for further discussion.

My point in all of this is simple. Anyone knowledgeable enough to employ the use of Form 1127 to obtain a payment extension must anticipate that the Service Center will bill him for taxes, failure to pay penalties, and interest, upon filing his tax return. After all, with an approved Form 1127, you will naturally submit the tax return without full payment. If a former Commissioner of the Internal Revenue Service is unaware that the right of a payment extension exists, how can we expect the Service Center minions to be aware of this right?

Therefore, when the bill for penalties arrives, you must fire off an affidavit substantially the same as that shown in Exhibit 3-3. The difference, of course, is that this affidavit will address the Form 1127, rather than the Form 4868. Your text would also address the fact that your return was timely filed, and under the terms of the Form 1127 extension, payment of your tax liability is *not* untimely.

4. The Form 2210

Doug's 1988 federal income tax return showed a tax liability of $7,181.65. He filed his return and paid the tax in full. Because Doug was self-employed, no federal withholding was taken from any checks he received during the year. However, Doug neglected to pay estimated tax payments during the year. Consequently, when it came to compute his tax liability, he was forced to add the penalty for underpaying his estimated tax liability.

The penalty was computed using Form 2210, Underpayment of Estimated Tax by Individuals. The penalty came to $390, and that amount was added to Doug's tax liability. A copy of Form 2210 was attached to Doug's federal income tax return and mailed to the IRS with a check in the amount of $7,571.85. That amount reflected the sum of the income tax liability, plus the underpayment penalty of $390. The income tax return with Form 2210 and the check were mailed to the IRS Service Center via certified mail, return receipt requested.

Within a few months of mailing the return and payment, Doug received a computerized statement from the IRS demanding more money. The bill stated that because Doug "underpaid estimated taxes" during 1988, the penalty was assessed. It certainly did not come as any surprise that Doug underpaid his estimated 1988 liability. He knew that at the time the return was prepared. However, it did seem rather strange that the IRS would bill him for the underpayment penalty *after* he submitted Form 2210 with the return. Since Doug paid the penalty when the return was filed, the IRS' notice constituted a double charge.

Doug responded with an affidavit. Please see Exhibit 3-4. Doug's affidavit included a copy of the Form 1040 which reflected the computation of the penalty, the Form 2210 which is the actual penalty computation, and a copy of the cancelled check used to pay the tax and penalty in full. Doug also included copies of the postal receipts to prove that he did in fact file the return and that the IRS received the submission. Lastly, he verbalized the ultimate declaration that the penalty was in fact paid, and that the additional assessment should immediately be abated.

In virtually no time at all, the IRS responded to Doug's affidavit with a notice. The notice indicated that the IRS reviewed his affidavit, and "for cause shown" cancelled the penalty originally demanded. In Doug's case, his savings exceeded $400 because of interest added to the original penalty assessment.

EXHIBIT 3-4

Doug _____
Address
City, State, Zip

Date:
SSN:

Internal Revenue Service
Regional Service Center
Kansas City, MO 64999

STATE OF _____)
) ss
COUNTY OF _____)

AFFIDAVIT OF DOUG _____

1. Reference is made to your Request for Payment, dated _____
(copy attached to this affidavit). The notice demands payment of
$421.83 in penalty and interest for underpaying my 1988 estimated
federal income tax liability. For the reasons stated in this
affidavit, the penalty is inappropriate and is due to be abated. The
facts are:

2. A timely federal income tax return was submitted by me for the
year 1988. A true and correct copy of my Form 1040 with all its
accompanying schedules, is attached to this affidavit. The federal
income tax liability shown on Form 1040 is $7,181.65. In addition to
the sum of $7,181.65, I included in my payment to the IRS the amount
of $390. As shown on page two of Form 1040, that amount was computed
as the penalty for underpayment of estimated taxes. It has already
been paid to the IRS. Form 2210, Computation of Estimated Tax Penalty
was used to compute the $390. It was attached to Form 1040. See
attached copy.

3. When the tax return was filed, I included full payment of the tax,
plus the $390 penalty. The total remitted to the IRS was $7,571.85.
Attached to this affidavit is a copy the check (front and back) used
to make the payment. The Form 1040, Form 2210, and the check for full
payment were mailed to the IRS via certified mail. Attached to this
affidavit are copies of the postal receipts showing that the IRS
received each of these documents.

4. Based upon these facts, it is clear that I have already properly
computed and paid the penalty for failure to make estimated tax
payments. Therefore, your notice and demand for payment is entirely
inappropriate and is due to be abated in full.

_____
Doug _____

Subscribed and sworn to before me
this ____ day of _____, 1989.

Notary Public: _____
My Commission Expires: _____

5. Your Tax Liability

When it came time for Greg to file his 1983 income tax return, he was $877 short. Greg was a factory worker, living, as many do, from paycheck to paycheck. As a result of under-withholding, he found himself in a jam on April 15. Wisely, rather than filing a return without full payment of the tax, he borrowed the money from his sister-in-law to pay the balance in full. Greg mailed his tax return to the IRS, together with a check from Chris in the amount of $877. As far as Greg knew, the matter was resolved.

By October of 1984, some six months after the return was filed and the tax was paid, Greg began receiving notices from the IRS to the effect that he owed $500 on the 1983 account. Greg consulted his return preparer, who also happened to be his uncle. Uncle Clarence learned that the $877 check written on Chris' account was processed by the IRS as a $377 check. More incredibly, it was processed by the IRS' bank which processed it as a $377 check. Now, please do not ask me how any of this happened. It just did. Because the initial check was processed for $377, rather than $877, a $500 balance indeed existed on Greg's 1983 account.

Uncle Clarence's solution to the problem seemed reasonable enough. He recommended that since the $877 was processed as a $377 check, the remaining $500 should simply be mailed to the IRS to end the matter. This was done. Greg obtained a cashier's check from Chris' bank in the amount of $500 and mailed it to the IRS. Now here is where it *really* gets weird. Somebody somewhere along the line noticed that the $877 check had been errantly processed as a $377 check. Therefore, the check was run through the system a second time, this time correctly. The problem, however, was that by the time it was presented to Chris' bank for payment, $500 had been withdrawn to cover the cost of the cashier's check. That left insufficient funds in Chris' account to cover the $877 check. The bank bounced the check back to the IRS. This happened in April of 1985, *one year* after the check was originally mailed to the agency, and six months after it initially processed the check as one written for $377. Again, I beg you, please do not ask me why!

Greg realized the check bounced when the IRS returned it to him with a short notice explaining that the bank returned the check unpaid. Shortly after that notice, the IRS issued a final demand to Greg, explaining that if the tax, which by now had risen to over $1,000 was not paid in full, his paycheck would be levied. Given

EXHIBIT 3-5

AFFIDAVIT OF (Your Name)

STATE OF _____)
) ss
COUNTY OF _____)

1. My name is _____. My address is _____. My
Social Security Number is _____.

2. By letter dated _____, the IRS notified me that my
federal income taxes for the year _____ have not been paid. This
statement is in error.

3. My taxes for the year in question were paid at the time my federal
income tax return was filed. The return was filed on (date), by
mailing it to the IRS Service Center at (address). The return and
payment were mailed via certified mail. Attached to this affidavit
are true and correct copies of the U.S. Postal Receipts showing the
date of mailing and showing that the IRS received my tax return and
check on (date).

4. My taxes in the amount of _____ were paid with my personal
check number _____. Attached to this affidavit is a true and
correct copy of the face and reverse sides my check number _____.
The copy shows the check was written on (date) and was processed by
the IRS through the (name of bank as shown on back of cancelled
check). The check then cleared my bank on (date). Also attached to
this affidavit is a true copy of my bank statement for the month of
_____, indicating that check number _____ was paid on
(date). (If taxes were partially paid through wage withholding, or
more than one check, copies of Form W-2 and all other checks should be
referred to by and included in the affidavit.)

5. Based upon these facts, it is clear that I have already properly
paid my federal income taxes in full. Therefore, your notice and
demand for payment is entirely inappropriate and is due to be abated
in full.

_____
Your Name

Subscribed and sworn to before me
this _____ day of _____.

Notary Public: _____
My Commission Expires: _____

Greg's modest income, such an act would be devastating. To add insult to injury, the IRS was ignoring the $500 payment made via cashier's check in late 1984.

Uncle Clarence fumbled with a letter or two in an effort to help out, but his request that the IRS "get to the bottom of this mix-up" was unheeded. By March of 1986, Greg's worst fears were realized when the IRS levied his paycheck. The IRS dipped into Greg's paychecks three separate times in an effort to collect the tax. By that time, Uncle Clarence packed it in, and Greg was desperate.

After reviewing the situation, I knew the first order of business was to persuade the IRS to release the levy. This was done by drafting an affidavit which explained the bizarre situation to the local Collection Division. I hesitate to display the affidavit Greg used, for the simple reason that Greg's facts were so off-the-wall. Normally, the dispute over whether taxes were paid are settled with a very simple affidavit which makes reference to the date of payment, the payment device, and which has attached to it a copy—both front and back—of the cancelled check. An example of a simple affidavit to this effect is shown in Exhibit 3-5. Please review it.

Greg's affidavit was submitted to the local revenue officer who reviewed it and the IRS' records. Later that week, Greg's employer received notice that the levy was released. As far as damage control was concerned, the problem was solved. All that remained was for Greg to pursue the IRS for the excess funds it gathered through the levy. This was done by filing a Claim for Refund.[2] By the time that claim was considered by the IRS, Greg had nearly $300 returned to him by the agency.

6. The Left Hand Versus The Right Hand

Doug was involved in an audit with the IRS for the years 1981 and 1982. The agency hotly contested his charitable contributions to various independent church organizations, contributions which were substantial. Doug was not getting along well with the auditor as the IRS had made the determination that Doug was somehow attempting to cheat the system. Such was not the case and the IRS was never able to sustain its claim to that effect.

During the course of the examination, the agent questioned Doug regarding the 1983 tax return. Doug responded to general inquiries by pointing out that he filed his 1983 return in a timely manner, and that yes, he did claim similar charitable contributions in that year as well. The agent explained that he would have to look into 1983 as a matter of policy.

Later during the course of the investigation, the agent made a peculiar statement to Doug. He declared that Doug misled him regarding 1983 and that, in fact, no 1983 return was filed. Doug could not understand the agent's claim since he clearly filed the return. We do not know where the agent learned that Doug supposedly did not file, but he was mistaken. Doug presented a file-copy of his 1983 return to the agent, but he was unimpressed. Since the document was not mailed via certified mail, there was no independent proof that Doug had in fact mailed the return. Moreover, because of the agent's views toward Doug and his contributions, there was little hope that the agent would ever believe Doug's word.

Consequently, rather than stand toe to toe with the agent over the issue, Doug made a request of the service center to produce the return he knew he filed. The request was made on IRS Form 4506, Request for Copy of Tax Form. Please see Exhibit 3-6. The one-page form is a simple request of the Service Center to provide a copy of your tax form, either 1040, W-2, 941, etc. The one hitch to the Form 4506 is that you must *have filed* the return in order for the Service Center to locate, copy and return it to you. But they did just that in Doug's situation.

Shortly after the completion of the 1981, 1982 and 1983 examination, in which the agent determined that Doug did not file for 1983, the Service Center returned a copy of Doug's 1983 income tax return to him. The beauty of the discovery was that the Service Center not only photocopied and returned the document to Doug, but certified that the document was a "true and correct" copy of the return on file with the IRS at its Service Center. Moreover, the copy boasted an impressive "official seal" of the Internal Revenue Service, and signature of the Service Center official responsible for maintaining the records. The entire package was so impressive that it was suitable for framing!

We have no knowledge as to why the tax examiner claimed and accused Doug of failing to file his 1983 income tax return. It was either a case of the left hand not knowing what the right hand was doing, or a case where the agent was purely attempting to harass and intimidate Doug. I find the former explanation to be suspect for the simple reason that if the Service Center had record of the return,

EXHIBIT 3-6

Form **4506** (Rev. November 1989) Department of the Treasury Internal Revenue Service	**Request for Copy of Tax Form** ▶ **Please read instructions before completing this form.** ▶ **Please type or print clearly.**	OMB No. 1545-0429 Expires 11-30-92

Note: *Do not complete this form to get **tax account information**. See instructions.*

1 Name of taxpayer(s) as shown on tax form (husband's and wife's, if a joint return)	**6a Social security number** as shown on tax form (*if joint return, show husband's number*)
2 Current name and address	**6b Wife's social security number** as shown on tax form
	7 Employer identification number as shown on tax form
	8 **Tax form number** (Form 1040, 1040A, 941, etc.)
3a If copy of form is to be mailed to someone else, show the third party's name and address. (See instructions.)	9 Tax period(s) (year or period ended date) (no more than 4 per request) See instructions.
3b If we cannot find a record of your tax form, check here if you want the payment refunded to the third party. ☐	10 Amount due for copy of tax form: a Cost for each period . . . . . $ 4.25 b Number of tax periods requested on line 9 . . . .
4 If name in third party's records differs from line 1 above, show name here. (See instructions.)	c Total cost (multiply line 10a by line 10b) . . . . $
	Make check or money order payable to Internal Revenue Service

5 Check the box to show what you want:

☐ Copy of tax form and all attachments (including Form(s) W-2, schedules, or other forms). The charge is $4.25 for each period requested.

Note: *If you need these copies for court or administrative proceedings, also check here.* ☐

☐ Copy of Form(s) W-2 only. There is no charge for this. See instructions for when Form W-2 is available.

		Telephone number of requester
Please ▶ **Sign** **Here** ▶	Signature (See instructions. If other than taxpayer, attach authorization document.) Date	( ) Convenient time for us to call
	Title (if line 1 above is a corporation, partnership, estate, or trust)	

Important: Full payment must accompany your request.

Instructions

Privacy Act and Paperwork Reduction Act Notice.—We ask for this information to carry out the Internal Revenue laws of the United States. We need the information to gain access to your tax form in our files and properly respond to your request. If you do not furnish the information, we may not be able to fill your request.

The time needed to complete and file this form will vary depending on individual circumstances. The estimated average time is:

Recordkeeping . . . . . .13 minutes

Learning about the law or the form . . . . . . 7 minutes

Preparing the form . . . .21 minutes

Copying, assembling, and sending the form to IRS . . . . .17 minutes

If you have comments concerning the accuracy of these time estimates or suggestions for making this form more simple, we would be happy to hear from you. You can write to the **Internal Revenue Service**, Washington, DC 20224, Attention: IRS Reports Clearance Officer, T:FP; or the **Office of Management and Budget**, Paperwork Reduction Project (1545-0429), Washington, DC 20503.

Purpose of Form.—Use Form 4506 to get a copy of a tax form or Form W-2 only.

Do not use this form to request Forms 1099. Copies of Forms 1099 are not available from IRS. If you need a copy of Form 1099, contact the payer.

Do not use this form to request tax account information.

Note: *If you had your tax form filled out by a paid preparer, check first to see if you can get a copy from the preparer. This may save you both time and money.*

Please allow at least 45 days for delivery. Be sure to furnish all the information asked for on this form to avoid any delay in our

sending your requested copies. (You must allow 6 weeks processing time after a tax form is filed before requesting a copy.)

Tax Account Information Only.—A listing of certain tax account information is available free of charge if you write or visit an IRS office or call the IRS toll-free number listed in your telephone directory.

Generally, tax account information is needed when students applying for financial aid are required to give the college a copy of their tax form. The school may, however, accept tax account information provided by the IRS instead. If so, the following information will be sent upon request:

(a) Name and social security number,

(b) Type of return filed,

(c) Filing status,

(d) Tax shown on return,

(e) Adjusted gross income,

(f) Taxable income,

(g) Self-employment tax, and

(h) Number of exemptions.

(Continued on back)

Form **4506** (Rev. 11-89)

EXHIBIT 3-6 (continued)

Form 4506 (Rev. 11-89) Page **2**

Mortgage Revenue Bonds.—States issuing mortgage revenue bonds are required to verify that the mortgage applicant did not own a home during the 3 previous years. As part of this verification, the mortgage lender may want proof that you did not claim interest or real estate tax deductions for a residence on your tax return. If you have a copy of your tax return, or if it was filled out by a paid preparer and you can get a copy, the mortgage lender can accept your signed copy.

If you filed Form 1040A or 1040EZ, you can request *tax account information* to help satisfy the verification requirement. To do this, **do not** complete this form. Instead, contact your local IRS office for this information.

If you filed Form 1040, you may have to get a copy of it to verify that you did not claim any itemized deductions for a residence. To get a copy, **complete** Form 4506 and write "Mortgage Revenue Bond" across the top.

Lines 3a and 3b.—If you have named someone else to receive the tax form (such as a CPA, scholarship board, or mortgage lender), show the name of an individual and the address on line 3a to ensure the copy gets to the right person. If you checked the box on line 3b, we will refund the payment for the copies to the third party.

Line 4.—Enter the name of the client, student, or applicant if it is different from the name shown on line 1. For example, line 1 may be the parents of a student applying for financial aid. Show the student's name on line 4 so the scholarship board can associate the tax form with their file. If we cannot find a record of your tax form, we will notify the third party directly that we cannot fill the request.

Line 5.—If you need only a copy of your Form(s) W-2, check the box for Copy of Form(s) W-2 only. Also, on line 8 show "Form(s) W-2 only" and on line 10c show "no charge."

Form W-2 is not available until 6 weeks after you file it with your tax return (for example, Form 1040). Otherwise, Form W-2 information is only available 18 months after it is submitted by your employer. (If you lost your Form W-2 or have not received it by the time you are ready to prepare your tax return, contact your employer.)

Lines 6a and 6b.—For individuals, enter the social security number as shown on the tax form. For jointly filed tax forms, show the husband's social security number on line 6a and the wife's on line 6b. If you do not furnish this information, there may be a delay in processing your request.

Line 7.—Enter your employer identification number **only** if you are requesting a copy of a **business** tax form. Otherwise, leave this line blank.

Line 9.—Enter the year(s) of the tax form you are requesting. For fiscal-year filers or requests for quarterly tax forms, enter the date the period ended; for example, 1986 for an annual filed tax form or 3/31/86, 6/30/86, etc. for a quarterly filed tax form. If you need more than four different tax periods, use additional Forms 4506. Tax forms that were filed 6 or more years ago may not be available for making copies. However, tax account information is generally still available for these periods. See **Tax Account Information Only.**

Line 10.—Write your social security number or Federal employer identification number **and** "Form 4506 Request" on your check or money order. If we cannot fill your request, we will refund your payment.

Signature.—*Form 4506 must be received by IRS within 60 days following the date upon which you signed and dated the request.*

Requests for copies of tax forms to be sent to a third party must be signed by the person whose name is shown on line 1.

Copies of jointly filed tax forms may be furnished to either the husband or the wife. Only one signature is required. Sign Form 4506 exactly as your name appeared on the original tax form. If your name has changed, **also** sign with your current name.

For a corporation, the signature of the president of the corporation, or any principal officer and the secretary, or the principal officer and another officer are generally required. Further rules on who may obtain tax information on **corporations, partnerships, estates,** and **trusts** are detailed in Internal Revenue Code section 6103.

If you are **not** the taxpayer shown on line 1, you must attach your authorization to receive a copy of the requested tax form. An authorization must specifically state what tax form and period(s) is covered, and that it may be supplied to the person designated authority. You may send a copy of the authorization document if the original has already been filed with IRS. This will generally be a power of attorney, or other authorization such as evidence of entitlement (for Title 11 Bankruptcy or Receivership Proceeding). If the taxpayer is deceased, you must send Letters Testamentary or other evidence to establish that you are authorized to act for the taxpayer's estate.

Where To File.—Mail Form 4506 with the correct total payment attached to the **Internal Revenue Service Center** for the place where you lived when the requested tax form was filed.

Note: *You must use a separate form for each service center from which you are requesting a copy of your tax form.*

If you lived in: ▼	Use this address: ▼
New Jersey, New York (New York City and counties of Nassau, Rockland, Suffolk, and Westchester)	P.O. Box 400 Holtsville, NY 11742
New York (all other counties), Connecticut, Maine, Massachusetts, New Hampshire, Rhode Island, Vermont	P.O. Box 3006 Woburn, MA 01888
Florida, Georgia, South Carolina	P.O. Box 47412 Doraville, GA 30362
Indiana, Kentucky, Michigan, Ohio, West Virginia	P.O. Box 145500 Cincinnati, OH 45214
Kansas, New Mexico, Oklahoma, Texas	3651 South Interregional Highway Photocopy Unit Stop 6716 Austin, TX 73301
Alaska, Arizona, California (counties of Alpine, Amador, Butte, Calaveras, Colusa, Contra Costa, Del Norte, El Dorado, Glenn, Humboldt, Lake, Lassen, Marin, Mendocino, Modoc, Napa, Nevada, Placer, Plumas, Sacramento, San Joaquin, Shasta, Sierra, Siskiyou, Solano, Sonoma, Sutter, Tehama, Trinity, Yolo, and Yuba), Colorado, Idaho, Montana, Nebraska, Nevada, North Dakota, Oregon, South Dakota, Utah, Washington, Wyoming	TPR/Photocopy C6 P.O. Box 9953 Mail Stop 6734 Ogden, UT 84409
California (all other counties), Hawaii	5045 E. Butler Avenue Photocopy Unit Stop 53260 Fresno, CA 93888
Illinois, Iowa, Minnesota, Missouri, Wisconsin	2306 E. Bannister Road Photocopy Unit Stop 53 Kansas City, MO 64131
Alabama, Arkansas, Louisiana, Mississippi, North Carolina, Tennessee,	P.O. Box 2501 Stop 46 Memphis, TN 38101
Delaware, District of Columbia, Maryland, Pennsylvania, Virginia, outside the United States	P.O. Box 920 Photocopy Unit Drop Point 536 Bensalem, PA 19020

which they certainly did, the data should have been transmitted to the IMF. And, if the agent consulted the master file record to determine whether Doug submitted his return, which I can only assume he did, as I am familiar with no other means of ascertaining one's filing status, I must conclude that he had full knowledge of the fact that Doug indeed filed his return for 1983. These facts render the agent's claims to be contrary and resultant accusations toward Doug, blatant harassment!

Thankfully, the Service Center, in response to the Form 4506 submitted by Doug, presented a signed and "sealed" copy of the return, complete with the trappings of officialdom inherent in all government productions. This "official record" of Doug's return laid to rest forever the claim that he did not file. Given the nature of the manner in which the Service Centers provide a copy of your return when requested on Form 4506, it is impossible for any authority to discount your claim of having filed same.

7. The Most Complete Approach

Each of the examples we have examined above show how one person solved his problem through the use of an affidavit. In each case, certain aspects of the affair made success more probable. However, no one person had "everything" going for him. Yet, each was successful. While very often we have no control over the circumstances of our case, particularly those aspects involving the IRS, there are steps that can be taken to manipulate events in order to ensure sucess. When this occurs, you are left with the most complete approach to a situation. Just such a case presented itself in the summer of 1989. What we did to solve the problem was indeed, the most complete approach.

In July of 1989, Dave was in the process of completing Form 1120S, *Income Tax Return of Small Business Corporation*. The corporation was on an extension to September 15, 1990. A Small Business Corporation is also known as an "S" corporation. This special corporate status is elected by small businesses as a means of simplifying their tax compliance burden, as well as their financial burden to the IRS. It is quite popular among small business corporations. However, in order to be treated by the IRS as an "S" corporation, certain requirements must be met, not the least of which is the filing of a proper "S" election. That election is made on

Form 2553.

Dave filed his corporation's Form 2553 with the Andover Service Center in February of 1988, shortly after his corporation was formed. Along with the "S" election, Dave applied to the IRS for the assignment of an Employer's Identification Number to his new business. A cover letter, along with the proper forms, including the Form 2553, were mailed to the IRS Service Center. Shortly thereafter, the IRS notified Dave that an EIN was assigned to his new business.

While Dave was immersed in the return preparation process, he was consulting regularly with his accountant. Before long, the accountant raised the question why the IRS had not sent Dave the forms package for the small business corporation. Instead, he received the forms kit for a regular corporation. "I have no idea," responded Dave. He probably did not know the difference.

This greatly disturbed the accountant, since he was quickly forming the opinion that the IRS never received Dave's "S" election. "What will happen if they didn't?" Dave asked.

"They will treat you as a regular corporation, and that will cost you money," responded the accountant.

Concerned, Dave phoned Taxpayer Assistance personnel in his city. Dave is a regular reader of my material, so he was aware of such things as a master file, document locator number, etc. During his conversation with the IRS representative, Dave explained how he mailed the Form 2553. He explained that it was sent with a cover letter, to which was attached *both* the application for EIN, *and* the Form 2553. "Is it possible that these became separated during processing?" Dave asked.

"That is not likely," responded the assister. But she went on to say that, "Because of the volume of work at the Service Center, data entry operators sometimes neglect to process multiple forms in a single filing. They may have overlooked the 2553."

Dave asked whether his master file record showed the assignment of the EIN. Surprised that a citizen would ask about a "master file record," she hesitated briefly, then punched the master file into her computer.

"It does show the filing of the SS-4 (application for EIN)," she explained.

Dave again explained that the Form 2553 was physically *attached* to the SS-4. Since she earlier stated that it was unlikely that the forms would become separated, Dave asked whether he could obtain a hard copy of the SS-4 and its attachment, one of which should be the 2553. She responded by saying that she did not know of a way that this could be done. Dave replied by asking, "Is there a document locator number shown there for the SS-4?" Again somewhat surprised that a citizen would ask such a probing question, she hesitated, then checked the computer file.

"Yes, here it is," she finally stated.

Dave recorded the DLN, then asked, "Why couldn't I make a Freedom of Information Act Request for the documents reflected by this DLN? When I receive them, the Form 2553 should be present."

The IRS employee was getting an education. She responded by agreeing that it probably "would work."

As the conversation progressed, Dave expressed great concern of the prospect of the IRS penalizing him for its failure to process his Form 2553. He questioned the employee extensively regarding the procedures for solving the problem *before* the IRS began making demands for money. Sadly, the IRS assister explained that there appeared to be nothing he could do but wait for the storm to commence. To make matters worse, she even reported that it was highly unlikely the IRS, or the courts for that matter, would ever permit Dave to make his "S" election retroactively.

Dave reported all his findings to the accountant. Frustrated but determined, Dave said, "There must be something we can do. We discovered the problem before the IRS did. We must be able to fix it!"

The accountant's response was simple: "I don't even think your friend Dan Pilla can get you out of this one."

The challenge having been made, Dave and I went to work!

The first order of business was for Dave to make a record of his conversation with the IRS assisters. As closely as possible, Dave wrote down his conversation in an "I said, she said" fashion. I cautioned that the notes should be as complete and as accurate as humanly possible. The notes could be used later to establish Dave's good faith effort to resolve the situation before it became a problem. By making a contemporaneous record of the conversation, he would be able to draw from that record months, or even years later, if necessary, to document his efforts.

Dave's notes were more than thorough. By the time he was done, his conversation with the IRS was recorded on five pages of typed, single-spaced sheets. He was careful to record the "admissions" made during the conversation, such as the IRS' propensity to err in data processing, as well as other statements tending to indict the IRS. Finally, the notes were dated and signed by Dave and placed in the file.

At the same time, we made a Freedom of Information Act request for the documents reflected by the DLN given to Dave by the agency representative.[3] The FOIA request went to the Service Center where the documents were mailed. If we were lucky, we would have the documents, including the Form 2553, in our hands before the due date of the return. With a copy of the Form 2553 returned to us by the IRS itself, it would be impossible for the agency to claim it never received it.

However, it would not be luck which would decide the issue. The due date for the 1120S approached rapidly, and the IRS still had not returned the forms. Moreover, we were informed by the agency that it needed *additional* time to locate the material. Clearly, we would not have it by September 15, the filing deadline.

As the filing deadline neared, it was determined that Dave would submit the 1120S and "let nature take its course." Naturally, we realized that the "natural course" would be for the IRS to claim that no "S" election was filed, and would disallow Dave's 1120S return. If this action were to stand, it would cost thousands of dollars in increased taxes and penalties. But we stood ready for the worst.

The return was filed in a timely manner. By November of 1989, just two months later, Dave received the dreaded notice. "We are sorry," the IRS began, "but we are unable to process the Federal income tax return filed by your S corporation." The letter pointed out that no "S" election was on file, but recognized that the agency may be in error. The letter explained, "If you filed Form 2553, please send us a copy of it with all shareholder's consents. If this copy does not have an Internal Revenue Service date of receipt stamp, we will need verification that your form was filed. Your verification can be a photocopy of the letter that told you the form was accepted or a receipt of certified mailing."

Unfortunately, Dave had neither. Now came the moment of truth. Dave would have to persuade the IRS that his Form 2553 was in fact filed, or it would cost him plenty. The only hope was a detailed affidavit. In the affidavit we carefully described the manner in which the Form 2553 was mailed with Form SS-4. Copies of each form, including the transmittal cover letter, were provided. Much earlier, the IRS acknowledged receipt of the SS-4 when it assigned the EIN. A copy of that acknowledgement was attached to the affidavit as well.

Dave went on to explain in the affidavit both his conversation with the accountant in which it was discovered that the IRS mailed the incorrect forms package, and the lengthy conversation with Taxpayer Assistance personnel. Copies of the detailed contemporary notes of that conversation were attached to the affidavit. Next, Dave explained that an FOIA request was made for all documents associated with the DLN given him over the phone. A copy of the IRS' acknowledgement of that request was attached to the affidavit.

Finally, Dave pointed out in the affidavit that he filed Form 2553 in a timely fashion, and that through oversight on the part of the IRS, it was not processed. He concluded his affidavit by stating, "the Form 1120S filed on September 15, 1989, should be accepted by the IRS as filed." The affidavit was, of course, signed and notarized. The original was copied and then mailed to the IRS via certified mail—then we waited.

On January 29, 1990, just a few weeks after we mailed the affidavit and all supporting attachments, Dave heard from the Service Center. Before even opening the letter, he called me. I listened as the envelope was torn open. A pause followed, then a loud sigh, as Dave began to read, "Your election to be treated as an S-corporation with an accounting period of December is accepted. The election is effective beginning Feb. 3, 1988."

We did it! Not only did we persuade the IRS to accept the 1120S as filed, but it recognized the "S" election made on Form 2553 retroactive to February 3, 1988!

In retrospect, it is certainly true that if the Form 2553 election had been mailed to the IRS via certified mail in the first place, the elaborate production described above would not have been necessary. However, the form was not mailed in that fashion. Therefore, the only alternative, short of paying thousands in added taxes and penalties, was to prove that the form was filed. Using Dave's experience with the IRS as a guide, we can identify several steps which proved essential to success.

First, as soon as the problem was identified, Dave began calling IRS officials for guidance on how to solve it before it escalated with the filing of his corporate return. As my regular readers know, I am not a fierce proponent of seeking answers to questions from the IRS. However, as in this case, some good can come from questioning

Taxpayer Assistance personnel. For example, we were able to obtain a DLN from the assister, which we later used to our advantage.

Second, Dave made careful, contemporaneous notes of his conversation with the IRS assister. The notes were important because they provided the opportunity to record and disclose to Service Center personnel the "admissions" made regarding the IRS' propensity to err regarding the processing of documents. Furthermore, the notes would serve admirably as a means to refresh Dave's recollection of the conversation months or years later, if necessary.

Third, the FOIA request was made for the master file. While success came in this case prior to our receiving the FOIA material by return mail, such is not usually the case. Ordinarily, FOIA material can be critical to winning a battle such as this. You should also recall that we had a DLN given us by the IRS assister. Under ordinary circumstances, a DLN cannot be obtained unless the FOIA request is made and honored.

Fourth, and most important, the affidavit signed by Dave was *specific, specific, specific,* as to the steps taken by him to file the Form 2553, and it described in detail the steps taken by him to resolve the problem. He attached copies of all relevant documents, including the IRS' assignment of his EIN, and the notes of the conversation with the telephone assister. Lastly, the affidavit boldly and clearly declared that the form was filed timely, and boldly and clearly asked that the IRS determine such to be the case, thereby affording Dave the treatment to which he claimed entitlement.

When the lessons learned from this account are applied, one can prevail in any dispute where the IRS has lost or otherwise claims that you did not file a particular tax form properly or timely.

Use A Cover Letter

Affidavits should never be transmitted to the IRS as "stand alone" documents. Previously, we discussed the use of the Form 843 as a transmittal form to be used when making written demands for abatement. (See Chapter Two.) In the case of the affidavit, it is advisable to use a cover letter when mailing the affidavit to the Service Center.

The substance of the cover letter is very simple. It should explain

EXHIBIT 3-7

Your Name
Address
City, State, Zip

Date

Internal Revenue Service
Regional Service Center
Address
City, State, Zip

RE: IRS Notice Dated _____
     SSN: _____

Dear Sir:

(Note: Your cover letter must set forth your facts.)

I received your letter referenced above regarding the status of Form
2553. The letter states that you "have no record of my filing Form
2553 and electing to be treated as an S corporation for income tax
purposes." The letter goes on to state that if I provide
"verification" that the form was filed on time, the Form 1120S will be
accepted as filed.

Attached to this letter as a means of verifying the filing of the Form
2553 you will find the Affidavit of David _____. The affidavit
sets froth all the facts and circumstances surrounding the filing of
the Form 2553 and constitutes verification that the Form 2553 was
filed in a timely amnner. Based upon the facts of this case as set
forth in the affidavit, I request that the 1120S filed on behalf of
_____ company be accepted as filed and that a permanent
record be made evidencing this fact.

Any questions you have regarding this matter or the facts stated in
the attached affidavit may be directed to me at the address shown in
this letter.

Sincerely,

(Signed) David _____

that the affidavit is submitted in response to the IRS' claim, whatever that may be, and constitutes proof that you filed your form or paid your taxes, contrary to the claim of the agency. The cover letter should repeat your demand that the IRS reverse its position. Reproduced as Exhibit 3-7 is the cover letter that Dave used to convey his affidavit to the IRS. It is simple but clearly communicates the vital points.

Given the track record of affidavits in resolving disputes with the IRS, I can state unequivocally that affidavits are truly the best defense for an innocent man. Through the affidavit, clear facts are established which must be considered by the agency in making its decision in your case. In absence of controverting evidence, which will never exist when the IRS is clearly mistaken, your affidavit will indeed carry the day.

Notes To Chapter 3

1. You can call 1-800-424-FORM to obtain copies of any IRS form—even those which do not exist!

2. Please see Chapter 5, *Taxpayers' Ultimate Defense Manual*, for details on the Claim for Refund.

3. Full details of these procedures are provided for in Chapter 3, *Taxpayers' Ultimate Defense Manual*.

CHAPTER 4

Letters and Affidavits That Will Help Win Your Audit

The Basics:
The Nine Most Important Facts To Know About An Audit

Have you ever been audited? What emotions were you experiencing when you opened the envelope containing the invitation?—fear, anxiety, apprehension, out-right panic?! If you have yet to be audited, project yourself into the hot seat. Are you an astute enough citizen to avoid the rush of these sentiments? Probably not. But do not despair. Very few citizens fully understand the nature of an audit, and consequently, very few citizens can avoid at least a little fear, if not full-fledged panic.

Much of what I have written in the past is addressed to those struggling through the quagmire of the audit. Little has been written by me, and almost nothing by others, to benefit those on the outside, terrified of looking in. As I declared on radio across the country, my goal is to remove the fear and ignorance associated with the tax audit process. I firmly believe that citizens who understand the audit process and their rights, as well as the powers and limitations of the IRS, present much less exposure than those who do not. Clearly, the ignorant and fearful are taken advantage of, while the knowledgeable and strong survive.

This chapter, read in conjunction with Chapter Two of *How Anyone Can Negotiate,* will put you far and away ahead of the crowd when it comes to understanding the audit process. It will remove you from the ranks of the weak, infirm potential audit targets. If and when the letter in the brown envelope finds its way to your doorstep, you wil not melt into a puddle, but will be prepared to stand tall in the knowledge that you can win.

Fact One: Assume You're Right

Have you ever spoken with someone just notified that he will be audited? In almost 100 percent of the cases, the most significant question plaguing him is, "What did I do wrong?" The feeling is no different than when you are pulled over by a traffic cop. The first statement from your lips is, "What did I do wrong, officer?" The assumption lining this question is that you did, in fact, do something wrong. To be successful in the audit, you must dispel this notion, and you must do it now.

Tax returns are not selected for audit because the IRS found a mistake in the return. Whe the IRS claims a mistake has been made, it will send a correction notice of the variety explored in Chapter Two. The face-to-face audit process is something entirely different. The audit process is undertaken by the IRS to *verify* the correctness of your return. By selecting your return for examination, the IRS is, in effect, asking you to demonstrate that your return is accurate. It does not overtly declare that you have made an error in the return.

As explained earlier in this work, the IRS selects the majority of its examination cases through a sophisticated computer program known as the Discriminate Function System (DIF). The DIF program compares each and every entry on your return with national and regional statistical averages for persons in your same income category and profession. If any line of your return is out of synchronism with those averages, the computer flags your document as having "potential for change." It *does not* conclude, nor can it at that stage, that the return is in error. That can only be determined *after* your records are examined.

By dispelling the notion that you are selected for audit because of a mistake and you have been "caught," you place yourself into a significantly more powerful position. Those still laboring under the misconception enter the tax audit environment with the attitude that holds, "I am going to minimize my losses and get out of here." That attitude will cost you money—guaranteed! The reason is that it is almost *assured* that the tax auditor will find some error—real or *perceived*—in your return. If you believe going in that an error existed, you are much more likely to accept his opinion, one which IRS statistics show to be *incorrect* 64 percent of the time!

On the other hand, if you enter the audit theater believing that your return is correct, and you can take affirmative steps to demonstrate that, your chances of winning a "no change" ruling on your return greatly increase. For example, if you understand and believe that you have acted properly, you will likely go the extra step, or offer the extra bit of argument necessary to assure your position. These small differences are usually the margin between the winners and losers.

Fact Two: Know What You Must Know

Stated another way, never, and I do mean *never*, walk into an audit blind. As explained, the audit process is the means by which the correctness of a tax return is determined. When you are selected for audit, you are called upon to demonstrate that all or part of the declarations contained in your filing are true and correct. Believe me when I say, you will be greatly handicapped in this regard if you have *no clue* what is claimed in your return!

Every tax return has two major components, the correctness of which you are responsible to illustrate. The first is the element of income. Any audit carries with it the potential that your income will be questioned. If this occurs, you will be required to prove that your declarations of income are complete. The second, and more common component of the audit is the element of deductions. In this regard, you must show *both* that the *amount* claimed as the deduction is accurate, and that the *character* of the expense qualifies as a legitimate deduction.

Neither of these is a particularly cumbersome or difficult project. Chapter Two of *How Anyone Can Negotiate With The IRS* contains step-by-step procedures to follow to ensure that you will be able to meet the challenge. Working with your tax professional more closely in the preparation process is one way of achieving this knowledge. If you prepared the return yourself, keeping careful records and storing the records in an organized fashion can take much or all of the pain out of this aspect of the test.

In all of the hundreds of audits with which I have been involved, I can honestly state that the one problem associated with the unsuccessful cases is that the citizen lacked a fundamental understanding of what was in his return. Without such an understanding, he was wholly unable to explain the nature of certain expenses, or to verify certain others.

Do not make the mistake of falling into the trap of saying, "I have a tax professional do my return. I don't need to know that stuff." Please recognize that all the tax professional can legally do is organize your raw material into the proper format required by the IRS and tax regulations. Your tax professional cannot create deductions for you which do not exist, and he cannot fabricate explanations of deductions he entered into the return. Make no mistake about it, *you* are ultimately responsible for the declarations in the return and you are ultimately responsible to prove your statement is accurate. Moreover, this burden is *non-delegable.*

Fact Three: Take Back The Power

If I were forced to select which of these *nine important facts to know about an audit,* was *the* most important fact, I would have to say the winner is, "Take Back The Power."

There can be little doubt that the public is terrified of the tax audit process. Even beyond that, they are terrified of tax auditors. The IRS, through a carefully orchestrated process of *disinformation,* has led the public to believe, or at best, *allowed* the public to believe that the tax auditor possesses substantial powers over the citizen. The truth be told, the IRS revenue agent, he who performs the face-to-face examination, has absolutely no power over you whatsoever. He has no power to lien, levy, or seize your assets. He has no power to send you to jail, and he has no power to even alter your tax return without your consent.

Certainly there are those within the IRS who possess such power, or are in a position to make your life less comfortable, but the revenue agent is *not* such a person. The task of the revenue agent is simple. He is assigned to examine your return to determine its correctness. The unwritten rule, of course, is to collect more money. As far as the revenue agent is concerned, that cannot be done unless the examination case is closed and *you* agree to pay more money.

Your Rights AS A TAXPAYER

As a taxpayer, you have the right to be treated fairly, professionally, promptly, and courteously by Internal Revenue Service employees. Our goal at the IRS is to protect your rights so that you will have the highest confidence in the integrity, efficiency, and fairness of our tax system. To ensure that you always receive such treatment, you should know about the many rights you have at each step of the tax process.

Free Information and Help in Preparing Returns

You have the right to information and help in complying with the tax laws. In addition to the basic instructions we provide with the tax forms, we make available a great deal of other information.

Taxpayer publications. We publish over 100 free taxpayer information publications on various subjects. One of these, Publication 910, *Guide to Free Tax Services*, is a catalog of the free services and publications we offer. You can order all publications and any tax forms or instructions you need by calling us toll-free at 1-800-424-FORM (3676).

Other assistance. We provide walk-in tax help at many IRS offices and recorded telephone information on many topics through our *Tele-Tax* system. The telephone numbers for *Tele-Tax*, and the topics covered, are in certain tax forms' instructions and publications. Many of our materials are available in Braille (at regional libraries for the handicapped) and in Spanish. We provide help for the hearing impaired via special telephone equipment.

We have informational videotapes that you can borrow. In addition, you may want to attend our education programs for specific groups of taxpayers, such as farmers and those with small businesses.

In cooperation with local volunteers, we offer free help in preparing tax returns for low-income and elderly taxpayers through the Volunteer Income Tax Assistance (VITA) and Tax Counseling for the Elderly (TCE) Programs. You can get information on these programs by calling the toll-free telephone number for your area.

Copies of tax returns. If you need a copy of your tax return for an earlier year, you can get one by filling out Form 4506, *Request for Copy of Tax Form*, and paying a small fee. However, you often need only certain information, such as the amount of your reported income, the number of your exemptions, and the tax shown on the return. You can get this information free if you write or visit an IRS office or call the toll-free number for your area.

If you have trouble clearing up any tax matter with the IRS through normal channels, you can get special help from our Problem Resolution Office, as explained later.

Privacy and Confidentiality

You **have** the right to have your personal and financial information kept confidential. People who prepare your return or represent you *must* keep your information confidential.

You also have the right to know why we are asking you for information, exactly how we will use any information you give, and what might happen if you do not give the information.

Information sharing. Under the law, we can share your tax information with State tax agencies and, under strict legal guidelines, the Department of Justice and other federal agencies. We can also share it with certain foreign governments under tax treaty provisions.

Courtesy and Consideration

You **are** always entitled to courteous and considerate treatment from IRS employees. If you ever feel that you are not being treated with fairness, courtesy, and consideration by an IRS employee, you should tell the employee's supervisor.

Representation and Recordings

Throughout your dealings with us, you can represent yourself, or, generally with proper written authorization, have someone represent you in your absence. During an interview, you can have someone accompany you.

If you want to consult an attorney, a certified public accountant, an enrolled agent, or any other person permitted to represent a taxpayer during an interview for examining a tax return or collecting tax, we will stop and reschedule the interview. We cannot suspend the interview if you are there because of an administrative summons.

You can generally make an audio recording of an interview with an IRS Collection or Examination officer. You must notify us 10 days before the meeting and bring your own recording equipment. We also can record an interview. If we do so, we will notify

  Department of the Treasury
Internal Revenue Service
Publication 1 (Rev. 6-89)

you 10 days before the meeting and you can get a copy of the recording at your expense.

Payment of Only the Required Tax

You have the right to plan your business and personal finances so that you will pay the least tax that is due under the law. You are liable only for the correct amount of tax. Our purpose is to apply the law consistently and fairly to all taxpayers.

If Your Return is Questioned

We accept most taxpayers' returns as filed. If we inquire about your return or select it for examination, it does not suggest that you are dishonest. The inquiry or examination may or may not result in more tax. We may close your case without change. Or, you may receive a refund.

Examination and inquiries by mail. We handle many examinations and inquiries entirely by mail. We will send you a letter with either a request for more information or a reason why we believe a change needs to be made to your return. If you give us the requested information or provide an explanation, we may or may not agree with you and we will explain the reasons for any changes. You should not hesitate to write to us about anything you do not understand. If you cannot resolve any questions through the mail, you can request a personal interview. You can appeal through the IRS and the courts. You will find instructions with each inquiry in Publication 1383, *Correspondence Process.*

Examination by interview. If we notify you that we will conduct your examination through a personal interview, or you request such an interview,

you have the right to ask that the examination take place at a reasonable time and place that is convenient for both you and the IRS. If the time or place we suggest is not convenient, the examiner will try to work out something more suitable. However, the IRS makes the final determination of how, when, and where the examination will take place. You will receive an explanation of your rights and of the examination process either before or at the interview.

If you do not agree with the examiner's report, you may meet with the examiner's supervisor to discuss your case further.

Repeat examinations. We try to avoid repeat examinations of the same items, but this sometimes happens. If we examined your tax return for the same items in either of the 2 previous years and proposed no change to your tax liability, please contact us as soon as possible so we can see if we should discontinue the repeat examination.

Explanation of changes. If we propose any changes to your return, we will explain the reasons for the changes. It is important that you understand these reasons. You should not hesitate to ask about anything that is unclear to you.

Interest. You must pay interest on additional tax that you owe. The interest is figured from the due date of the return. But if our error caused a delay in your case, and this was grossly unfair, we may reduce the interest. Only delays caused by procedural or mechanical acts not involving the exercise of judgment or discretion qualify. If you think we caused such a delay, please discuss it with the examiner and file a claim for refund.

Business taxpayers. If you are in an individual business, the rights covered in this publication generally apply to

you. If you are a member of a partnership or a shareholder in a small business corporation, special rules may apply to the examination of your partnership or corporation items. The examination of partnership items is discussed in Publication 556, *Examination of Returns, Appeal Rights, and Claims for Refund.* The rights covered in this publication generally apply to exempt organizations and sponsors of employee plans.

An Appeal of the Examination Findings

If you don't agree with the examiner's findings, you have the right to appeal them. During the examination process, you will be given information about your appeal rights. Publication 5, *Appeal Rights and Preparation of Protests for Unagreed Cases,* explains your appeal rights in detail and tells you exactly what to do if you want to appeal.

Appeals Office. You can appeal the findings of an examination within the IRS through our Appeals Office. Most differences can be settled through this appeals system without expensive and time-consuming court trials. If the matter cannot be settled to your satisfaction in Appeals, you can take your case to court.

Appeals to the courts. Depending on whether you first pay the disputed tax, you can take your case to the U.S. Tax Court, the U.S. Claims Court, or your U.S. District Court. These courts are entirely independent of the IRS. As always, you can represent yourself or have someone admitted to practice before the court represent you.

If you disagree about whether you owe additional tax, you generally have the right to take your case to

Income Tax Appeal Procedure

At any stage
☐ You can agree and arrange to pay.
☐ You can ask for a notice of deficiency so you can file a petition with the Tax Court.
☐ You can pay the tax and file a claim for refund.

*Further appeals to the courts may be possible, except there is no appeal under the Tax Court's small tax case procedure.

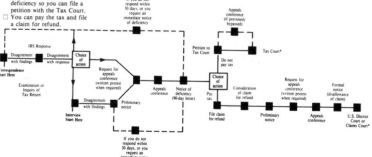

the U.S. Tax Court if you have not yet paid the tax. Ordinarily, you have 90 days from the time we mail you a formal notice (called a "notice of deficiency") telling you that you owe additional tax, to file a petition with the U.S. Tax Court. You can request simplified small tax case procedures if your case is $10,000 or less for any period or year. A case settled under these procedures cannot be appealed.

If you have already paid the disputed tax in full, you may file a claim for refund. If we disallow the claim or do not take action within 6 months, then you may take your case to the U.S. Claims Court or your U.S. District Court.

Recovering litigation expenses. If the court agrees with you on most issues in your case, and finds that our position was largely unjustified, you may be able to recover some of your administrative and litigation costs. To do this, you must have used all the administrative remedies available to you within the IRS. This includes going through our Appeals system and giving us all the information necessary to resolve the case.

Publication 556, *Examination of Returns, Appeal Rights, and Claims for Refund,* will help you more fully understand your appeal rights.

Fair Collection of Tax

Whenever you owe tax, we will send you a bill describing the tax and stating the amounts you owe in tax, interest, and penalties. Be sure to check any bill you receive to make sure it is correct. You have the right to have your bill adjusted if it is incorrect, so you should let us know about an incorrect bill right away.

If we tell you that you owe tax because of a math or clerical error on your return, you have the right to ask us to send you a formal notice (a "notice of deficiency") so that you can dispute the tax, as discussed earlier. You do not have to pay the additional tax at the same time that you ask us for the formal notice, if you ask for it within 60 days of the time we tell you of the error.

If the tax is correct, we will give you a specific period of time to pay the bill in full. If you pay the bill within the time allowed, we will not have to take any further action.

We may request that you attend an interview for the collection of tax. You will receive an explanation of your rights and of the collection process either before or at the interview.

Your rights are further protected because we are not allowed to use tax enforcement results to evaluate our employees.

Payment arrangements. You should make every effort to pay your bill in full. If you can't, you should pay as much as you can and contact us right away. We may ask you for a complete financial statement to determine how you can pay the amount due. Based on your financial condition, you may qualify for an installment agreement. We will give you copies of all agreements you make with us.

If we approve a payment agreement, the agreement will stay in effect only if:

You give correct and complete financial information,

You pay each installment on time,

You satisfy other tax liabilities on time,

You provide current financial information when asked, and

We determine that collecting the tax is not at risk.

Following a review of your current finances, we may change your payment agreement. We will notify you 30 days before any change to your payment agreement and tell you why we are making the change.

We will not take any enforcement action (such as recording a tax lien, or levying on or seizing property), until after we have tried to contact you and given you the chance to voluntarily pay any tax due. Therefore, it is very important for you to respond right away to our attempts to contact you (by mail, telephone, or personal visit). If you do not respond, we may have no choice but to begin enforcement.

Release of liens. If we have to place a lien on your property (to secure the amount of tax due), we must release the lien no later than 30 days after finding that you have paid the entire tax and certain charges, the assessment has become legally unenforceable, or we have accepted a bond to cover the tax and certain charges.

Recovery of damages. If we knowingly or negligently fail to release a lien under the circumstances described above, and you suffer economic damages because of our failure, you can recover your actual economic damages and certain costs.

If we recklessly or intentionally fail to follow the laws and regulations for the collection of tax, you can recover actual economic damage and costs.

In each of the two situations above, damages and costs will be allowed within the following limits. You must exhaust all administrative remedies available to you. The damages will be reduced by the amount which you could have reasonably prevented. You

must bring suit within 2 years of the action.

Incorrect lien. You have the right to appeal our filing of a Notice of Federal Tax Lien if you believe we filed the lien in error. If we agree, we will issue a certificate of release, including a statement that we filed the lien in error.

A lien is incorrect if:

You paid the entire amount due before we filed the lien,

We made a procedural error in a deficiency assessment, or

We assessed a tax in violation of the automatic stay provisions in a bankruptcy case.

Levy. We will generally give you 30 days notice before we levy on any property. The levy may be given to you in person, mailed to you, or left at your home or workplace. We cannot place a levy on your property on a day on which you are required to attend a collection interview.

Property that is exempt from levy. If we must seize your property, you have the legal right to keep:

Necessary clothing and schoolbooks,

A limited amount of personal belongings, furniture, and business or professional books and tools,

Unemployment and job training benefits, workers' compensation, welfare, certain disability payments, and certain pension benefits,

The income you need to pay court-ordered child support,

Mail,

An amount of weekly income equal to your standard deduction and allowable personal exemptions, divided by 52, and

Your main home, except in certain situations.

If your bank account is levied after June 30, 1989, the bank will hold your account up to the amount of the levy for 21 days. This allows you to resolve your tax bill before the bank turns over the funds to the IRS.

We generally must release a levy issued after June 30, 1989, if:

You pay the tax, penalty, and interest for which the levy was made,

The IRS determines the release will help collect the tax,

You have an approved installment agreement for the tax on the levy,

The IRS determines the levy is creating an economic hardship, or

The fair market value of the property exceeds the amount of the levy and release would not hinder the collection of tax.

If at any time during the collection process you do not agree with the collection officer, you can discuss your case with his or her supervisor.

If we seize your property, you have the right to request that it be sold within 60 days after your request. You can request a time period greater than 60 days. We will comply with your request unless it is not in the best interest of the government.

Access to your private premises. A court order is not generally needed for a collection officer to seize your property. However, you don't have to allow the employee access to your private premises, such as your home or the non-public areas of your business, if the employee does not have court authorization to be there.

Withheld taxes. If we believe that you were responsible for seeing that a corporation paid us income and social security taxes withheld from its employees, and the taxes were not paid, we may look to you to pay an amount based on the unpaid taxes. If you feel that you don't owe this, you have the right to discuss the case with the collection officer's supervisor. Also, you generally have the same IRS appeal rights as other taxpayers. Because the U.S. Tax Court has no jurisdiction in this situation, you must pay at least part of the withheld taxes and file a claim for refund in order to take the matter to the U.S. District Court or U.S. Claims Court.

The Collection Process

To stop the process at any stage, you should pay the tax in full. If you cannot pay the tax in full, contact us right away to discuss possible ways to pay the tax.

Start here

First notice and demand for unpaid tax

10 days later

Enforcement authority arises

Up to 3 more notices sent over a period of time asking for payment

Notice of intent to levy is sent by certified mail (final notice)

30 days later

Enforcement action to collect the tax begins (lien, levy, seizure, etc.)

Publications 586A, *The Collection Process (Income Tax Accounts)*, and 594, *The Collection Process (Employment Tax Accounts)*, will help you understand your rights during the collection process.

Refund of Overpaid Tax

Once you have paid all your tax, you have the right to file a claim for a refund if you think the tax is incorrect. Generally, you have 3 years from the date you filed the return or 2 years from the date you paid the tax (whichever is later) to file a claim. If we examine your claim for any reason, you have the same rights that you would have during an examination of your return.

Interest on refunds. You will receive interest on any income tax refund delayed more than 45 days after the *later* of either the date you filed your return or the date your return was due.

Checking on your refund. Normally, you will receive your refund about 6 weeks after you file your return. If you have not received your refund within 8 weeks after mailing your return, you may check on it by calling the toll-free *Tele-Tax* number in the tax forms' instructions.

If we reduce your refund because you owe a debt to another Federal agency or because you owe child support, we must notify you of this action. However, if you have a question about the debt that caused the reduction, you should contact the other agency.

Cancellation of Penalties

You have the right to ask that certain penalties (but not interest) be cancelled (abated) if you can show reasonable cause for the failure that led to the penalty (or can show that you exercised due diligence, if that is the applicable standard for that penalty).

If you relied on wrong advice you received from IRS employees on the toll-free telephone system, we will cancel certain penalties that may result. But you have to show that your reliance on the advice was reasonable.

If you relied on incorrect written advice from the IRS in response to a written request you made after January 1, 1989, we will cancel any penalties that may result. You must show that you gave sufficient and correct information and filed your return after you received the advice.

Special Help to Resolve Your Problems

We have a Problem Resolution Program for taxpayers who have been unable to resolve their problems with the IRS. If you have a tax problem that you cannot clear up through normal channels, write to the Problem Resolution Office in the district or Service Center with which you have the problem. You may also reach the Problem Resolution Office by calling the IRS taxpayer assistance number for your area.

If you suffer or are about to suffer a significant hardship because of the administration of the tax laws, you may request assistance on Form 911, *Application For Assistance Order to Relieve Hardship*. The Taxpayer Ombudsman or a Problem Resolution Officer will review your application and may issue a Taxpayer Assistance Order (TAO). You can get copies of Form 911 in IRS offices or by calling toll-free 1-800-424-FORM (3676).

Protection of Your Rights

The employees of the Internal Revenue Service will explain and protect your rights as a taxpayer at all times. If you feel that this is not the case, you should discuss the problem with the employee's supervisor. Your local Problem Resolution Officer will assist you if you are unable to resolve the problem with the supervisor.

Taxpayer Assistance Numbers

You should use the telephone number shown in the white pages of your local telephone directory under U.S. Government, Internal Revenue Service, Federal Tax Assistance. If there is not a specific number listed, call toll-free 1-800-424-1040. You can also find these phone numbers in the instructions for Form 1040.

You may also use these numbers to reach the Problem Resolution Office. Ask for the Problem Resolution Office when you call.

U.S. taxpayers abroad may write for information to:

Internal Revenue Service
Attn: IN:C:TPS
950 L'Enfant Plaza South, S.W.
Washington, D.C. 20024

You can also contact your nearest U.S. Embassy for information about what services and forms are available in your location.

That is right! You must *agree* with the auditor. If you do not, the case is moved to a higher authority within the IRS, an authority known as the Appeals Division.

Most citizens do not realize that they have an absolute right to appeal any and all decisions made by tax auditors in connection with an examination. Rather, these citizens are led or allowed to believe that when the auditor issues his findings, the matter is closed and all that remains is for the citizen to sign on the dotted line. However, you are not *required* to sign, and you cannot be *forced* to sign. Furthermore, no unholy terror will befall you should you refuse.

The one and only eventuality you can expect is for the IRS to issue its "formal notice," which you have a complete and absolute right to appeal. This right is simple and is explained in IRS Publication 1, *Your Rights as a Taxpayer.* On page two of that publication, we read, "If you don't agree with the examiner's findings, you have the right to appeal them"—period, end of discussion! Because I refer to Publication 1 extensively, I have reproduced a copy on the next four pages for your reference.

Understanding the right of appeal is critical to success in the audit. The reason is this: The IRS declares that 87 percent of all returns audited are incorrect. Of those determined to be incorrect, just 11 percent appeal their case. However, of those who do appeal, in excess of *60 percent* win their case! That tells me that the vast majority of persons experiencing an audit pay taxes *they do not owe,* and they pay these taxes because they are ignorant of their right to appeal. The process is discussed in IRS Publication 5, *Appeal Rights.* Please see Exhibit 4-1.

I have described the examination and appeals processes in this manner: The tax auditor is responsible to *create* problems, while the appeals officer is responsible to *solve* problems. Now you tell me, which would you rather do business with?

Fact Four: Know Who You Are Dealing With

Some months ago, I was speaking with a man who mentioned that he was contacted by the IRS regarding certain items in his return. I began the conversation by asking what the IRS' letter said. "There was no letter," he responded.

"What do you mean, there was no letter?" I countered.

"I didn't receive a letter. She called me on the phone."

EXHIBIT 4-1

Appeal Rights and Preparation of Protests for Unagreed Cases

Department
of the
Treasury
**Internal
Revenue
Service**

**Publication 5
(Rev. 3-86)**

If You Agree

If you agree with the examiner's findings in the enclosed examination report, please sign the agreement form and return it with our transmittal letter. By signing, you are agreeing to the amounts shown on the form.

If the agreement shows you owe additional tax you may pay it without waiting for a bill. Include interest on the additional tax and on any penalties at the applicable rate from the due date of the return to the date of payment. Figure the interest as shown in the enclosed Notice 433, Yearly Interest and Certain Penalty Rates.

If you do not pay the additional tax when you sign the agreement, you will receive a bill for the additional tax. Interest is charged on the additional tax from the due date of your return to the billing date. However, you will not be billed for more than 30 days interest from the date you sign the agreement. No further interest or penalties will be charged if you pay the amount you owe within 10 days after the billing date.

Please make your check or money order payable to the Internal Revenue Service and include on the check or money order your social security number or employer identification number, the tax form number, and the tax period for which payment is being made. Do not send cash through the mail.

If the examination report shows a refund is due you, you should sign and return the agreement form promptly so the Service can send your refund sooner. You will receive interest on the refund.

If You Don't Agree

If you decide not to agree with the examiner's findings, you have the option of requesting a meeting with the examiner's supervisor to discuss the findings. If you still do not agree, we urge you to appeal your case with the Service. Most differences can be settled in these appeals without expensive and time-consuming court trials. (Appeals conferences are not available to taxpayers whose reasons for disagreement do not come within the scope of the internal revenue laws. For example, disagreement based solely on moral, religious, political, constitutional, conscientious, or similar grounds.)

If you do not want to appeal your case in the Service, however, you can take it to court.

The following general rules tell you how to appeal your case.

Appeal Within The Service

Appeals within the Service are handled by the Office of Regional Director of Appeals. If you decide to appeal, address your request for a conference to your District Director in accordance with our letter to you enclosing these instructions. Your District Director will forward your request to the Appeals Office, which will arrange for a conference at a convenient time and place. However, a consolidated Appeals conference may be held for all producers in certain windfall profit tax cases. See the heading for procedures on these cases if you are appealing a windfall profit tax issue.

If agreement is not reached with Appeals, you may, at any stage of these procedures, take your case to court. See the back of this publication concerning Appeals to the courts.

Written Protests

Along with your request for a conference you may need to file a written protest with the District Director. You don't have to file a written protest if:

- The proposed increase or decrease in tax, or claimed refund, does not exceed $2,500 for any of the tax periods involved; or
- Your examination was conducted by correspondence or in an IRS office by a tax auditor.

If a written protest is required, you should send it within the period granted in the letter transmitting the report of examination and include in it:

1. A statement that you want to appeal the findings of the examiner to the Appeals Office;

2. Your name and address;
3. The date and symbols from the letter transmitting the proposed adjustments and findings you are protesting;
4. The tax periods or years involved;
5. An itemized schedule of the adjustments with which you do not agree;
6. A statement of facts supporting your position in any contested factual issue; and
7. A statement outlining the law or other authority on which you rely.

The statement of facts, under 6 above, must be declared true under penalties of perjury. You may do this by adding to the protest the following signed declaration:

"Under penalties of perjury, I declare that the facts presented in my written protest, which are set out in the accompanying statement of facts, schedules, and other attached statements, are to the best of my knowledge and belief, true, correct, and complete." If your representative sends us the protest for you, he or she may substitute a declaration stating:

- That he or she prepared the protest and accompanying documents; and
- Whether he or she knows personally that the protest and accompanying documents are true and correct.

Representation

You may represent yourself before Appeals, or you may be represented by an attorney, certified public accountant, or an individual enrolled to practice before the Internal Revenue Service. Your representative must be qualified to practice before the Internal Revenue Service. If your representative appears without you, he or she must file a power of attorney or a tax information authorization before receiving or inspecting confidential information. Form 2848, Power of Attorney and Declaration of Representative, or Form 2848-D, Tax Information Authorization and Declaration of Representative (or any other properly written power of attorney or authorization) may be used for this purpose. You can get copies of these forms from an Internal Revenue Service office.

EXHIBIT 4-1 (continued)

You may also bring witnesses to support your position.

Procedures for Crude Oil Windfall Profit Tax Cases

The Statement of Procedural Rules allows the Service to provide a single consolidated Appeals conference to address all oil items arising in connection with a property or lease whenever the Service determines that a consolidated procedure is necessary for effective administration of the windfall profit tax law. Generally, oil items are items taken into account in computing the windfall profit tax that can be more readily determined at the property or lease level such as:

- The tier or tiers of the crude oil;
- The quantity of crude oil in each tier;
- The adjusted base price and removal price; and
- The severance tax.

All producers having an interest in the property or lease will be permitted to participate in this conference if a written request to attend is made within 60 days of the mailing of the letter proposing the adjustment. If a written protest is required, it should also be sent within the 60-day period. If you do not agree with the adjustments but decide not to attend the conference, and the issue is appealed by the other owners, your case will be held in suspense until the final administrative determination is made.

The determination by the Appeals Office is the final administrative determination with respect to all oil items arising in connection with the property or lease for the period under examination.

These procedures do not affect the producers' administrative appeal rights with respect to producer items, that is, items more readily determined at the producer level such as exemptions and independent producer status. All unagreed producers are still entitled to a separate Appeals conference to resolve producer item issues. A separate notification of appeal rights relating to producer items will generally be issued following the final administrative determination of the oil items.

Any person who receives a 60-day letter with respect to oil of which another person is the producer and who is not autho-

rized to act on behalf of or represent that other person shall, within 10 days of the receipt of the 60-day letter, furnish to that other person a copy of the 60-day letter, including the proposed adjustments. Any person forwarding a 60-day letter shall notify the Service of the name, taxpayer identification number, mailing address, type of interest owned, and ownership percentage of the person to whom the letter is forwarded. This information shall be furnished to the Service at the return address shown on the 60-day letter.

Appeals To The Courts

If you and the Service disagree after your conference or if you skipped our appeals system, you may take your case to the United States Tax Court, the Unites States Claims Court, or your United States District Court. (However, if you are a nonresident alien taxpayer, you cannot take your case to a United States District Court.) These courts are independent judicial bodies and have no connection with the Internal Revenue Service.

Tax Court

If your case involves a disagreement over whether you owe additional income tax, estate or gift tax, or certain excise taxes, you may go to the United States Tax Court. To do this, ask the Service to issue a formal letter, called a notice of deficiency. You have 90 days from the date this notice is mailed to you to file a petition with the Tax Court (150 days if addressed to you outside the United States). If you do not file the petition within the 90-day period (or 150 days as the case may be), the law requires that we assess and bill you for the deficiency.

If you discuss your case with the Internal Revenue Service during the 90-day period (150-day period), the discussion will not extend the period in which you may file a petition with the Tax Court.

The Court will schedule your case for trial at a location convenient to you. You may represent yourself before the Tax Court, or you may be represented by anyone permitted to practice before that Court.

If you dispute not more than $10,000 for any one tax year, there are simplified procedures. You can get information about

these procedures and other matters relating to the Court from the Clerk of the Tax Court, 400 Second St. N.W., Washington, D.C. 20217.

District Court and Claims Court

You may take your case to your United States District Court or to the United States Claims Court. Certain types of cases, such as those involving manufacturers' excise taxes, can be heard only by these courts. Generally, your District Court and the Claims Court hear tax cases only after you have paid the tax and have filed a claim for refund. You can get information about procedures for filing suit in either court by contacting the Clerk of your District Court; or the Clerk of the Claims Court. If we haven't acted on your claim within 6 months from the date you filed it, you can then file suit for refund. If we have disallowed your claim, a suit for refund must be filed no later than 2 years from the date of our disallowance.

Litigating Expenses

If certain conditions are met, you may be entitled to recover from the Government reasonable litigation expenses incurred. These include, for example, court costs, expert witness fees, cost of engineering reports, and attorneys' fees. To recover these expenses, you must:

1. Substantially prevail in your case with respect to the amount or issues;
2. Show that the Government's position was unreasonable; and
3. Exhaust your administrative remedies with the IRS.

These provisions apply to civil litigation in a court of the United States, including the Tax Court. Expenses incurred solely for administrative appeal purposes within the IRS are not recoverable from the Government.

Penalty

Whenever it appears to the Tax Court that proceedings before it have been instituted or maintained by you primarily for delay or that your position in such proceedings is frivolous or groundless, damages in an amount not in excess of $5,000 shall be awarded to the United States by the Tax Court in its decision.

✰U.S. GOVERNMENT PRINTING OFFICE: 1988 202-004/81510

"The IRS agent called you on the phone?" I asked, puzzled.

"Yes," he said, "she called and asked for social security numbers for my wife and children, and some other documents."

"What did you tell her?" I queried.

"I didn't know what to say," he confessed. "I just told her I'd get back to her."

"Does she expect you to just mail this material to her?" I asked.

"Yes," he replied. "She gave me an address—a post office box to send it to."

"Listen," I said, "you can't be mailing that kind of material to a post office box, based on just a phone call."

"She said she was from the IRS," he explained.

After hearing this, I asked, "How do you know who that person is? Even if she is from the IRS, you have no idea what her problem is and no way of knowing what she intends to do with the material."

His response was, "But she said she was from the IRS."

I countered his point with a question. "Who are you talking to right now?"

"I'm talking to Dan Pilla," he quickly answered.

"We've never met," I pointed out. "You've never seen me before. You couldn't pick me out of a crowd of two, could you? You have no way of knowing whether I'm Dan Pilla or not, do you?"

Laughing, he responded. "You're right. I see your point, but what should I do?"

"Send a letter to the address she gave you. In the letter, explain that it is not your practice to respond to requests for personal information over the phone. Ask the lady to submit her request to you in writing, and you will respond in a timely fashion."

There is nothing unreasonable about seeking some measure of protection, security and privacy in your dealings with the IRS. Believe it or not, it is fairly common for the IRS, particularly the Examination Division, to solicit information over the phone. My recommendation has always been that one should never provide any information as sensitive as tax data over the phone or in response to a phone call. Even if it is safe to assume that the caller is indeed an employee of the IRS (which is *not* a valid assumption), you are entitled to a notice in writing of the nature of the inquiry.

One should never provide information without the benefit of such a notice. At the very least, the notice should give basic information regarding the nature of the claim, the year in question and the intended use of the information. This will enable you to determine your requirement to provide the material and otherwise formulate an accurate and correct response.

Fact Five: Pin Down The Issue

The first cousin to the IRS telephone contact is the audit letter which is vague and general in its request for an examination and records. Generally speaking, the IRS' audit notice is specific as to the matters at issue, and is specific as to the nature of records requested in the audit.

When the IRS does mail an audit letter which, like the verbal contact, is vague, overly broad and non-committal as to the issues, my recommendation is that you respond in writing with a request for specificity. IRS Publication 1, *Your Rights as a Taxpayer,* declares that:

"You also have the right to know *why* we are asking you for information, exactly *how* we will use any information you give, and what might happen if you do not give the information."

Publication 1, page 1 (emphasis added).

When the IRS notifies you of an audit with an unspecific letter, I have used the letter shown in Exhibit 4-2 as a means to pin down the issue. I believe this kind of letter is critical if you are contacted with vague requests by the IRS. When the request is vague, it is the practice of tax examiners to manipulate the situation in a direction which best serves the interests of the IRS. On the other hand, when you have a clear statement as to the issues in question, you are in a position to ensure that the examination does not stray from the course initially set. This can be important.

The next point we shall discuss involves Jan, who, through certain statements and maneuvers prevented herself from being forced into a premature audit. But Jan was also able to greatly reduce the burden placed on her by the IRS' initial request. When presented with the demand to "appear for an audit," Jan responded by writing a letter similar in substance to the one shown in Exhibit 4-2. When the examiner responded with details, she learned that the IRS intended to examine returns for the years 1984, 1985 and 1986. She received her letter in December of 1988.

Immediately, by pinning the IRS down on the issues, Jan was able to reduce the burden of her audit by one-third. The reason is this. The IRS has just three years from the date a return is filed in which

EXHIBIT 4-2

Your Name
Address
City, State, Zip

Date:
SSN:

Dear Sir:

On (date) I was contacted via telephone by a person claiming to be a representative of the Internal Revenue Service. That person asked me to provide certain information and data regarding my personal affairs. However, I should make it clear that I received no written notice from the IRS regarding this matter. I am reluctant to provide sensitive information to any person based merely on a phone call.

IRS Publication 1, Your Rights as a Taxpayer, acknowledges my right to privacy and states that I have the right "to know why we are asking you for information, exactly how (the IRS) will use any information (I) give, and what might happen if (I) do not give the information." Pub. 1, page 1.

In light of the fact that the request for information in my case was made via telephone, I have no way of knowing any of the information which Publication 1 states I am entitled to know. Therefore, I request that the IRS provide me with a detailed statement of the purpose of your request, why the information is requested, the use to which it will be put, and whether I must comply with the request. I also ask that you explain what may happen if I refuse to provide the requested data.

I would like you to provide a detailed statement of the issues, if any, which are in question on my return. You should also explain which year or years are in question. If your request for information does not involve my tax return, please state specifically the purpose of the request.

Please provide this information at your earliest convenience.

Thank you.

Your Signature

to conduct a civil examination of that return.[1] The filing date of Jan's 1984 return was April 15, 1985. She was notified by the IRS of its desire to audit that return in December of 1988. However, the three-year statute of limitations covering 1984 *expires* on April 15, 1988! Thus, the IRS was late and had no lawful authority to examine her 1984 return. When she informed the agent of this fact, he promptly dropped 1984 from consideration. Jan was left to contend with just two years.

Fact Six: Don't Be Pushed Around

A common reason why the IRS' "success" rate in audits is so high is simple. Many people allow themselves to be forced into an audit for which they are either ill-prepared, or wholly unprepared. Without the necessary understanding of your return and the records upon which it is based, one cannot hope to meet with full success in the audit encounter. Worse is the situation where you lack records, either because they were lost or because you have not been able to spend adequate time to find and organize them.

When you are unable to fully prepare for an audit, do not allow yourself to be forced into a meeting with the IRS. It is essential to financial health that you postpone your examination until such time as you are fully prepared. You may ask, "How can *I* tell the *IRS* when *its* audit will take place? Won't they tell *me* when I must be there?" Certainly the IRS will flex its administrative muscle and "order" you to appear at a given place and time, usually a time which does not allow ample opportunity to prepare. However, they do not possess the authority to *enforce* this directive.

Earlier I stated that you must "take back the power." I explained that revenue agents lack the authority to alter your tax return without your consent, and that you have the absolute right to appeal *any* decision of a tax examiner. This axiom applies equally to the decision of the examiner to hold an audit at a time which is inconvenient for you. First of all, let us consider the language from IRS Publication 1, *Your Rights as a Taxpayer.* On page two, the document declares:

"If we notify you that we will conduct your examination through a personal interview, or you request such an interview, you have the right to ask that the examination take place at a reasonable time and place that is convenient for both you and the IRS. If the time or place we suggest is not convenient, the examiner will try to work out something more suitable. However, the IRS makes the final determination of how, when, and where the examination will take place."

As a general principle, you cannot be forced into an audit for which you are ill-prepared by reason of prior commitments of your time. Still, a common power-play by the IRS is to *demand*, under vague and ambiguous threats, that you appear at a given time and place.

Jan recently encountered this very problem. Her audit was set for the latter part of April, 1989. After receiving the notice, she immediately wrote the revenue agent, explaining that she would not be availabe until the end of June. Demands upon her time in connection with her job made even the most common of daily tasks impossible. There would be no way she could take sufficient time to prepare for a tax audit.

To Jan's shock and surprise, however, (and in violation of the Taxpayers' Bill of Rights Act and the language of Publication 1), the agent responded to her letter by explaining that her request for additional time had been *denied*. She would have to go through with the examination of her return as scheduled, "or else."

By now, you should understand the implication of the statement "or else." It means if you do not agree, *appeal!* Knowing this, Jan stuck to her guns. She continued to assert that an April appearance would be impossible. If the IRS agent were indeed interested in examining her return and obtaining accurate information, he would simply have to wait. The next communication Jan received from the IRS was very disheartening. The agent mailed the so-called 30-day letter, Report Explaining Changes to Tax Return. The report indicated that the two specific deductions in question on Jan's return had been completely *disallowed*. She had not even been given the opportunity to present her records to the auditor because she continued to insist on changing the date of the audit.

As I have explained many times before, the 30-day letter is not final on the issue of your tax liability. It only reflects the Examination Division's attitude on the question. In this case, the attitude clearly was, "Do it my way or don't do it at all." Unfortunately for the Examination Division, however, their attitude is irrelevant! In response to the 30-day letter, Jan wrote a letter of protest as described in IRS Publication 5 (see Exhibit 4-1). The letter which Jan wrote demanding an Appeals Conference is shown in Exhibit 4-3.

EXHIBIT 4-3

Jan _____
Address
City, State, Zip

Date:
SSN:

Dear Sir:

Reference is made to the 30-day notice and examination report which
were mailed to me on (date). The letter states that if I do not agree
with the proposed changes set out in the report, I should so state in
writing.

Please be advised that I do not agree with the findings and
recommendations in regard to the tax liability in question. The
reason is that my deductions were arbitrarily disallowed without
giving me the opportunity to prove their correctness.

I have been in contact with the revenue agent assigned to this case.
I attempted to make arrangements to postpone the date of our original
meeting. Due to several factors out of my control, including being in
the middle of an extremely busy period at work, I was unable to go
forward with the meeting at the time originally scheduled. Pursuant
to my right to have the audit conducted at a convenient time (see
Publication 1, page page 2), I requested that the conference be
rescheduled. However, this request was denied and the 30-day letter
mentioned above was issued.

I am in possession of the records and testimony which are necessary to
prove my entitlement to the various deductions I claimed.
Disallowance of those deductions without consideration of my proof is
arbitrary and a denial of due process. For these reasons, I request a
reconsideration of the examination report, or in the alternative, an
Appeals Conference.

Sincerely,

Jan _____

Jan mailed the letter and awaited notification from the IRS that an appeals conference was scheduled. But events took another interesting turn. Rather than receive a letter from the Appeals Division regarding the conference, she received a phone call from the revenue agent who issued the initial report. His news seemed, on its face, to be negative. The agent informed Jan that she "did not have a right to an appeals conference in this case."

"What can you possibly mean by that?" she asked. "My deductions have been disallowed and I don't agree with your report."

"Well," responded the agent, "you never met with me to discuss the issues. Therefore, you can't appeal."

Boldly, Jan responded, "Of course I never met with you. You refused to honor my request for a postponement. I told you I could not meet with you until June. You didn't seem to think that was important. It wasn't *my* fault we didn't meet."

"Nevertheless," the agent continued, "the case has been returned to me by the Appeals Division. They will not consider the matter until after you have discussed all of the issues with me."

"I was willing to do that in the first place," barked Jan. "I just can't do it before the end of June."

"I have rescheduled the audit conference," explained the agent in a stern voice. "I hve determined that the best time for this examination is (get this!) the *end of June*. I will expect you to be present at that time."

Laughing, Jan agreed and hung up the phone.

In case you might have missed the point, what the agent in effect told Jan is, "You can't fire me! I quit!"

What the agent did not bother to explain to Jan, but what is painfully obvious from the context of the conversation, is that the Appeals Division returned the case to the agent for further development because *he failed to do his job!* It is not the function of the Appeals Division to *audit* tax returns. Why should an Appeals Officer be forced to assume the responsibility of another division of the IRS, simply because one agent refused to act reasonably with a citizen?

In the final analysis, Jan's desire to postpone the examination to a time convenient to her was honored, as it had to be. It is worth noting, however, that her request was honored *only* because she stood her ground and refused to be pushed into a compromising situation. You should also note, that in the vast majority of cases, you will not be required to go to the lengths Jan did in order to preserve your rights. All that will be required of you is a simple letter to the IRS agent explaining that you are unable to appear at the time and date suggested for given reasons. You should suggest alternative times and dates more convenient. I find it helpful if you politely refer to the language of Publication 1 in making your request. In this way, you will ensure that you are never pushed into a premature meeting with the IRS that certainly could cost you money.

Fact Seven:
If You're Not Comfortable, Stay Away

Are you good under pressure? Do you talk too much? Or do you have a propensity to freeze up or babble when presented with questions and demands by an authority figure? Certainly, many people fall apart at the seams when confronted by any authority figure, and most assuredly, the IRS. When I suggest that one has the ability to deal with the IRS without the need of an expensive attorney or accountant, the typical response is, "There is no way I can confront those sharks and win. They will trap me and that will be the end of it."

Without a doubt, a large segment of the IRS' audit habits and techniques revolve around asking questions and seeking information designed to "trap" the citizen. By this I mean that the agent knows in advance the purpose of a particular line of questioning he may pursue while at an audit, but will not as a general matter, reveal his purpose to the poor citizen. Instead, he will merely ask the questions and demand answers without providing answers of his own. Not only is this practice unfair, but it has the effect of rattling an ignorant citizen. If you fall into this category of one who is easily rattled or intimidated, or afraid that you will "talk too much," staying out of danger is simple. Merely *stay away* from the audit!

I am not suggesting that you refuse to be audited. On the contrary, as I declared earlier, you have the obligation to prove that the disclosure of income and deductions in your return are true and correct. I am suggesting, however, that there is an alternative to your physical presence at the audit. In either case, you will have complied with your requirement to prove the correctness of your return *without* subjecting yourself to a painful and intimidating confrontation with the tax authorities.

Larry was a person of the kind I have described here. He was naturally nervous at the very thought of dealing with the IRS and the last thing he wanted to do was face an auditor, even if he did not have to take time off work. Consequently, when he received his audit notice for 1986, he was adamant that he did not want to personally appear. Under these circumstances, Larry merely demanded that his examination be handled via correspondence. The so-called "correspondence examination" is very common, and the IRS routinely uses this process to verify returns. The following statement appears in Publication 1, *Your Rights as a Taxpayer*, on page 2:

> "We handle many examinations and inquiries by mail. We will send you a letter with either a request for more information or a reason why we believe a change needs to be made to your return. If you give us the requested information or provide an explanation, we may or may not agree with you and we will explain the reasons for any changes. You should not hesitate to write to us about anything you do not understand. If you cannot resolve any questions through the mail, you can request a personal interview."

This language indicates, though not as plainly as I might have written it, that your audit may be handled *purely* through the mail. Larry's letter pointed out that he did not wish to appear personally before the agent. He further explained that he would answer all questions presented in wrting and would provide copies, with written explanations of all documents and receipts necessary to verify the correctness of his return. An example of Larry's letter is shown in Exhibit 4-4.

As the audit progressed, Larry was called upon to present copies of bank statements, cancelled checks and other data relevant to the examination. Each time this occurred, he responded in writing by submitting the applicable material with any needed explanations. When all was said and done, Larry's audit was completed over a period of nearly one year, but in that entire time, Larry never set foot in an IRS office. He never laid eyes on any tax examiner, and never lost one hour of work. Most importantly, Larry never placed himself in a situation or environment where his own fear and ignorance would come back to haunt him.

EXHIBIT 4-4

Larry _____
Address
City, State, Zip

Date:
SSN:

Dear Sir:

On (date) I received notice from you that my return for (year) is now
under audit. The notice indicated that the following deductions (list
them) are under examination. Lastly, your letter asks that I appear
on (date) to discuss these issues.

Please be advised that it is my desire and intent to fully cooperate
to resolve each of your questions. I am in possession of records and
testimony which will demonstrate that my return is true and correct in
all respects. I stand prepared to present that evidence in order to
resolve this matter. I am aware of my responsibility to present
adequate proof of my deductions and income.

However, I am also aware, as explained in IRS Publication 1, that many
tax examinations are conducted via correspondence. For various
reasons, not the least of which is a grueling work schedule which will
not permit any time off (or list all other appropriate reasons), I
will not be able to meet with you face-to-face. Nevertheless, I stand
ready and willing to provide any and all necessary information and
will answer any and all relevant questions regarding the same, through
the mail.

Pursuant to your request of (date) I am enclosing true and correct
copies of all records which pertain to the following items (list items
of income or deductions flagged by IRS). The records consist of
(provide explanation for each document, including issue to which it
relates).

If you have any questions regarding these matters, please write me at
the above address. I will provide prompt responses by return mail.

Sincerely,

Larry _____

Fact Eight: Stop The Steamroller

One of the most troubling phenomenon I have experienced with average citizens dealing with the IRS is the apparent lack of willingness, or knowledge of the ability to say "Stop" to the IRS. By this, I am referring to the situation where, in the course of an examination, the IRS raises an issue for which there is no current answer. But rather than inform the agent that additional time is needed to obtain further information and provide answers, the citizen is content to allow the agent to make an adjustment disallowing the expense or item. Naturally, this has effects adverse to the citizen's pocketbook.

The tendency of the IRS is to complete an examination in the first interview. The obvious reason for the expedited treatment of your case is that the sooner the IRS completes your examination, the sooner it can accommodate those patiently awaiting their opportunity for fun and frivolity. Unfortunately, a *fast* examination is not always an *accurate* examination, particularly when the citizen has not fully prepared himself for the affair. In this situation, when presented with demands or questions for which there are no apparent answers *at the moment,* one *must not* be shy about his right to suspend the interview to avail yourself of the opportunity to obtain the information, or find an answer.

I was once involved in an audit with a woman who was asked to provide evidence of the purchase prices of several stocks she owned, then sold during the year in question. The IRS was attempting to determine whether she reported the correct profit from the sale of her stock. In order to do this properly, we were asked to provide proof of the purchase price, or basis, in the stock, so that the difference between the purchase and sale prices could accurately be computed.

The proof we offered was the woman's ledger used to record the purchase price and sale price and dates of all her holdings. Unfortunately, the agent was not impressed with the woman's record-keeping. He wanted to see copies of the confirmation slips, or statements issued by the brokerage firm each time a buy or sell order was executed. The confirmation slips would contain the date, purchase or sale price of the stock, the number of shares involved and the total amount of the trade. Without the confirmation slips, he would "adjust" the profit claimed on the stock sales.

We explained that the confirmation slips were not saved. The only record possessed by the woman was the contemporaneous ledger she created for the purpose of memorializing these very facts. The agent responded that in light of the fact that no confirmation slips existed, he would disallow the claimed basis in the stock, asserting that the sale price of the stock represented *100 percent profit*. "That assumes she obtained the stocks for free," I argued. "You know that didn't happen."

"That may be true," he badgered, "but you have the burden to prove your basis and I don't accept this ledger." He then indicated that he would make the adjustment.

At that stage of the proceedings, I indicated that we wanted the examination suspended until such time as the confirmation slips could be produced. "You said you didn't have them. What would be the use of suspending the audit?" he countered. "I intend to make the adjustment."

"The purpose of this audit," I countered, "is to determine the correctness of this woman's income tax return. Clearly, we cannot determine its correctness by merely drawing the assumption that she obtained expensive stocks free of charge. Obviously that is ridiculous, and that did not happen. In the interest of fairness, we must be provided an opportunity to present adequate proof on this point." While the agent did see it my way in the wake of this speech, what he did not know is that absent his consent, we intended to suspend the audit *unilaterally*. I have declared many times that tax examiners lack the authority to alter your return without your consent. You saw what happened in Jan's case when the examiner attempted to play hard ball. These facts place the power firmly in our hands. We must use it to ensure that the outcome of the audit is fair and just, and not based upon the arbitrary whim of a self-styled authority. In short, take back the power!

With the audit in a suspended state, we took time to gather the needed information, both from the library and through the brokerage house itself. Without much effort, we were ready to head back downtown to face the monster. This time, the audit was indeed concluded, but on our terms, not those of the auditor. He did accept our proof and the result was a "no change" audit as to the stock transactions. If we did not "stop the steamroller" when the agent made it clear that he intended to disallow the claimed basis in the stocks, my client would have been presented with a bill for tens of thousands of dollars in additional taxes, penalties and interest.

Fact Nine: Prevent Audit Abuse

Since my first book, *The Naked Truth,* was released in October of 1986, I have been a guest of something in the neighborhood of 500 radio and television talk shows. During these numerous broadcasts, I have spoken with Americans across the country concerning their problems with the IRS. It is not uncommon, during these shows, that we find ourselves discussing these nine "most important" things to know about an audit. Of the nine points and techniques discussed, the one which *usually* generates the most surprise is this one. The reason is because it is so simple to prevent audit abuse through the technique I am about to describe, yet each time I suggest it, I am presented with this response: "I didn't know I could do that."

What is my "trade secret" for preventing audit abuse and keeping the IRS tiger firmly under control? Simple...tape record the audit. That is right. Bring a cassette tape recorder to the audit and record the festivities! In response to your question, "I didn't know I could do that," let me again draw from IRS Publication 1, *Your Rights as a Taxpayer.* At page 1, the document reads:

"You can generally make an audio recording of an interview with an IRS Collection or Examination officer. You must notify us 10 days before the meeting and bring your own recording equipment. We also can record an interview. If we do so, we will notify you 10 days before the meeting and you can get a copy of the record at your expense."

What could be a simpler way of both keeping in line the IRS agent with whom you are paired, as well as making a permanent, accurate record of what transpires during the interview. Believe me when I say that the agent will be much less inclined to deliberately and overtly intimidate you, or to deceive or mislead you, if your recorder is running!

As early as the writing of *The Naked Truth,* I spoke of the right to tape record an audit. However, the IRS was generally reluctant to allow this during those years. Since then, Congress ratified the Taxpayers' Bill of Rights Act, and its provision that citizens be permitted to tape record an audit at their own expense. Thus, we have a firm right, expressed by the IRS' own literature, to ensure that your rights are protected and to obtain a true record of the proceedings.

Publication 1 speaks of notifying the IRS "10 days before the meeting" of your intention to record the audit. The notice to the IRS must be in writing. Exhibit 4-5 is an example of a simple letter informing the IRS that you will tape record the audit. By taking this step, you cannot be deprived of your right to record the audit. Moreover, by doing so, you can believe that your audit will be substantially devoid of abusive remarks and behavior on the part of the examiner.

EXHIBIT 4-5

```
Your Name
Address
City, State, Zip

Date:
SSN:

Dear Sir:

On (date) I received notice from you that my return for (year) is now
under audit. According to my right as explained in IRS Publication 1,
I wish to record the examination which will take place on (date). I
will bring my own recording equipment. Please note that this request
is made within the time period required.

Thank you.


Your Signature
```

Using affidavits to win your audit

Chapter Three was dedicated to demonstrating the value of affidavits in proving that certain steps were taken by you when questioned by the IRS. I pointed out that affidavits are sworn statements, which, when presented to the IRS, must be accepted as true in the absence of controverting evidence. Not only are affidavits valuable tools in proving that your return was filed, or your taxes were paid properly, they can be equally beneficial in solving audit disputes. In fact, in some situations, affidavits can be the *difference* between the allowance or disallowance of a deduction claimed in your return.

Throughout this chapter, I have been referring to Publication 1 to support certain of my statements, observations and declarations. By now, you should know that Publication 1 is the IRS' statement as to what your rights are as a "taxpayer." While I have drawn upon certain remarks made within Publication 1, I in no way acknowledge the publicatoin as a *complete* statement of your rights. As I have already declared in the previous chapter, I believe Publication 1 to be deficient in several important ways.

My largest complaint levied at the examination process is that agents of the Examinaton Division have no clear guidelines as to what constitutes adequate proof of a deduction, and what does not. Consequently, the audit process is riddled with broad variances in the way in which certain individuals verify the correctness of their returns. In one case, an agent will accept a cancelled check as adequate proof of a deduction, while another agent will demand *both* a cancelled check *and* an invoice to support the same claim. This disparity in handling such critical and basic points of concern no doubt contributes greatly to the high rate of incorrectness found by the IRS in individual income tax returns. It seems all an agent need do to disallow a deduction is demand more and more proof until at some point, the paper trail ends. When it does, he merely lowers the boom on your deduction. The result, your return is added to the list of those found wanting, and you are billed accordingly.

One of my concerns with Publication 1 is that the important subject of your burden of proof and the manner in which you may legitimately prove the claims made on your return is not afforded *one word* in the four-page diatribe. I think you will agree that any document professing to be a statement of your "rights" should contain at least some basic data in this regard. Because of the deficiency in information on this topic, I spent much time and effort in *How Anyone Can Negotiate* to fill the gap. Chapter Two of that book, entitled, "10 Ways to Prove Deductions and Verify Income" lists the ways in which one can accomplish the sometimes clumsy task of proving his return is correct.

Among the ways to "prove your deductions," we discuss the use of your own testimony, or sworn word. While the IRS will never tell you this, it is not necessary that you provide a slip of paper of one kind or another in order to establish your entitlement of a deduction. The law requires only that you *prove* that you expended the amount of money claimed as a deduction, and that the deduction is permissable under the law. Proving these facts does not always involve the production of a slip of paper.

In the past, affidavits have been most useful in carrying your burden to prove not only your entitlement to certain deductions, but in verifying the correctness of the income claimed on your return as well. This is a critical area, because nowhere else in the tax law do we find a less defined, less structured area, thus giving rise to the potential for the most IRS abuse.

Affidavits which verify income

Paul was a commissioned salesman. He received checks once per month from a store for which he had sold merchandise. In 1988, his 1986 tax return came under scrutiny by the IRS. Among the many questions with which Paul was presented, one of the more troubling was, "How did you live on just $18,300 per year?" Paul's answer was simple: "I couldn't," he said. "That's why I got another job."

But the IRS examiner was not satisfied. She wanted Paul to prove that he earned no more than the $18,300 claimed in the return. "Please provide copies of your bank statements," she asked, intending to compare bank deposit with income claimed. When the bank deposits are higher than the declared income, the IRS assumes the difference is unreported income and adjusts the return accordingly.

"I didn't have a bank account," Paul answered, "I cashed my checks each month and used cash." Before the audit was complete, the agent arbitrarily tacked an additional $3,900 of income to Paul's return, claming that he "must have" earned that much additional income in order to live. In order to defeat the agent's claim that Paul earned unreported income in this amount, we used an affidavit. An example of Paul's affidavit is shown in Exhibit 4-6.

Paul's affidavit was presented to the auditor and it declared that the income shown on the return was all the income earned by Paul during 1986. This statement was presented with a matching declaration from the president of the company for whom Paul worked. Between the two statements, the IRS agent was wholly without authority to increase the amount of income shown in Paul's return. When the affidavit was mailed to the agent, we accompanied

EXHIBIT 4-6

AFFIDAVIT OF PAUL _____
SSN: _____

STATE OF _____)
) ss
COUNTY OF _____)

My Name is Paul _____. During the year 1985, I was employed by (name of company) as a commissioned salesman. I was paid solely on the basis of the sales that I made. I did not receive a fixed salary or an hourly wage.

During 1985, my total commission income was $18,300. This amount was determined by adding all the commission checks paid to me by (name of company) during 1985. Submitted together with this affidavit is the affidavit of (name), the owner of (name of business). His affidavit also verifies that the total commissions paid to me during 1985 equal $18,300.

I filed a timely federal income tax return for 1985. On the return, I accurately reported all income earned by me for all sources. The total gross income shown in the return is $18,300. I did not earn any income from any other source. I did not earn in excess of $18,300 during 1985.

_____
Paul _____

Subscribed and sworn to before
me this ____ day of _____.

Notary Public _____
My commission expires: _____

it with a demand that the additional $3,900 in unreported income be dropped from the audit report. By letter dated just a few days after we mailed the affidavit, the agent agreed that the additional income would be dropped, and all corresponding penalties were similarly abandoned.

Another fine example of the use of an affidavit to verify one's income is illustrated with Dennis' case. Dennis operated his own small business. Dennis was not an accountant but he kept his own records, handled all his own billing, and prepared his own income tax returns. When one of Dennis' returns came under audit, he thought he was prepared to manage the situation.

During the course of the examination, the auditor believed she discoverd a discrepancy in Dennis' tax return, but never discussed the issue. Rather, she kept her imagined discovery to herself, springing it only after the examination was complete and the report was issued. In the report, we learned that the auditor was under the impression that Dennis underreported his income by many thousands of dollars. She added the phantom income to Dennis' return, and calculated the corresponding tax and penalties. Naturally, we appealed the decision.

When the issue of Dennis' income was presented to the appeals officer, we used ledgers prepared by Dennis contemporaneously with his receipt of the income to establish that his income was as shown on the return. Ledgers are nothing more than your own records which reflect the receipt of income as it is earned or received. In addition to the ledgers themselves, Dennis submitted an affidavit similar to Paul's (Exhibit 4-6) which supported Dennis' claim that the ledgers were true and correct reflections of his income, that they were made contemporaneously with earning or receiving the income, and that all of the income earned by him during the year in question is shown in the ledgers.

The affidavit was signed by Dennis and notarized, and was submitted to the IRS with copies of the letters attached. After reviewing the affidavit and the ledgers attached, the IRS was forced to modify the report issued by the revenue agent. Dennis was able to show, with the use of his affidavit, that the income reported in his tax return for the year in question was true and accurate. Moreover, with the fall of the phantom income, the interest and penalties charged Dennis for the supposed underreporting were concomitantly reduced. The few minutes it took to draft the simple affidavit and to have it signed and notarized, saved Dennis countless thousands of dollars in taxes, interest and penalties which clearly, he did not owe.

Affidavits Which Prove Deductions

We have covered the first of your two primary obligations with regard to the correctness of your return. You bear the burden to prove that the income shown in the return is true and complete, and that the deductions shown are correct. At this juncture, we shall examine the manner in which affidavits have been used in the past to support or verify certain itemized deductions when called upon to do so by the IRS.

Dan was a stockbroker. Dan also was a self-described "cashman." What that means is that like many people, Dan preferred to use cash rather than checks and credit cards to conduct his business. Of course, there is nothing illegal or immoral about using cash over paper and plastic, but when it comes to proving deductions, one can be faced with difficulty if he does not go through the motions of collecting receipts.

When Dan's tax return came under audit, there were a number of areas which needed verification. On Schedule A, Dan had reported about $450 in charitable contributions. Dan also filed Form 2106, *Employee Business Expense*. There, he showed several thousand business miles, fees for parking, etc., and over $1,000 in meals and entertainment expenses. He also showed some miscellaneous expenses associated with his brokerage activities. With the exception of several restaurant receipts, Dan had no documentation to show his mileage, his business expenses, or the charitable contributions. Based upon this absence of "proof," Dan asked the obvious question, "Will I have to give up these expense deductions because of my lack of receipts?" My answer shocked him.

"No," I said pointedly.

"How will I prove these deductions without receipts?" he asked.

"We will use what are called 'reconstructions' and your testimony," I explained. "A reconstruction is nothing more than the process by which you retrace your steps involving the particular deduction, showing on paper how much money you spent, and what it was spent on. Your testimony is your 'word' as to the manner and amounts of money which you spent. These methods are perfectly valid and acceptable ways in which deductions can be proven."

I went on to explain exactly how the reconstruction would be accomplished. The procedures apply whether we are proving mileage and business expenses, or any other deduction claimed on a return. The success of a reconstruction depends upon the starting point. One must have some type of constant reference to turn to which will provide the raw material upon which the reconstruction is built.

In Dan's case, the starting point was his appointment book for the year in question. Through the notations within his book, he was able to determine whom he had seen and where they met. For example, if a notation showed that he was to meet client X at the ABC restaurant, he could safely assume that he drove to the restaurant from his office, thus resulting in deductible business miles. He could also assume that he paid the cost of the lunch, something he always did for clients, thus resulting in deductible entertainment expenses. Lastly, he could assume that the purpose of the discussions with this client were solely business related. Why else would he be meeting this person during business hours?

The appointment book provided the raw material. From there, Dan reconstructed a mileage log showing his business miles, and the purpose of the travel. He was also able, using the few receipts he had and the notations within his book, to determine how much money was spent on the business lunches. Based upon the particular establishment in question and its location, he could determine whether parking fees were expended or not.

The reconstructions were written out long-hand, each on a separate sheet of paper. Not only were the particular expenses shown, but so was the manner in which the expenses were arrived at. Dan then signed and dated the documents, plainly indicating that they were reconstructions. When it came time for our meeting with the IRS, we had completed all of the reconstructions. In addition to the other forms of documentation which Dan did have, much of which related to the purchase of his home, we submitted the reconstructions.

In addition to the reconstructions, Dan provided an affidavit explaining just exactly how these reconstructions were prepared. The affidavit stated clearly and plainly that the expenses shown in the worksheets, copies of which were attached to the affidavit, were expenses incurred in the ordinary course of business. Dan stated that as a stockbroker, he regularly entertained clients and incurred business miles to do so. He explained the purpose of the entertainment, and most importantly, the manner in which the

EXHIBIT 4-7

AFFIDAVIT OF JACK _____

STATE OF _____   )
) ss
COUNTY OF _____   )

1. My name is Jack _____. My address is _____. My Social Security Number is _____.

2. In February of 1990, Revenue Officer _____ made the claim that my federal income tax return for the year 1988 was not filed. This statement is in error.

3. As a matter of fact, my return was filed on November 3, 1989. The return was filed together with returns for 1986 and 1987. An envelope containing the three returns was mailed via certified mail, return receipt requested, to the IRS Service Center in Kansas City, MO. Attached to this affidavit as Exhibit A is a true and correct copy of the receipt for certified mail, item No. P 058 674 123, dated at (City, State) on November 3, 1989. Also in Exhibit A is the Post Office Domestic Return Receipt for Item No. P 058 674 123, bearing the "received" stamp of the IRS at 2306 Bannister Road, Kansas City, MO. (the address of the IRS Service Center).

4. All three returns were mailed to the IRS in the same envelope on November 3, 1989, with first class and certified mail postage pre-paid.

5. From this evidence it is shown that the IRS received my return for 1988 on November 6, 1989.

6. Attached to this affidavit is a true and correct copy of my retained copy of the original 1988 income tax return filed with the IRS on November 3, 1989. The original was mailed to the Service Center as indicated above.

7. The IRS' claim that I failed to file an income tax return for 1988 is incorrect. The return, as shown, was filed by mailing the same via certified mail to the IRS' Service Center in Kansas City. Based upon these facts, the claim of failure to file a 1988 made by the IRS should be set aside as invalid.

_____

Jack _____

Subscribed and sworn to before me
this _____ day of February, 1990.

Notary Public: _____

My Commission Expires: _____

reconstructions were accomplished. An example of Dan's affidavit is shown in Exhibit 4-7.

The IRS official received the reconstructions and carefully reviewed the affidavit. The agent's questions focused on the *merits* of the reconstructions, how the facts were arrived at and the business purpose of the expenses. Dan was careful to answer each question specifically and fully, making sure that all the details were clear. When all was said and done, Dan was given the benefit of *every dime* supported by his reconstructions and affidavit. Despite the fact that Dan did not have contemporaneous records to back up the claimed expenses, the reconstructions and affidavit provided all the proof needed to settle the audit dispute in Dan's favor.

Bruce's tax return came under audit much in the normal course of IRS affairs. His return contained a deduction of $750 for contributions made to his church. Bruce did not have receipts for the money given, because as many do, he donated cash by dropping it into the collection plate each week. In order to establish the deduction and avoid increased taxes, interest and penalties, we structured a simple affidavit which, when presented with an explanation on the part of Bruce and his wife, proved their entitlement to the deduction.

The affidavit declared pointedly that Bruce and his wife attended church each and every week, 52 weeks per year. The affidavit also declared pointedly that each week, they gave $15 in cash by dropping it into the collection plate. Next, it was explained that on Friday of each week, after depositing one-half of her paycheck into the bank, and taking the remaining portion in cash, Bruce's wife would do the grocery shopping. When completed, she would have money for the weekend which included money for the weekly church contribution.

The simplicity, clarity and lack of ambiguity in this affidavit, indeed any affidavit, is the key to success. One cannot expect to meet with success using this technique if the affidavit is vague or in any way ambiguous. It must state the facts clearly, simply and to the point. It must avoid equivocation and generalities. Lastly, it must draw the ultimate conclusion based upon the facts presented. In Bruce's case, the ultimate conclusion was that he did in fact contribute $750 to his church during the year in question.

In another case, Kathy was faced with a situation much the same as Dan's. She was a sales representative for a line of clothing. She travelled throughout much of the Midwest. Her returns for three years during which this activity was at its zenth came under examination by the IRS. Unfortunately, Kathy did not have *one scrap* of paper for those earlier years. Therefore, it was necessary to reconstruct those years and to establish that the travel expenses shown in Kathy's tax return were legitimate deductions.

Unlike Dan, Kathy had one factor present in her case which provided an advantage. She used a charge card extensively in her travels. The first step was to send a letter to the card issuer and request copies of all monthly statements for the years in question. In time, these were provided and proved most helpful in structuring both an affidavit and reconstructions. In addition, Kathy did possess her address book which showed the names and addresses of the companies and persons on whom she called during the course of business. The charge statements would tell us the city that Kathy travelled to, and the address book revealed who she would have seen while there. From her experience and the statements, we were able to ascertain how much time was spent in each city, and how much money was spent on meals, hotels and gasoline.

To be sure, not each and every expense Kathy incurred was paid for with plastic. But we were able to fill in the gaps based upon her experience, and those details were presented to the IRS in the form of an affidavit. Kathy's affidavit was very similar in form and substance to Dan's affidavit. (See Exhibit 4-7.) After conversations with the IRS regarding her travel, the charge slips, and the affidavit, Kathy's expenses as shown in the reconstructions were allowed, to the penny.

While the audit process has historically been a fearful and intimidating one, it need not be. When one fully understands the nature of the examination process, his obligations and rights throughout the process, and most importantly, that he truly can "take back the power" from the IRS, the tax audit process can be relegated to the ranks of the mundane. Indeed it should be, because when the public is terrified of the IRS and the audit process, the IRS profits greatly through citizens who consent to pay thousands of dollars in tax not lawfully owed, merely as a kind of salve for their fears. If you cannot afford the expense of an audit, you must understand your rights and the power of the affidavit process.

Notes To Chapter 4

1. See *The Naked Truth*, pages 66-68; and *How Anyone Can Negotiate With The IRS—And WIN!*, pages 150-151.

CHAPTER 5

How To Short Circuit
The Audit Selection Computer

Earlier in this discourse, I explained the manner in which returns are selected for examination by the IRS. The IRS will select the return on the basis of its variance with statistical averages (the DIF system) or it will be kicked out for a line-by-line examination of the entire return (the TCMP audit). This is done for the purpose of building and updating the IRS' statistical data base. Both of these processes generally involve a face-to-face meeting with the IRS, the kind that usually strikes terror into the hearts of the unsuspecting citizen. However, another method of audit can be equally as costly and does not always involve a face-to-face confrontation with a tax examiner. We have identified that method of audit in Chapter Two (the computerized examination) and have explored several methods of neutralizing the potential adverse effects of such an effort.

What we have not yet addressed, and which will be explored here, is an answer to the most often asked question I face when discussing IRS matters with the public. That question is, "How can I make my tax return 'audit-proof'?" You may be asking that question yourself by now, and you may have seen or read articles or reports written by the "experts" on how this may be accomplished. In the past, I have answered this question in a fashion which seems to constitute an abandonment of hope by me in apparent recognition of the IRS' computerized omnipotence. However, such is not the case.

Historically, I have declared that in light of the IRS' 1984 *Strategic Plan* to audit every citizen for every year and to intensify computer-generated contacts to increase "presence," it would be functionally impossible to audit-proof your return. Drawing from observations made by the "experts," I have pointed out that in essence, the only method which could be marginally effective in reaching this goal would be to forego claiming your deductions entirely, or greatly reduce the amount claimed. Naturally, the fewer deductions claimed, both in terms of dollar amount and character, the more diminished the likelihood of suffering a face-to-face audit. Still, as shown in Chapter Two, even short form filers with less than $10,000 in annual income run the risk of an audit and those audits have proven to be quite expensive.

The real question, therefore, is not whether we can *avoid* an audit, but rather, whether we can avoid the face-to-face audit. After all, most citizens will admit that the face-to-face confrontation is intimidating and troublesome because of being forced to take time from work, disrupting their daily affairs, and most importantly the acknowledged fear that the audit will *cost them money* which in most cases, they simply do not have.

I will not labor here to disprove any of my earlier statements regarding the probability of an audit of your return. I will, however, demonstrate that with a few very basic precautions, precautions which, frankly, just one in a million citizens will *ever* take, you can transform your return's *red flags* into the IRS' *white flags* of surrender!

The "One-in-a-Million" Precaution

Marie was an employee of a major corporation during the first three months of 1989. During the remaining months, she was self-employed as a sales and marketing consultant. As part of the weekly payroll withholding formality, Marie's employer paid approximately $1,000 to the state because of her state income tax liability.

After Marie left the employ of the corporation and struck out on her own, she made regular quarterly installment payments to both the state and the IRS to satisfy her obligation to make estimated payments of her liability. All the estimated payments to the state were mde in 1989 so that the full amount could be deducted on her 1989 federal income tax return. For reasons we will not examine here, Marie's accountant instructed her to make large payments to the state as estimated state income tax installments. By the time she made her final estimated payment in December of 1989, she had paid exactly *twice as much* in state income taxes as the law required.

On her 1989 federal income tax return, Marie claimed a Schedule A deduction of all state income taxes paid in 1989. That amount was approximately $13,000. However, Marie's state income tax liability amounted to just $5,300. Thus, Marie *overpaid* the state by some $7,700. Naturally, she was entitled to a refund from the state, which she received in 1990 after filing the 1989 return. But she also was entitled to claim as a deduction the *full amount* paid to the state in 1989, which was $13,000.

Now you tell me—what is wrong with this picture? We know that the IRS' most common technique for selecting tax returns for examination is the discriminate function system (DIF). Under that system, the IRS' computer compares every line of your tax return with national and regional statistical averages for persons in your same income category and profession. If any one line of your return does not fall within permissable tolerances, your return will be selected for audit. Can you predict what the likely outcome will be with Marie's return when it is run through the DIF score?

If not—let there be light! Because Marie's claimed deduction for state income taxes is over *twice as high* as it should be for persons in her same income bracket, the likely result of the DIF analysis is for her return to be selected for audit. However, Marie *knew this* at the time she filed the return. She knew how the IRS selected items for audit, and she knew that her claim of state income tax deductions was over twice what statistical averages dictated it should be. But she claimed the deduction anyway! Was Marie crazy? Was she asking for trouble? Or, did she know something that you do not?

The answer, frankly, is the latter. Let me tell you what Marie knows that just one in a million citizens know.

First of all, Marie knew that the mere selection of her return by the DIF program was not a determination that there was an error in her return. As explained in the previous chapter, the fact that your return is selected means only that you are called upon to demonstrate that your return is correct as filed. But you knew that after having read the previous chapter.

Marie, however, also knew that before the return would be *assigned* for face-to-face examination, it would be reviewed by an individual within the IRS' Examination Branch at the Service Center *subsequent* to the computer audit. Only if that individual found it necessary or appropriate to conduct a face-to-face examination would the matter be referred to the district office. Therefore, Marie took measures which would *ensure* that it *would not* be found necessary to refer her return to the district office.

Knowing that her deduction for state income taxes would be viewed as exceptionally high, and knowing that the DIF program would likely identify the deduction as such, and further, knowing that Service Center personnel would review her return prior to any examination assignment, Marie made copies of the cancelled checks used to pay the state income taxes claimed. She *attached* those copies of the checks—both front and back—directly to the tax return which she filed with the IRS!

Doesn't that seem miraculously simple?! If and when Marie's return is selected by the DIF program as having potential for audit because of the seemingly high amount of state income taxes claimed, any person examining the return will find, as part of the return, self-contained *proof* of the accuracy of her deduction. One need only review the photocopied checks which were provided as part of her return to know that her claim of approximately $13,000 in state income taxes was entirely legal and proper.

Without a doubt, this technique will function as a major component in determining whether Marie will ever be required to face the music of an audit. The only questionable entry on her return was proved by her at the time she filed. By employing this one-in-a-million secret, she has disarmed the IRS' audit machine. With the wind removed from its sails, the IRS' audit ship is adrift at sea vis-a-vis Marie's 1989 income tax return.

Turn Your "Red Flags"
Into Their "White Flags"

What is the character of deductions or claims in a tax return that raises "red flags" with the IRS? This is probably the *second* most commonly asked questions with which I am presented. The theory behind asking the question is, "If I know which issues constitute the 'red flags,' I will avoid claiming those deductions in my return."

Though the *logic* of this observation may be indisputable, there is a major disadvantage. By foregoing the claim to a deduction to which you are legally entitled, you have "protected" yourself into paying *more money* to the IRS than you are legally required to pay. By invoking that measure, you have cost yourself the money you were attempting to save by reducing your return's potential for audit. Stated another way, you just threw the baby out with the bath water!

Rather than "protect" yourself by increasing your income tax liability, why not "protect" yourself by heading the audit off at the pass? That is accomplished by using the technique described above. Marie headed the audit off at the pass and at the *same time*, enjoyed the full benefit of her perfectly legal and proper deduction. If she succumbed to the logic of many as expressed above, her tax liability would have been increased by exactly 33 percent of $13,000, which is $4,290.

Let us attempt to identify some of the "red flags" and the kind of material which could be attached to your return in order to transform the "red flags" into the IRS' "white flags" of surrender.

1. **Medical Expenses.** Because medical expenses are only deductible to the extent that they exceed 7.5 percent of your adjusted gross income, one's medical expenses must be somewhat excessive in order to be deductible. Therefore, a medical expense deduction in excess of the 7.5 percent limitation should be supported by cancelled checks paid to physicians or hospitals, or ideally, a statement from the person or institution to whom paid indicating the total amount paid.

2. **Charitable Contributions.** Charitable contributions generally become excessive when they exceed 10 percent of your income. Below that level, IRS will not consider the contribution to be statistically out of line. Above that level, however, the computers will begin to wonder. A statement from the church or organization to whom the gifts were made will simplify the process by greatly reducing the number of attachments to the return. This is especially true, if as most do, you make your donations on a weekly basis rather than in one or two lump sums.

3. **State Income or Real Estate Taxes.** Averages for these amounts are quite simple for the computer to determine. Any payment of these taxes in excess of the state or county rates (ala Marie) will cause the computer to hesitate when examining your

submission. As explained above, Marie submitted copies, front and back, of the four checks used to pay the state income tax installments. Naturally, her Form W-2 provided the remaining proof of the total paid to the state during 1989.

4. **Travel and Entertainment Expenses.** Frankly, it is impossible to know exactly where the point of safety ends and trouble begins with many deductions. The IRS' DIF scores are a carefully guided secret. So much so that I believe you might sooner obtain the plans to a Titan submarine than you will the DIF scores. Therefore, an undefined standard must be applied when determining whether to engage the use of the technique described here for heading off a potential audit. That undefined standard is the test of "reason and common sense." That in itself may be trouble, because everyone knows that the IRS is devoid of reason and common sense, or so it seems!

Still, this measure can be applied to the travel and entertainment expense issue, as well as all others discussed here. If, for example, your tax return reveals that your profession is that of a travelling salesman, perhaps a deduction of 15 percent of your income as travelling expenses is not excessive. However, if your job is that of a sales clerk in a local department store, just five percent may be extremely excessive. What is or is not excessive can only be determined by you, based upon your circumstances, and it is a judgment call. When in doubt, if you are concerned about an audit, include the proof with your return.

My task here is to identify the "red flag" areas, but I hope you understand that I cannot definitively identify the *level* at which a particular deduction becomes potentially troublesome in the eyes of the IRS.

5. **Meals.** Recent legislation has placed a cap upon the amount of business meals which can be deducted. That cap is 80 percent of the total business meals incurred during the course of the year. Stated another way, if you incur $100 in business meals during 1990, you are permitted to deduct just $80 as a business expense. The area of meals can be a red flag when the amount of meals deducted appears excessive under the circumstances. As with the previous example, a person required to travel extensively during the course of his business affairs can be expected to incur a fairly substantial amount of business meals, while the same deduction would be suspect for a person of whom little or no travel is required. You must be the judge (because the precise DIF scores are unavailable) as to what may

appear abnormal in this regard.

6. **Office in Home Deduction.** Schedule C, the form used by self-employed persons to report their income and expenses, contains the following question: "Are you deducting expenses for business use of your home?" If the answer is "yes," you are asked to check the appropriate space provided in the form. Historically, the deduction for business use of your home, the so-called "home office" deduction, has been an area to which the IRS has paid much attention in the past. When your home office deduction, if disallowed, has the potential to cause problems with your financial future, you may be well advised to provide proof of this deduction in your return. This should include, as a minimum, a worksheet demonstrating the manner in which the deduction was computed, evidence showing the value of your home (used as a starting point to determine the deducton) and the square footage of your home and that of the area used for business.

7. **Automobiles, Personal Computers, Recreational Vehicles:** Form 4562, the form used to compute depreciation of business property, under Part III, *Automobiles, Certain Other Vehicles, Computers, and Property Used for Entertainment, Recreation or Amusement,* the IRS asks the following question. "Do you have evidence to support the business use claimed?" You are asked to indicate your answer by checking the appropriate box. If you answer "yes," the next question asks, "Is the evidence written?" Again, you are asked to indicate your answer by checking the appropriate box.

Clearly, the answers to these questions provide notice of a "red flag" to the IRS for use in screening potential audit candidates. One way of preventing a face-to-face confrontation regarding the depreciation of business property would be to attach to the return evidence of the date of purchase and cost of the item being depreciated, as well as any documentary evidence indicating the business use of the property. Whenever documents are attached to the return to support one or more deductions claimed, it is a good idea to identify on the face of the documents the form or schedule and line number to which the evidence applies. This will eliminate the potential for confusion when it comes to reviewing the material.

8. **Business Losses.** I have previously explained that income and expenses incurred as a result of self-employment are reported on Schedule C. The difference between your income and expenses constitutes the gain or loss from self-employent. When a loss is reported on the Schedule C, the form requires that certain questions

be answered. First, you must declare whether all your investment is "at risk." That is to say, whether the loss incurred will directly affect your personal income. If your investment is "not at risk," the IRS will treat your loss differently, and attempt to limit the amount you can deduct as a result of the business loss. Even when your investment is wholly "at risk," the IRS is wont to label the business a "hobby" when a loss is sustained, thereby limiting the deduction substantially. When your Schedule C shows a business loss, particularly if your investment is not wholly "at risk," a "red flag" is certainly raised and you may wish to substantiate your losses in the return itself in an effort to short circuit the audit, of which there is a clear risk.

9. **Employee Business Expenses.** Employees (persons not working for themselves) who incur expenses which are ordinary and necessary business expenses have a form on which these deductions are computed. Form 2106, Employee Business Expenses, is used to compute the deduction for mileage, meals, travel expenses, etc. The points made earlier in this discussion regarding meals and travel are valid and relevant to this discussion. To those, I will add another factor: mileage expenses. One of the more heavily scrutinized deduction items in a return is the mileage expense claim, particularly when that claim is made on Form 2106. Mileage is troublesome, for both the IRS and citizens, because the law is clear that mileage incurred as a result of commuting from home to work or office is *not* deductible. Thus, when an employee not required to travel over the road reports deductible business mileage, the question is immediately raised in the IRS' mind, "Is this person claiming commuting mileage on his return?" Believing the worst, the agency's tendency is to call for an examination. In another scenario, when a seemingly high percentage of business use of an auto is claimed, such as 80 or 90 percent, questions are raised regarding the propriety of such a claim. While a claim of 90 percent business use of an auto is entirely proper *under some circumstances,* it is difficult for the IRS to imagine what such circumstances may be. Therefore, when business use of an auto is claimed, with an apparently high percentage of business use associated with it, one may be well advised to provide proof of the business miles, such as copies of the mileage log, as part and parcel of the return.

After reading the above discourse, you are probably asking yourself what standard should be applied when considering the types of documents to attach to your return. That question is answered with this simple rule: any data which you would present to the IRS in a *face-to-face* examination should be attached to your return to support any potential "red flag" deductions. You may be quick to respond that by attaching *all* necessary documentation, your return may become somewhat voluminous. While this may be true, you must also acknowledge that the bit of extra effort needed at the time of filing is well worth it if that effort later saves you the hassle of a face-to-face confrontation.

In addition to the necessary documentation, you should include a simple letter with your return which explains the purpose of the supplemental material. The letter should contain your name and should explain that you are attaching proof of a particular deduction. You should make reference to the Schedule and line in your return to which the proof relates, and should include a brief explanation of the proof supplied. An example of Marie's letter is shown in Exhibit 5-1.

EXHIBIT 5-1

Marie _____
SSN:

Letter Explaining Deduction

On Schedule A, Line 5, I claimed an itemized deduction for State Income Taxes paid during 1989. The deduction was in the amount of $13,000. I am attaching documents to this income tax return which will verify that I am entitled to claim the deduction in that amount.

Attached to this letter, and made a part hereof, please find true and correct copies of four personal checks. The checks were written to (name of party) and are in the following amounts (enter amounts). The checks were written on (give dates). The sum of the amounts shown in these checks is (enter amount).

(NOTE: When your proof is not in the form of checks, you should be careful to explain more precisely the nature of the proof. For example, with respect to charitable contributions, you may wish to state that the proof is a receipt from the ABC Church. Whenever documents are attached which are not self-explanatory, be sure to provide an explanation of their substance. Do not expect the IRS to figure it out on its own.)

_____
Signature of Marie

DATE:

Another "One-in-a-Million" Precaution

Each year, we are faced with the burden to correctly prepare and submit an income tax return which comports with countless tax laws and regulations. The difficulty, however, is that nobody, it seems, knows exactly how to prepare an income tax return correctly. Study after study has shown that both the IRS and the private sector accountants and return preparers have not found the combination to the complete tax code and regulations. For example, *Money* magazine has, each year for the past three years, submitted a hypothetical family financial profile to 50 tax accountants and return preparers with simple instructons: determine the tax liability for this family based upon the facts provided by *Money*. The results of each of the three studies are startling. Each of the 50 experts arrived at a different conclusion with respect to the tax bill. Not one of the 50 expert opinions matched that of any other. And this was true in *all three* studies!

Moreover, the GAO has studied the IRS' problems with complex tax information for years. In the June, 1990, issue of *Pilla Talks Taxes*, I reported that the latest GAO report[1] on the topic showed that the IRS' answers to citizens' questions were incorrect in 37.2 percent of the cases. That is to say, more than one in every three citizens phoning the IRS with questions will receive *incorrect* information. The pie chart in Exhibit 5-2 is taken from page 12 of the

EXHIBIT 5-2

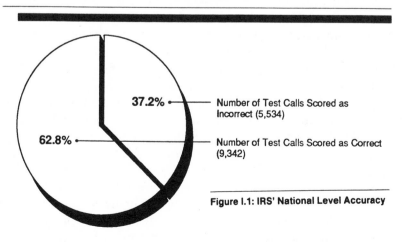

37.2% ●——— Number of Test Calls Scored as Incorrect (5,534)

62.8% ●——— Number of Test Calls Scored as Correct (9,342)

Figure I.1: IRS' National Level Accuracy

GAO report and indicates the percentage of correct versus incorrect information provided.

It is no secret that incorrect income tax returns lead to substantial penalties and interest assessments. While the subject of penalties in a broader sense will be more fully explored in the next chapter, here we will examine a one-in-a-million technique for avoiding most penalties which can be attributed to confusing and shifting tax laws, regulations and murky IRS publications, not to mention confused professionals and lost IRS employees. One of the more crushing of these penalties is the so-called "substantial understatement penalty."[2]

The understatement portion of the "accuracy-related" penalty applies when a citizen makes a "substantial" understatement of his tax liability on the tax return. When this occurs, a penalty of 20 percent of the understatement is added to the tax due.[3] An "understatement" is defined by the Code as the difference between what was reported on the return as the tax liability, and what *should have been reported* as the tax liability. An understatement is considered "substantial" and hence, subject to the 20 percent penalty if, "the understatement for the taxable year exceeds the greater of (1) 10 percent of the tax required to be shown on the return for the taxable year, or (2) $5,000."

To illustrate an example under which the former circumstances would apply, suppose you reported an income tax liabilty of $400 on your 1989 return. Suppose further that after audit, the IRS has determined your tax to be $1,500. The difference between the tax shown ($400) and that required to be shown ($1,500) is $1,100. Since $1,100 is greater than "10 percent of the tax required to be shown on the return," the IRS *will consider* the understatement to be "substantial," and will tack the 20 percent penalty to the bill.

The manner in which the tax laws operate serve to put the citizen at a distinct disadvantage where this penalty is concerned. A person with questionable income or questionable deductions, who seeks advice from a professional or from the IRS, will come away with varying answers equal to the number of persons whose advice he sought. Desiring to be honest, he is forced to choose between claiming the questionable item on the return and risking the price of an audit, with penalties, or not claiming the item and losing the tax benefit, which he may very well be perfectly entitled to claim. More often than not, the IRS prevails in this debate, primarily because citizens do not wish to risk even the chance of an audit, much less the penalties inherent with the disallowed deductions.

Recently, I spoke with two persons facing this kind of decision. Both situations involved questions of income, rather than deductions. In the first situation, the man, a pastor, was given a gift from his congregation. The gift, $2,200 was erroneously included as income on his W-2 by the church secretary. In the second case, a salesmen was given bonuses by his company during the year. When he received is Form 1099 reflecting his commission income, the bonuses were included. However, the company had erroneously *overstated* the value of the bonuses to a significant degree.

Both men were faced with the obvious choice: file the forms as prepared and pay more taxes than were due, or claim a lesser amount of income than shown on the forms and risk the penalty assessment.[4] My solution to the dilemma finds its origin within Revenue Regulation 1.6661-4. That regulation reads in part as follows:

> "Items...for which there is *adequate disclosure* are treated as if such items *were shown properly* on the return for the taxable year in computing the amount of tax for purposes of section 6662, shown on the return. Thus, the tax attributable to such items is *not included* in the understatement for the year. Disclosure is adequate with respect to the tax treatment[5] of an item on a return only if it is made on such return or in a statement attached thereto." (Emphasis added.)

The key, then, to avoiding the "substantial understatement" penalty where the issue involves questionable items of either income or expenses, is to make full disclosure of the item in the tax return itself, then explaining to the IRS exactly how you arrived at your tax treatment you assigned to the item. As you see, by making full disclosure in your return, you have avoided the dilemma presented by confusing and chaotic laws.

There are two ways in which to make full disclosure, either of which is adequate to avoid the penalty. The first is to prepare and submit with your tax return IRS Form 8275, *Disclosure Statement*. That form is the document on which you explain all of the facts and circumstances surrounding the questionable item. While writing this treatise, I did some research concerning Form 8275. I found that while the form is obviously critical to the tax preparation process, it is *not* discussed in IRS Publication 1, *Your Rights as a Taxpayer*. More importantly, Form 8275 is *not* found among the 79 specific tax forms and publications which the IRS considers to be the minimum, most important forms to be stocked by the IRS' over 600 walk-in

EXHIBIT 5-3

Form **8275** (Rev. May 1990) Department of the Treasury Internal Revenue Service	**Disclosure Statement** ► Attach to your tax return. ► See separate instructions.	OMB No. 1545-0889 Expires 4-30-93
Name(s) shown on return		Identifying number shown on return

Part I General Information

(a) Detailed description of item (or group of similar items) being disclosed and the location of the item(s) on your return, including schedule and line (e.g. Schedule A, line 21).	**(b)** Amount of disclosed item described in column (a)
1	
2	
3	
4	

Part II Detailed Explanation

1 ....

....

....

2 ....

....

....

3 ....

....

....

4 ....

....

....

Part III Information About Pass-Through Entity (To be completed by partners, shareholders, beneficiaries, or residual interest holders.)

Note: *A pass-through entity is a partnership, an S corporation (as defined in section 1361(a)(1)), an estate, a trust, a regulated investment company (as defined in section 851(a)), a real estate investment trust (as defined in section 856(a)), or a real estate mortgage investment conduit* **(REMIC).**

(Complete this part only if you are making adequate disclosure with respect to a pass-through item.)

1 Name, address, and ZIP code of pass-through entity	2 Identifying number of pass-through entity
	3 Tax year of pass-through entity / / to / /
	4 Internal Revenue Service Center where the pass-through entity filed its return

For Paperwork Reduction Act Notice, see separate instructions. 　¤ U.S. Government Printing Office: 1990-262-151/00166 　Form **8275** (Rev. 5-90)

EXHIBIT 5-3 (continued)

Department of the Treasury
Internal Revenue Service

Instructions for Form 8275

(Revised May 1990)

Disclosure Statement

(Section references are to the Internal Revenue Code unless otherwise noted.)

General Instructions

Paperwork Reduction Act Notice

We ask for this information to carry out the Internal Revenue laws of the United States. We need it to ensure that taxpayers are complying with these laws and to allow us to figure and collect the right amount of tax. You are required to give us this information if you wish to use this form to make adequate disclosure to avoid the portion of the accuracy-related penalty due to a substantial understatement of income tax, negligence or disregard of rules or regulations, or certain preparer penalties.

The time needed to complete and file this form will vary depending on individual circumstances. The estimated average time is:

Recordkeeping . . . . . 3 hrs., 7 min.
Learning about the law
or the form . . . . 48 min.
Preparing and sending
the form to IRS . . . . . 53 min.

If you have comments concerning the accuracy of these time estimates or suggestions for making this form more simple, we would be happy to hear from you. You can write to both the IRS and the Office of Management and Budget at the addresses listed in the instructions of the tax return with which this form is filed.

Changes to Note

Under section 6662, the Revenue Reconciliation Act of 1989 combined a number of penalties into a single **accuracy-related penalty.** These include the penalty for substantial understatement of income tax and the penalty for negligence or disregard of rules or regulations. The accuracy-related penalty, which applies to returns due after December 31, 1989, is imposed at 20% of the portion of the underpayment attributable to a substantial understatement of income tax or to negligence or disregard of rules or regulations.

Under amended section 6694, income tax return preparer penalties have been increased to $250 for understatements due to unrealistic positions and $1,000 for willful or reckless conduct.

Although regulations have not been issued for the accuracy-related penalty, Notice 90-20, 1990-10 I.R.B. 17 provides guidance for making disclosure to avoid the portions of the penalty attributable to the substantial understatement of income

tax or negligence or disregard of rules or regulations as well as for the income tax return preparer penalties.

Purpose of Form

Form 8275 is used by taxpayers and income tax return preparers to disclose items on a tax return for purposes of avoiding certain penalties. Specifically, the form is used for disclosures relating to the portions of the accuracy-related penalty due to negligence or disregard of rules or regulations or to a substantial understatement of income tax. It can also be used for disclosures relating to the preparer penalties for understatements due to unrealistic positions or for willful or reckless conduct.

Caution: *Disclosure on Form 8275 will not avoid the portion of the accuracy-related penalty due to a substantial understatement of tax on a tax shelter item.*

Who Should File

Form 8275 is filed by individuals, C corporations, pass-through entities, and income tax return preparers.

For items attributable to a pass-through entity, disclosure should be made on the tax return of the entity. If the entity does not make the disclosure, the partner (or shareholder, etc.) may make adequate disclosure of these items.

When To File

Exception to Filing Form 8275.—For purposes of the substantial understatement portion of the accuracy-related penalty, items that meet the requirements of Revenue Procedure 90-16, 1990-10 I.R.B. 24 are considered adequately disclosed on your return without filing Form 8275. For example, you will have adequately disclosed a charitable contribution deduction if you complete the contributions section of Schedule A (Form 1040), and you supply all required information. If you make a contribution of property other than cash, the statement required by the Schedule A instructions must be attached to your return.

Note: *This exception does not apply to the negligence or disregard of rules or regulations portion of the accuracy-related penalty or the preparer penalty for willful or reckless conduct.*

Carrybacks, Carryovers, and Recurring Items.—If you have **carryover** items which you disclosed on a prior year tax return, you do not have to file another Form 8275 for those items in subsequent tax years.

If you have **carryback** items which you disclosed on a tax return filed for the year in which the carryback originated, you do not have to file another Form 8275 for those items in prior tax years.

However, if you are disclosing items that are of a **recurring nature** (such as depreciation expense), you still need to file Form 8275 for each tax year in which the item occurs.

Where To File

File all Forms 8275 with your original tax return. Keep a copy for your records.

If you are making adequate disclosure for items received from a pass-through entity, send a second copy to the Internal Revenue Service Center where the pass-through entity filed its return. Attach to this copy a notation that the statement is to be associated with the return of the entity. If you have items from more than one pass-through entity, you must complete and file a separate Form 8275 for items received from each pass-through entity.

Negligence or Disregard of Rules or Regulations

The penalty on underpayments attributable to negligence or disregard of rules or regulations for returns due after December 31, 1989, is different from that applicable to returns due prior to January 1, 1990, in that:

• The rate of the penalty has increased from 5% to 20% and

• The penalty is only imposed on the portion of the understatement attributable to negligence or disregard of rules or regulations rather than on the entire underpayment. The penalty will not be imposed on any part of the underpayment for which it can be shown that there was reasonable cause for your position and that you acted in good faith with respect to the position.

Disclosing a position taken on your return by filing a properly completed Form 8275 will avoid the negligence or disregard of rules or regulations portion of the accuracy-related penalty. However, your disclosure must be complete and specifically identify the item which is being disclosed.

Your position will not be considered sufficiently disclosed by just completing and filing a form, schedule, or line item according to the applicable instructions.

You cannot avoid the penalty by disclosure if you failed to keep proper books and records or failed to substantiate items properly. Disclosure will never avoid the penalty for a frivolous position.

EXHIBIT 5-3 (continued)

Substantial Understatement

Generally, if there is a substantial understatement of income tax for returns due after December 31, 1989, you may be subject to a penalty of 20% on the amount of the understatement. For returns due before January 1, 1990, the penalty is 25%.

There is a substantial understatement of income tax if the amount of the understatement for any tax year exceeds the greater of 10% of the tax required to be shown on the return for the tax year, or $5,000 ($10,000 for a corporation other than an S corporation or a personal holding company as defined in section 542).

An **understatement** is the excess of:

• The amount of tax required to be shown on the return for the taxable year; **over**

• The amount of tax shown on the return for the taxable year, reduced by any rebates.

For purposes of the substantial understatement portion of the accuracy-related penalty, the amount of the understatement will be reduced by the part that is attributable to:

• An item (other than a tax shelter item), for which there was substantial authority for the treatment claimed at the time the return was filed or on the last day of the taxable year to which the return relates.

• An item (other than a tax shelter item) that is adequately disclosed on this form.

• A tax shelter item, if (1) there was substantial authority for the treatment claimed at the time the return was filed or on the last day of the taxable year to which the return relates, and (2) you held the reasonable belief that the tax treatment of the item was more likely than not the proper tax treatment.

Tax Shelter Items.—A tax shelter, for purposes of the portion of the accuracy-related penalty due to a substantial understatement of tax, is a partnership or other entity (such as a corporation or trust), an investment plan, an investment arrangement, or any other plan or arrangement, if the principal purpose of the entity, plan, or arrangement is the avoidance or evasion of Federal income tax.

A tax shelter item is any item of income, gain, loss, deduction, or credit which is directly or indirectly attributable to the principal purpose of the tax shelter to avoid or evade Federal income tax.

Income Tax Return Preparer Penalties

Under amended section 6694, the penalties imposed on income tax return preparers have been increased.

A preparer who files an income tax return or claim for refund is subject to a $250 penalty for taking a position which understates any part of the liability if:

• the position has no realistic possibility of being sustained on its merits, and

• the preparer knew (or reasonably should have known) of the position, and

• the position is frivolous or not adequately disclosed on the return or on Form 8275 .

The penalty will not apply if it can be shown that there was reasonable cause for the understatement and that the preparer acted in good faith.

In cases where any part of the understatement of liability is due to a willful attempt by the return preparer to understate the liability, or if the understatement is due to reckless or intentional disregard of rules or regulations by the preparer, the preparer is subject to a $1,000 penalty.

As with the negligence or disregard of rules or regulations and the substantial understatement portions of the accuracy-related penalty, the preparer penalties under section 6694 may be avoided in cases where a position is sufficiently disclosed and is not frivolous.

Note: *For further information concerning the accuracy-related penalty and preparer penalties, and disclosure as a means of avoiding these penalties, see Notice 90-20, 1990-10 I.R.B. 17.*

Specific Instructions

Be sure to supply all of the information requested in Parts I and II, and, if applicable, Part III. Your disclosure will be considered adequate if you supply the information requested in detail.

Part I

Column (a).—Enter a complete description of the item(s) you are disclosing. If you are claiming the same tax treatment for a group of similar items in the same tax year, enter a description identifying the group of items you are disclosing rather than a separate description of each item within the group.

If you are disclosing more than one item and one (or more) is a pass-through item, please identify which item(s) is from the pass-through entity. If you are disclosing items from more than one pass-through entity, a separate Form 8275 must be completed for each entity. Also, see **Where To File** instructions on page 1.

Part II

Enter either:

• A description of the relevant facts affecting the tax treatment of the item and the nature of the potential controversy concerning the tax treatment of the item; **or**

• A concise description of the legal issues presented by such facts.

Note: *Disclosure will not be considered adequate unless the information you provide in Part II reasonably identifies the item, its amount, the location of the item(s) on your return, and the nature of the potential controversy to which the disclosure relates. For example, if instead of supplying the information asked for above, you attach a copy of an acquisition agreement to your return to disclose the issues involved in determining the basis of certain acquired assets, your disclosure generally will not be considered adequate.*

Part III

Line 4.—Contact your pass-through entity if you do not know where its return was filed. However, for partners and shareholders in an S corporation, information for this item can be found on the Schedule K-1 (Form 1065) or on the Schedule K-1 (Form 1120S) that you received from the partnership or S corporation.

☆ U.S. Government Printing Office: 1990-262-151/00147

sites across the United States. Even worse, the IRS' *Package X,* the two-volume, 622-page package of hundreds of tax forms and instructions provided to accountants and return preparers, *does not* contain Form 8275 nor its instructions. A more paranoid citizen might be inclined to draw the conclusion that the IRS *does not* want you to know about Form 8275, and the protection it affords. For this reason, I have included a copy of Form 8275 and its instructions for your review. Please see Exhibit 5-3.

Because Form 8275 is not readily available from the IRS, you may wish to prepare a simple letter which will function effectively in lieu of the IRS' form. Should you do so, such a letter must include the following information:

(1) A caption identifying the letter as disclosure under §6662;

(2) An identification of the item or items to which the disclosure relates. Reference should be given to the specific form or schedule and line of the item(s) in question;

(3) The amount of the item or items, and

(4) The facts affecting the tax treatment of the item or items that reasonably may be expected to apprise the IRS of the nature of the potential controversy concerning the tax treatment of such items.[6]

As a word of caution, the IRS warns in an applicable regulation that:

> "Disclosure *is not adequate* with respect to an item (or group of similar items) if it consists of undifferentiated information that is not arranged in a manner that reasonably may be expected to apprise the IRS of the identity of the item, its amount, and the nature of the potential controversy concerning the item (or items). For example, attachment to the return of an acquisition agreement generally will not constitute adequate disclosure of the issues involved in determining the basis of certain assets." Ibid. at (b)(3).

Following the four points mentioned above, and using our pastor as an exaple, his letter regarding full disclosure might look something like what is shown in Exhibit 5-4. Please see Exhibit 5-4.

The "substantial understatement" penalty can not only relate to items of "income" which are omitted from your return, but also is routinely applied to deductions which are disallowed. As you well know, the matter of what is and what is not deductible is always subject to heated debate. When the IRS prevails, it naturally desires to stick the unfortunate citizen with all appropriate penalties, thus making him a two-time loser. Whenever you are faced with a

EXHIBIT 5-4

Pastor's Full Name
Social Security Number

                    Letter of Disclosure under Code §6662

1. This disclosure relates to items of alleged income which have been
omitted from this return, but which are reflected in the attached Form
W-2. (Attach copy of Form. In the case of deductions, all proof of
the expense should be attached.)

2. The amount of the item in question is $2,200.

3. The amount of $2,200 was presented to me as a gift from my
congregation. The congregation voted on the issue and as a body
elected to present a gift to me in that amount. The Church Board
issued a minute reflecting the fact of the election, and the decision
to issue the gift in that amount. When the Form W-2 was issued, the
amount of $2,200 was erroneously included as income. Since the $2,200
was a gift and not income, it is not included as income in this tax
return. Attached to this letter and made a part hereof is a true and
correct copy of the official minute of the Board of Directors of the
Church. This Letter of Full Disclosure is provided to explain the
difference between the amount shown as income on the Form W-2, and
amount shown as income on the Form 1040 as all income.

(NOTE: In the case of deductions, a full and complete explanation of
the facts and circumstances surrounding the deduction should be
provided, including a statement which explains your reasoning in
support of the deduction.)

_____
Pastor's Signature
DATE:

questionable deduction, the act of making full disclosure on your return will help to avoid the penalty. When the question is one of a deduction, your letter of full disclosure should include, at a minimum, these items:

1. An explanation of the *nature* of the expense;

2. A full and complete explanation of the *purpose* of the expense (if a business expense, your explanation should include a statement as to why the expense is "ordinary and necessary" to the operation of your business);

3. Copies of all documentary proof available to support the deduction; and

4. If the IRS has a particularized form covering the deduction, such as Form 4684 for Casualty and Theft Losses, or Form 8283 for Non-Cash Charitable Contributions, these forms should be completed and attached to your letter.

Be sure to follow the four points mentioned above when drafting your letter, and be careful to incorporate these items into that format.

If full disclosure is made as discussed above and shown in Exhibit 5-4, one will *eliminate* the potential threat of the "substantial understatement" penalty, even if the IRS were to ultimately disagree with the tax treatment you assigned to the item in question. Through this process, certain crushing penalty provisions of the Code can be entirely avoided, *before* your return is even filed. Perhaps the single most terrifying aspect of all the tax law changes to which we have been treated during the past several years is the fact that the IRS is trigger-happy when it comes to penalties. One of my hottest criticisms of the IRS has come in this area, where they routinely assess civil penalties without regard to the facts of the case.

This chapter contains two important prospective measures you can employ *before* filing your return. These techniques are so important that either can actually reduce or eliminate the risk that you will even be forced to face the IRS in an audit. What is that kind of assurance worth to you, the average citizen who, like most, is terrified of the prospect of an audit? Despite the great advantage gained through these measures, barely one in a million citizens will use either this year. I find it hard to believe that any citizen cannot afford to take these kinds of protective measures against IRS abuse.

Notes To Chapter 5

1. GAO/GGD-90-37, IRS' Test Call Survey.

2. See Code §6662. Prior to 1989, the penalty was assessed Under Code §6661. Penalty reform, discussed in Chapter Six, altered many of the penalty provisions of the Code. At present, the "substantial understatement" penalty is a segment of the "accuracy-related penalty" contained within Code §6662.

3. For returns filed prior to January 1, 1989, penalty is computed at the rate of 25 percent, and the IRS is permitted to "stack" the negligence penalty, which is another five percent. Please see Chapter Six for full discussion of penalties and penalty reform.

4. For reasons not relevant, neither man was successful in obtaining a corrected form.

5. The term "tax treatment" as used here refers to the manner in which an item of income or expense is handled in your return. Under the example of the pastor, if he *included* the income in his return, the "tax treatment" would be that the gift was "income" and thus, taxable. However, if he did not report the gift whatsoever, the "tax treatment" would be that the item (the gift) was not income and hence, not taxable.

6. See Rev. Reg. §1.6661-4(b)(1).

CHAPTER 6

How You Can Rain
On The IRS'
"Penalty Parade"

Penalties are *big business* for the IRS. For years, oppressive penalties, never mind interest, have made it extremely difficult, and sometimes impossible, for honest citizens striving to comply with the law to pay the taxes the IRS says must be paid. The trend in legislation in the decade of the 1980's was to increase the penalty burden placed upon the citizen. Thus, while the law has become more and more complicated and troublesome, one's financial risk at all levels of tax law has grown as well. This is one reason more and more citizens each year turn to professionals for assistance in preparing their returns.

Unfortunately, the professionals, as repeatedly shown, do not always get it right. Worse, the obligation to file a *correct* income tax return is non-delegable. That is to say, you cannot avoid your legal obligation to file an accurate return merely by employing a professional. Regardless of whether you prepare your own return, a top notch preparation or accounting firm tackles the chore, or your brother-in-law returns a long-awaited favor, you and you alone are held accountable by the IRS.

This sobering fact makes it mandatory that you understand some of the basic concepts surrounding the IRS' penalty arsenal. I have written regarding penalties many times in the past, pointing out that with approximately 150 *different* penalties available in the Code, the

IRS has a virtual potpourri of options available to accomplish the task of separating you from your money.

And separate you it does! In 1988, the IRS assessed over 26.5 *million* penalties, collecting over $2 *billion* from individual return filers alone—people just like you and me.[1] By 1989, net penalty assessments against individuals rose by 19 percent, with a concomitant increase of 26 percent in the dollar amount collected. In 1989, the IRS tacked over $2.5 billion in penalties to the tax assessments of individual return filers.[2]

Penalties, Past and Present

Historically, penalties have been extremely burdensome for citizens, not only because of the sheer number of options available to the IRS, but also because the agency has been permitted to engage in a practice known as "stacking." Penalty stacking is nothing more than the practice of assessing one penalty on top of another in order to achieve the highest possible punitive effect in a given case. This led to a condition which I have complained of for years, that being that resultant penalties could double, or when interest is considered, even triple a tax bill, rendering payment by an otherwise well-intentioned citizen all but impossible.

For example, in the typical situation where a citizen has failed to file a tax return, the IRS would asses the negligence penalty of five percent, the failure to file timely penalty of up to 25 percent, the substantial understatement penalty of up to another 25 percent, the failure to pay penalty of one-half percent per month, and the underpayment of estimated tax penalty computed based upon the interest rate applicable at the time. To these penalties we must now add the *second* negligence penalty which is equal to *50 percent* of the interest due on the tax. When one has completed the calculation necessary to tally these various amounts, what might have begun as a $2,500 tax bill is quickly and dramatically transformed into a $5,000 *or more* tax bill! Is it any wonder that former IRS Commissioner Lawrence Gibbs stated in testimony before Congress in February of 1989, that these penalties, "when taken together. . .sometimes produce unintended results and have a combined impact that can be too severe." Gibbs observed that penalty provisions enforced in such a manner "have produced tensions that are counterproductive to the goals of tax administration."

As early as July, 1988, I decried the injustice of a penalty system which doubled or tripled a tax bill. I pointed out in the July issue of *Pilla Talks Taxes,* that:

> "In virtually every collection case I've ever seen, the problem of payment was not created by the tax, it was created by the interest and penalties. This element makes the average bill almost impossible to pay. The result is the levy upon, and seizure of wages and property which usually leave the citizen destitute. The irony is that when the levies and seizures render the citizen insolvent, the IRS ends up with very little, or even nothing."

Shortly after that written indictment of the IRS' draconian penalty system, former Commissioner Gibbs called upon Congress to overhaul the system, calling for "considerably fewer penalties."

Fortunately, today, there are two important factors to consider which weigh in favor of the citizen facing what could be crushing penalty assessments. The *first* is a matter of which I spoke extensively in the past. That is, penalty assessments, which can be oppressive, are a matter over which you have a large measure of control. While the IRS generally did not explain this fact in the past, you have the absolute right to demand an abatement, or cancelation, of all penalties which are added to your bill. Each and every penalty provision of the Code contains what is referred to as a "good faith" or "reasonable cause" provision. What that means is simply this: if you acted in good faith, or based upon a reasonable cause to believe that your actions or failures to act were proper and justified, the penalties assessed against you *do not apply.*

Some time ago, I was a guest on a nationwide satellite radio broadcast originating in Dallas. I was on the show several times in the past, so a segment of the audience was familiar with my message. While on the subject of penalties, we took a call from a woman with a success story to relate. She and her husband were assessed over $1,000 in various penalties on account of inadvertent errors in their return. When they received the bill, they phoned the IRS asking what could be done about the penalties. They were told by the dutiful IRS employee that the penalties were "automatic" and "nothing could be done." They were told they would just have to pay.

After hearing my description of the right to demand an abatement of penalties when a "good faith, reasonable cause" defense is applicable, they immediately purchased my book and followed the steps described (details on the applicable procedures are discussed below). After mailing their "demand for abatement," they anxiously awaited the IRS' response. Within a matter of weeks, they were notified by the Service Center in Austin, Texas, that their request for abatement was being honored, and that *all penalties,* in excess of $1,000, were duly *cancelled.* With the total investment of a postage stamp and just a few constructive minutes at the typewriter, that Texas couple saved over $1,000 in additional penalties which they clearly did not owe.

Though in the past, the IRS was *silent* on the right to abate penalties, it now speaks in general, if not vague terms, regarding this important alternative to full payment of penalties. Consider the following language from Publication 1, *Your Rights as a Taxpayer:*

"Cancellation of Penalties

"You have the right to ask that certain penalties (but not interest) be cancelled (abated) if you can show reasonable cause for the failure that led to the penalty (or can show that you exercised due diligence, if that is the applicable standard for that penalty).

"If you relied on wrong advice you received from IRS employees on the toll-free telephone system, we will cancel certain penalties that may result. But you have to show that your reliance on the advice was reasonable.

"If you relied on incorrect written advice from the IRS in response to a written request you made after January 1, 1989, we will cancel any penalties that may result. You must show that you gave sufficient and correct information and filed your return after you received the advice." Publication 1, page 4.

In spite of the IRS' marginal explanation of your right to abatement, the statistics show a continued high level of ignorance of this right. In 1988, just $371.71 million in penalties were abated by the IRS, about 16 percent of the gross amount assessed. In 1989, the ratio of assessments did not increase. Clearly, we are making just a small dent in the total penalties assessed and collected by the IRS. It is equally clear that in order to preserve the financial sanctity of American citizens, it is necessary to understand your rights to demand a full abatement, and the manner in which they are implemented.

The *second* major factor weighing in your favor in the penalty dispute finds its genesis in legislation. Shortly after my July, 1988, indictment of the oppressive penalty system which arguably led to Commissioner Gibbs' call for penalty reform, Congress began considering a somewhat extensive package of penalty reform legislation known as the Improved Penalty and Compliance Tax Act of 1989 (IMPACT). IMPACT passed through Congress rather quickly with the support of the Commissioner and broad bipartisan support of lawmakers. On the heels of the Taxpayers' Bill of Rights Act, it seemed fitting and appropriate for Congress to continue the work it began one year earlier. IMPACT was signed into law on December 19, 1989, as part of the Revenue Reconciliation Act of 1989.[3]

Penalty Reform—How It Figures

The provisions of IMPACT apply to tax returns and other documents due to be filed (without regard to any extensions), and actions or failures to act taken by citizens *after* December 31, 1989. Thus, your 1990 income tax return, due to be filed on or before April 15, 1991, will be covered by the penalty reform provisions of IMPACT.

One of the primary concerns of IMPACT was to prevent penalty stacking. In this regard, if no other, I believe that the intent of the law is achieved through its structure. Of paramount interest is the new "accuracy-related penalty," Code §6662. The accuracy-related penalty combines many of the previous, individual penalties bearing individual penalty rates into one penalty with one rate. In creating the new accuracy-related penalty, Congress repealed five other penalties routinely "stacked" against citizens in common audit situations. The five separate penalty provisions repealed and re-codified as Section 6662, the "accuracy-related penalty" are:

1. Negligence or disregard of rules or regulations;
2. Substantial understatement of income tax;
3. Substantial valuation overstatements;
4. Substantial overstatement of pension liabilities; and
5. Substantial estate or gift tax valuation understatements.[4]

The penalty rate provided under new Code §6662 is 20 percent. It applies when any one *or more* of the five conditions exist with regard to a tax return. Significant, however, is that the IRS is *limited* to 20 percent as the total applicable penalty, even if *all five* of the above conditions are present in a given case.

Under previous law (Code §6653(a)(1)), the first negligence

penalty was computed at the rate of just five percent of the underpayment of tax. However, as discussed briefly above, a *second* negligence penalty (Code §6653(a)(2)) was "stacked" on top of the five percent. That penalty was equal to *50 percent* of the interest charged on the underpayment. Interest, as you may well know, when computed under the IRS' rules and regulations, is substantial. When the second negligence penalty is added to a bill, it far exceeds any other penalty. Thus, the new 20 percent cap on negligence represents a substantial reduction in the overall rate charge for negligence.

Another important limitation we realize with IMPACT is that Congress made it clear that Code §6662 applies *only* when a return is filed by the citizen. Under §6664, added to the Code by IMPACT, Congress declared that the accuracy-related penalty applies only "in cases when a return of tax is filed..." Under previous law, if a citizen failed to file a return, or filed his return late, not only was the failure to file penalty of up to 25 percent included in the assessment, but *both* negligence penalties were "stacked," increasing substantially the total penalty. Under new Code §6664(b), this practice must now end, limiting the penalty in cases of failure to timely file to a total of 25 percent.

The new accuracy-related penalty contains still another limitation which I am sure will act to reduce the overall financial burden on citizens. Under previous law, both applicable negligence penalties were applied to the *total* amount of the underpayment determined by the IRS, when *any portion* of that underpayment was due to negligence. Under the new law, however, the penalty is *limited* to only the portion of the underpayment attributable to negligence. Perhaps the explanation of the House Committee will clarify this point:

"If an underpayment of tax is attributable to negligence, the negligence penalty is to apply *only* to the portion of the underpayment that is attributable to negligence rather than, as under present law, to the entire *underpayment* of tax. This is a significant change from present law. Under present law, if *any portion* of any underpayment is attributable to negligence, the negligence penalty applies to the entire underpayment (*both* the portion attributable to negligence *and* the portion not attributable to negligence). Thus, under present law, a taxpayer who has an underpayment, only a *small portion* of which was attributable to negligence, is subject to the same penalty as a taxpayer with the same underpayment, *all* of which is attributable to negligence, even though the behavior of the first taxpayer is arguably less culpable than the behavior of the second taxpayer. The bill *rectifies* this inequity by applying the negligence penalty *only* to the portion of the underpayment attributable to negligence." House Committee Report on H.R. 3299 (emphasis added).

Stated another way, when multiple issues are raised in a tax audit, and those multiple issues give rise to an increased tax liability, the IRS may not impose the accuracy-related penalty (20 percent) upon the *entire* additional tax bill. Rather, only that portion of the increased tax liability which is directly the result of one's negligence or intentional disregard of IRS rules or regulations, may be subjected to the penalty. This limitation will surely reduce the amount of penalties assessed in a given audit situation.

A final limitation upon the accuracy-related penalty is a reflection of prior law, but is more easily applied. The exception of which I speak here is the "reasonable cause" exception. As I declared earlier, a citizen's saving grace with regard to penalties has always been that each of the numerous penalty provisions of the Code contain the good faith, or reasonable cause exception. When the citizen can demonstrate that he acted in good faith, based upon reasonable cause for his actions, rather than out of an intentional or negligent disregard of the IRS' rules and regulations, the penalty does not apply. This axiom is rightfully carried forward into the new accuracy-related penalty. See Code §6664(c).

In drawing the following conclusion, I believe that Congress may well have been influenced by my repeated remarks that the IRS was trigger-happy with regard to the imposition of penalties in all circumstances:

"The committee is concerned that the present law accuracy-related penalties (particularly the penalty for substantial under-statements of tax liability) have been determined too *routinely and automatically* by the IRS. The committee expects that the enactment of standardized exception criterion will lead the IRS to consider fully whether imposition of these penalties is appropriate before determining these penalties." House Committee Report on H.R. 33299 (emphasis added).

This final observation on the accuracy-related penalty makes it plain, I believe, that Congress intended to place a burden on the IRS to more carefully consider, on a case by case basis, whether to impose any penalty at all. This directive represents a departure, in my judgment, from the previous Congressional attitude reflected in prior enactments, that penalties should be employed as a means of increasing revenue collections, as opposed to the auspicious presumption that penalties were to be employed solely as a deterrent to improper and unlawful conduct. I am persuaded that Congress' additional language, while not codified in the law but present as a clear reflection of Congressional intent, will aid substantially in the ability of the average person to fight back against any penalty improperly assessed.

What Are The Penalties You Now Face?

As this chapter progresses, we shall address specific circumstances under which the IRS has and can be expected to assess penalties, and the manner in which those penalties may be challenged and abated through the use of a simple letter. Before proceeding, however, the point must be made that the new penalty provisions expressed in IMPACT apply only to returns filed, and actions or failures to act which occur *after* December 31, 1989. Up through that period, the IRS may continue to assess penalties under the prior law. Therefore, without becoming overly technical or unduly verbose or burdensome, I shall attempt to clarify the penalties and procedures which apply both *before* and *after* enactment of IMPACT.

1. Negligence

The negligence penalty as it existed prior to IMPACT will remain operative for all returns and documents filed with the IRS before January 1, 1990. Thus, tax returns covering tax years 1988 and prior will be open to treatment under the old law until the statute of limitations on assessment (generally, three years from the date the return is filed) is closed. The negligence penalty under Code §6653(a) is five percent of the total underpayment, plus 50 percent of the interest due on the total underpayment.[5] However, as discussed above, the prior law did contain a "good faith" or "reasonable cause" provision.

The burden, either under the prior negligence or the current accuracy-related penalty, rests with the citizen to demonstrate that his underpayment of tax was not due to negligence or disregard of the IRS' rules or regulations. This must be done with specific evidence which supports the citizens' claim of good faith, reasonable cause. The manner in which this burden is carried out is rather simple. When the IRS assesses a negligence penalty, a notice is generally mailed to the citizen informing him of the good news. When faced with a penalty notice, a citizen has a right, as shown in Publication 1, to demand an abatement or cancellation of that penalty.

Any and all demands for abatement must be in writing and should be made in a prompt fashion. While the penalty statutes are silent on the time in which the demand for abatement should be lodged, experience has shown that the likelihood of the success of your demand seems to decrease as time increases from the date of notice by the IRS to the time of your demand. Your demand should be mailed to the IRS via certified mail and should include a copy of the IRS' original notice for reference. As with all IRS correspondence, you should retain a copy of your written demand for future reference.

Naturally, the mechanics of making the demand for abatement are quite simple. However, the serious question is, what do I say in my written demand? This, of course, depends upon the facts and circumstances of your case. But I have some simple, easy to apply rules of thumb which must govern. First of all, do not lose sight of the fact that you must provide *evidence* which demonstrates that you did not act or fail to act out of a deliberate effort to avoid the IRS' rules or regulations, and that you did not act "negligently" in connection with your duty to comply with the IRS' regulations. Any evidence, including your own testimony supported by an appropriately drafted affidavit, which tends to demonstrate these facts, is appropriate.

More specifically, you must show that your actions or failures to act, as the case may be, were occasioned—not by negligence or intentional disregard—but rather, by a good faith belief based upon reasonable cause, that you were acting correctly and properly. You must declare specifically, and buttress that declaration with facts, which show that you did all you were capable of doing to comply with the law or meet your obligations. Care should be taken to *document* as fully as possible all claims of good faith, reasonable cause.

What are some specific examples of good faith? Permit me to provide some *specific* examples. Please consider the following:

(a) Citizens generally ignorant of the complicated tax laws and the myriad of regulations to implement them are not required to "know the law" in the same way that a lawyer is required to "know the law." The old maxim that "ignorance of the law" is no excuse, does not apply to the tax laws. Because the laws are so complex, a citizen is considered to have met his obligation to "know the law" if he seeks the advise of qualified counsel, and based upon a full and accurate disclosure of all facts, follows the advice of counsel. Counsel can include an income tax preparer, attorney, accountant or other tax planner or expert upon whose advice the citizen relied in good faith. Even though that advice may later prove to be inaccurate, giving rise to an increased tax liability, negligence is not a factor.

(b) Reliance upon the advice of the IRS, if that can be demonstrated, is also a defense to the negligence penalty. As a matter of fact, the *Taxpayers' Bill of Rights Act* added the provision which holds that the negligence penalty does not apply to any erroneous advice provided by the IRS in writing, based upon a full and accurate disclosure of the facts, and upon which the citizen fully relied. See Code §6404(f). Unfortunately, not all advice provided by the IRS is in writing. The IRS will only provide advice in writing when the citizen makes his *request* in writing. The vast majority of citizens seek advice from the IRS via its toll-free telephone system. When the citizen seeks advice in this fashion, he would do well to record the date he phoned, the person he spoke with, the questions asked and, as completely as possible, the answers received. This will help greatly to prove later that the advice was received from the IRS and hence, the negligence penalty is subject to abatement. GAO statistics show that about four out of every 10 persons receiving advice in this fashion will be faced with challenges in the future.

(c) Generally speaking, the citizen must be "on notice" that the position taken in his return is erroneous before the negligence penalty will apply. I do not mean by this that the IRS is under any obligation to phone or write every citizen with an opinion of the adequacy of his return. We know this will not happen, nor is it required. However, the IRS punishes all its regulations, statutes and court rulings and other authority covering the laws, rules of law and operational guidelines in volumes of reference materials. When the IRS or the courts have not expressed any opinion as to the tax treatment of a particular item, and it is shown by the citizen that no such negative opinion existed at the time the treatment is elected, the negligence penalty cannot apply. When a published negative opinion as to the tax treatment of a particular item is on the books, the citizen is considered to be "on notice" as to the official position, even though he may not have personally *read* that opinion or ruling. Consequently, when questionable or sensitive issues are in question, one would do well to either research the law himself, or commission a professional to do so. When this is done, any subsequent claim of negligence is without merit.

(d) "Reasonable cause" is an aspect of the statute which is important. Reasonable cause is nothing more than a "good reason," based upon common sense and existing circumstances, for treating an item one way or another. Reasonable cause exists when the citizen can show a causal link between his actions or failures to act, and the circumstances claimed as reasonable cause. For example, Bernard made a contribution of certain paintings to charity. He deducted the value of the paintings on his return. However, before donating the paintings, he had them appraised by a member of a reputable appraisal association with expertise in the area of paintings. Copies of the appraisals were attached to Bernard's tax return as described in the previous chapter. Later it was shown that the appraisals in fact *overvalued* the worth of the paintings, and a portion of Bernard's deduction was disallowed. However, Bernard argued that he had "reasonable cause" for the value shown on the return, in that the value was determined by a qualified appraiser. Bernard argued that he relied upon the appraisal in "good faith," believing it to be accurate. As it turned out, the appraisal was inaccurate, but that did not justify the IRS' demand for the negligence penalty. Bernard's reliance in good faith on the appraisal was held to constitute "reasonable cause" justifying his actions, thereby vitiating the negligence penalty.

(e) One critical aspect of the "good faith" argument is that the citizen must make full disclosure to the IRS of all applicable facts. This is where the "one-in-a-million" precautions discussed in Chapter Five come into play. When full disclosure of the facts is made, this is a major factor in determining whether good faith exists. David was living abroad for several years during the 1980's. Having received much income through overseas sources, David was under the impression that certain of his receipts were excludable from his income, hence, not subject to our tax laws. On his return, David showed the amount of the income and its source, and explained fully why he believed it was not subject to taxation. He computed his tax liability without regard to that income, and filed his returns. This was done for two years running. After the second return was filed, the IRS challenged David's treatment of the income, and asserted the negligence penalty. David argued that he made full disclosure of the facts, and set forth his position clearly in the return. He argued that his act of full disclosure was evidence of good faith, and the explanation in the return set forth "reasonable cause." Furthermore, in the face of these disclosures, the IRS mailed David a refund for the first year. It was ruled that David's act of full disclosure on the return did indeed show "good faith," justifying abatement of the negligence penalties assessed against him.

Suffice it to say at this point that the facts argued as reasonable cause must bear a direct relationships to the issue the IRS challenges. It would be inappropriate to suggest, for example, that a death in your family in 1989 was "reasonable cause" for an error on your 1991 income tax return. In my second book, *How Anyone Can Negotiate*, I reproduced a portion of the IRS' manual which discusses "reasonable cause" criteria, and points out many of the issues which the IRS will consider and questions it will raise when faced with demands for abatement such as discussed here. I strongly recommend that one review that manual segment in connection with this discourse.

2. Late Filing or Failure to File

The late filing, or failure to file penalty, assessed under §6551 of the Code, generally has not been changed by IMPACT. But IMPACT did create a new type of classification of failure to file. Under prior law, the penalty for fraud could and routinely was ascribed to a failure to file, increasing the penalty to 75 percent. However, IMPACT does not allow the fraud penalty, now Code §6663, to be imposed on one's failure to file. Despite this, the failure to file statute, §6651, now distinguishes between "negligent" failures to file and "fraudulent" failures to file. In the case of the former, the old law and standards apply. In the case of the latter, the penalty is increased from five to 15 percent per month, with a cap of 75 percent, up from 25 percent. The "fraudulent" failure to file will be discussed more in detail later in this chapter.

In light of IMPACT, the accuracy-related penalty (new Code §6662 discussed earlier) may not be stacked with the failure to timely file penalty after January 1, 1990. Hence, when you are penalized for failure to file a return, you may not be simultaneously slapped with the negligence penalty. Thus, *currently,* the maximum exposure for a negligent failure to file under §6651 is 25 percent (five percent per month up to five months). For returns due to be filed *prior* to January 1, 1990, the maximum exposure is 30 percent (25 percent for failure to file and five percent for negligence).

Before embarking upon further discussion of the negligent failure to file penalty, let me point out an assumption we will operate under within this section. That assumption is that you *did not* in fact, file your return in a timely manner. If that assumption is inaccurate in your particular case, yet the IRS has accused you of failing to file in a timely manner, you must address the question in the fashion outlined in Chapter Two.

Section 6651 of the Code provides a penalty of five percent per month, or 25 percent total, in the case of failure to file any return on its due date. The penalty is not applicable when it is shown that the "failure is due to reasonable cause and not willful neglect..." This provision of the Code provides the angle required to win an abatement of the failure to file penalty when a good faith, reasonable cause for the failure can be shown. In this case, as with the negligence penalty itself, the citizen and not the IRS will bear the burden to prove that the failure was due to good faith, and not willful neglect.

IRS regulations written to interpret this provision of the Code provide that the delay in filing a return is due to reasonable cause and not willful neglect if the citizen can show that he exercised "ordinary business care and prudence" and was nevertheless unable to file the return. Thus, when the failure is due to no fault of your own, or circumstances beyond your control, and these facts are clearly documented, the failure to file penalty will be abated. See Rev. Reg. §301.6651-1.

The IRS Manual[6] provides the following list of items which are said to establish reasonable cause for a filing delinquency:

(a) The return is mailed timely but not delivered by the post office in time;

(b) The return is filed in time, but in the wrong IRS office, such as when a return required to be mailed to Ogden, Utah is mailed to Kansas City;

(c) When the delay is due to erroneous information provided by the IRS, or when the citizen requests necessary forms and instructions from the IRS but the IRS fails to provide them within sufficient time to file on the due date;

(d) When the delay is caused by the death or serious illness of the citizen or a member of his immediate family;

(e) When the delay is caused by unavoidable absence of the citizen, thereby preventing his completion and submission of the return;

(f) When the delay is caused by fire, flood, civil disturbance, or other casualty of the citizen's home, business or business records;

(g) When the citizen demonstrates that he personally visited an office of the IRS for the purpose of securing assistance in the preparation and filing of his return, but through no fault of his own, was unable to secure such assistance;

(h) When the citizen is unable, through reasons beyond his control, to secure all the records necessary to complete the return accurately prior to the due date; and

(i) When the citizen receives advice from a competent tax advisor, such as an attorney or accountant, to the effect that a return is not required to be filed. As a side note, all must realize that the duty to file timely is placed upon you, the citizen. The fact that you have delegated the preparation of your return to a paid professional will not by itself relieve you of the penalty in the event of the preparer's failure to complete the return in time for filing by the due date.

The above list is a sampling of those reasons which the IRS has accepted and will accept, provided they are documented or supported with specific facts. As I have already explained, when requesting an abatement of penalties, the facts and circumstances must be clearly and expressly set forth in a fashion which will allow the reader to conclude that you took all reasonable steps necessary to ensure that the return would indeed be filed in a timely manner, but through no fault of your own, were unable to do so.

A clear example of this is Ed, who filed his return nearly one year late. He was not under the protections of an extension, so when the return hit the Service Center, the IRS bounced a penalty letter back into Ed's hands. The demand called for the payment of in excess of $6,000 in penalties for failure to file the return in a timely manner.

Ed quickly responded with a request for abatement which demonstrated that his failure to file was based upon a reasonable cause, and not due to a deliberate effort on his part to avoid or defeat the IRS' rules and regulations. More specifically, Ed showed clearly that he exercised ordinary business care and prudence in connection with the preparation of his return, but through no fault of his own, was unable to file the return in a timely manner. Please see Exhibit 6-1.

You will note from Exhibit 6-1 that Ed took great care to *fully explain* the circumstances behind his failure to file a timely return. He set forth facts and circumstances which will allow the IRS to draw the conclusion that the failure to file timely was not a deliberate act on his part, but rather, was due to circumstances beyond his control. Care must be taken to avoid any vague or generalized references to events or circumstances. A letter which is not specific, illustrating a causal relationship between the events in question and the failure to file, the IRS willl afford your request in short shrift.

Please also note the final paragraph of Ed's letter. That paragraph declares that the facts contained in Ed's letter are true and correct. This is effectively tantamount to creating an affidavit. It may be advisable, however, to have your written statement notarized.

3. Late Payment of Tax

The penalty for late payment of taxes is an element of Code §6651. Your taxes are required to be paid in full on or before the due date of the return. When your tax return is due by April 15, the payment for any taxes shown due on the return is also required at that time. Section 6651 provides a penalty of up to one percent *per month* for a maximum of 25 months when the tax is not paid in full by the due date. The penalty is computed based upon the balance due. The penalty, like all those discussed, is assessed by the IRS and the citizen is billed for the increase. However, the law provides that the penalty will be abated when "it is shown that such failure is due to reasonable cause and not willful neglect..."

The standards for winning an abatement of the failure to pay the tax penalty are much the same as those already discussed, with one important exception. In order to prevail on this issue, we must take the showing of good faith a bit further. IRS regulations on the subject provide the following guidance:

"***A failure to pay will be considered to be due to reasonable cause to the extent that the taxpayer has made a satisfactory showing that he exercised ordinary business care and prudence in

EXHIBIT 6-1

Edward B.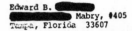
Mabry, #405
Tampa, Florida 33607

May 23, 1988

Internal Revenue Service
Regional Service Center
Atlanta, Georgia 39901

RE: Penalty Notice Dated April 25, 1988

Dear Sir:

This letter is in response to your notice dated April 25, 1988, (copy
enclosed) which assesses and demands payment of the sum of $6,687.31
for tax year 1986. The assessment is for late filing and late payment
penalties, plus interest.

This letter is a protest to the assessment of said penalties, and
request for abatement under 26 USC §6213(b). Under Rev. Reg.
§301.6651-1(c)(1), this letter contains facts which constitute the
showing of "reasonable cause" necessary to have the penalty assessment
abated.

FACTS -- I was under the effect of an Automatic extension of time in
which to file return, which form was timely filed on April 15, 1987.
The extension took the time for filing up to and including August 15,
1987. The purpose for filing the extension was that records necessary
for the accurate and truthful preparation of the return in question
were not all in my hands by April 15, 1987. A request for automatic
extension was filed.

The needed records included documents showing the receipt of income
and payment of deductible expenses in connection with a limited
partnership of which I have been a limited partner for a number of
years. The transmittal of the necessary tax information from the
general partner to the limited partners is perenially late. Ordinary
business care and prudence dictate that before my return can be
accurately prepared to correctly reflect my income and expenses, I
must have this information in hand.

Next, in December of 1986, my address had changed by reason of a move.
After the move, I was unable to locate all of the other personal
records which were necessary to correctly prepare the tax return.
These records were lost through no fault of my own. After having gone
through every box and searching in every conceivable possible
location, I located the records and immediately brought them to my tax
return preparer. This was in January of 1988, several months after
the extension had run out. I did not believe that I had any right to
file another request for extension, but was unable to file a correct

EXHIBIT 6-1 (continued)

income tax return by August 15, 1987, due to the missing records.
Once those records were located, I took immediate and prompt steps to
have the return prepared and to pay the tax shown due thereon, in a
prudent business manner.

I believe and so state that I did not act in a "willfully negligent"
manner as that phrase is used in IRS Code §6651(a). My reason for not
filing or paying on time was due, as shown above, to "reasonable
cause." I delayed filing the return to be sure that such return, once
filed, would be true and accurate in all respects. It was impossible
to file such a return without the information mentioned above. My
actions of filing late were a direct result of the knowledge of the
legal requirement to file a truthful return, and not an inaccurate
one. Ordinary business care required that I not file an incorrect tax
return. For this reason, I have acted in a reasonable manner, and not
due to willful neglect.

Under all of the facts and circumstances, I submit that the assessed
penalties for failure to file timely and failure to pay are due to be
abate. I hereby request, under the language of the regulations cited
above, the penalties be, in all things, abated.

Under penalty of perjury, I declare that all of the facts contained in
this demand for abatement are true and correct in all respects.

Sincerely,

Edward B. ▄▄▄▄▄

encl.

providing for paymet of his tax liability and was nevertheless either unable to pay the tax or would suffer an undue hardship (as described in Rev. Reg. §1.6161-1(b)[7] if he paid on the due date. In determining whether the taxpayer was unable to pay the tax in spite of the exercise of ordinary business care and prudence in providing for the payment of his tax liability, consideration will be given to all the facts and circumstances of the taxpayer's financial situation, including the amount and nature of the taxpayer's expenditures in light of the income (or other amounts) he could, at the time of such expenditures, reasonably expect to receive prior to the date prescribed for the payment of the tax. Thus, for example, a taxpayer who incurs lavish or extravagant living expenses in an amount such that the remainder of his assets and anticipated income will be insufficient to pay his tax, has not exercised ordinary business care and prudence in providing for the payment of his tax liability. Further, a taxpayer who invested funds in speculative or illiquid assets has not exercised ordinary business care and prudence in providing for the payment of his tax liability unless, at the time of the investment, the remainder of the taxpayer's assets and estimated income will be sufficient to pay his tax or it can be reasonably foreseen that the speculative or illiquid investment made by the taxpayer can be utilized (by sale or security for a loan) to realize sufficient funds to satisfy the tax liability. A taxpayer will be considered to have exercised ordinary business care and prudence if he made reasonable efforts to conserve sufficient assets in marketable form to satisfy his tax liability and nevertheless was unable to pay all or a portion of the tax when it became due." Rev. Reg. §301.6651-1(c).

The key to defeating this penalty is the requirement to show that you did in fact exercise ordinary business care and prudence in providing for your tax liability, but were nevertheless unable to do so. In this regard, you must set forth facts which clearly demonstrate the actions you took to provide for your tax liability, and the factors or events which made it impossible for you to do so. Great care must be taken to illustrate a causal link between the events allegedly out of your control, and your inability to pay your taxes in a timely manner.

Chris and her husband lived an entirely normal existence in all respects. Unfortunately, their world was shattered when Chris' husband suddenly lost his job. By reason of major work force reductions in his industry, there simply was no further work, not only with his current employer, but within the entire city in which he lived. Hoping for the best, he continued to search for work, did odd jobs, and fed his family with their modest savings. When it came time to file their tax return, the document was mailed to the IRS, but without full payment for the tax liability. The family just did not have sufficient funds to pay the tax, due to no fault of their own.

Within a very short period of time, the IRS' notice and demand for payment, togther with the accrued penalty for failure to pay, found its way to Chris' door. As though the several months of no work and katsup sandwiches was not depressing enough, they now had the impatience of the IRS with which to contend. Chris responded with a demand for abatement of the penalty, based upon reasonable cause. Following the lead established by the regulation we just read, Chris drafted her letter setting forth the specific facts which would demonstrate to the IRS that she and her husband exercised ordinary business care and prudence in providing for the payment of their taxes, but through no fault of their own, were unable to do so. Much time was spent painting a picture of the facts and circumstances in order to clearly illustrate the link between the unfortunate events of life and their inability to pay the tax in full. Please see Exhibit 6-2.

The late payment of the tax penalty is very common, but a demand for abatement of the variety shown in Exhibit 6-2 is not. Most citizens simply accept without question the addition to the tax of one percent per month, without ever realizing the penalty is merely contingent, and is fully subject to cancellation. When successful with a demand for abatement, substantial savings can result even when the underlying tax bill is but minimal.

4. Underpayment of Estimated Taxes

During the course of the year, every individual has an obligation to make estimated payments on his tax liability. Persons employed by others make these payments through the withholding system, in which a percentage of their weekly paycheck is forwarded by their employer to the IRS. The Form W-2 provided at the end of the year is a statement to both the IRS and the employee as to the amount of wages paid, and the amount subjected to both federal and state income tax and social security withholding requirements.

Self-employed persons do not have the luxury, if you wish to call

EXHIBIT 6-2

Chris and Dennis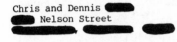
Nelson Street

November 10, 1989

Internal Revenue Service
Service Center
Kansas City, MO 64999

RE: Your Notice dated October 29, 1989
     Tax Year 1988
     SSN:

Dear Sir:

On October 29, 1989, we received notice from the IRS (see copy
enclosed) that a penalty for failure to timely pay income taxes is
assessed against us. The amount of the bill is $156, plus interest.
The bill represents five months of the penalty for failure to pay.

This letter is a protest to the assessment of that penalty and a
request for abatement under all applicable Code sections. In
accordance with Tax Regulation §301.6651-1(c), this letter contains
facts which constitute a showing of "reasonable cause" and "ordinary
business care and prudence" necessary to have the penalty for failure
to pay taxes abated.

THESE ARE THE FACTS:

For six years, from February, 1983, to July of 1988, I worked as a
computer programmer and systems analyist for   Inc., in
     . My job with the company was highly specialized. My work
involved exclusively defense contracts. During each and every year
while employed there, I filed my returns on time and paid all taxes
due. My taxes were always paid through wage withholding. Each year I
would either have a refund due me, or would have to pay just a few
hundred dollars in taxes. I never faced a large tax bill when filing.
The reason is I have always been careful to be sure that wage
withholdings were enough to cover my liability.

Since the mid 1980's, the computer firms in the   and
surrounding areas have steadily decreased their work forces. One by
one, each firm, including   Inc., laid off workers. In
July of 1988, I was laid off and have not worked since. At the time
of the layoff, I made efforts to find other employment. I searched
for jobs with every potential employer in my industry. I applied for
jobs both directly related, and entirely unrelated to my previous
employment. I was shocked to learn that there is literally no
employment to be had in this area for my particular skills.

EXHIBIT 6-2 (continued)

From the time of my layoff, I drew unemployment for 26 weeks. After
26 weeks, the unemployment benefits ran out. At the time of my
layoff, we had just $2,000 in savings. The unemployment compensation
was just $800 per month, while our monthly living expenses for a
family of four were over $1,200 per month, including our house
payment. We were required to use our savings in order to live from
month to month. When the savings ran out, we had to borrow money to
make up the difference.

At the time of the layoff, because I had no further employment, no
withholding taxes were paid. So when our income tax return for 1988
was filed in April of 1989, we owed over $3,000 in federal income
taxes. We filed the return without the paying the tax, because we
were told by our tax preparer that we had to.

Our failure to pay taxes in April was not because we failed to save
enough money. We were unable to save enough money because of being
laid off. All funds I received from the 26-week unemployment
compensation period were used to feed my family including two young
children. We have no equity in our house and so we were unable to
borrow any funds against the house to pay the taxes. After our $2,000
savings ran out, we were forced to borrow money from my father in
order to live.

We did exercise ordinary business care and prudence in providing for
the payment of our 1988 income taxes. This done by filing a W4 form
with my employer. I was always careful to be sure that enough money
was taken from my check through withholding to cover my federal and
state taxes. But there was no way to anticipate that I would be laid
off when I was. During the period of time in question, I made every
reasonable effort to conserve sufficient funds to pay my taxes, but
through no fault of my own, was unable to. I was unable to for the
simple reason that we simply did not have enough money to pay our
mandatory living expenses. We were living on unemployment, our small
savings which quickly ran out, and then money borrowed from my father.

Under the harsh circumstances which we suffered during the past year,
it was impossible to save any money for any thing. I made every
reasonable effort to pay our taxes. But through no fault of our own,
we just did not have the money. We did not squander our funds, all
available funds were needed to survive and feed two small children.

Under the circumstances of this case, we did exercise ordinary
business care and prudence in providing for payment of the tax, but
through no fault of our own, were unable to. Based upon the facts
shown above, we submit that "reasonable cause" exists to have the
failure to pay the tax penalty abated in full.

We declare under penalty of perjury that the facts contained in this
letter are true and correct in all respect.

Chris ▇▇▇   Dennis ▇▇▇

it that, of a wage withholding program. They must discipline themselves to make quarterly estimated income tax installment payments. The IRS provides Form 1040ES, actually a coupon, for this purpose. The estimated payment is due within 15 days after the close of each calendar quarter.

Section 6654 of the Code, unaffected by IMPACT, establishes the amount which is to be paid as the estimate for the year and provides a penalty for failure to make such estimated payments. Thankfully, the statute also creates an exception to the imposition of the penalty in certain cases. The exception is somewhat different than the "good faith, reasonable cause" standard we have been examining. Still, the defenses available under the statute are equally effective. As a matter of fact, upon examining the standard, it is my opinion that it may be much broader than the "good faith, reasonable cause" standard applicable in other statutes.

Section 6654(d)(1) establishes the amount of the installments which must be made on an annual basis in order to avoid imposition of the penalty. The statute provides that one must make installment payments equal to the *lesser* of 90 percent of the tax shown due on the current return, or 100 percent of the tax paid the previous year. To illustrate the requirements of the statute, let us assume a few hypothetical facts:

(a) In 1989, you paid federal income taxes of $3,000;

(b) In 1990, your federal tax liability will be $4,000.

In order to avoid the penalty, you must pay either 90 percent of the current liability, which is $3,600 ($4,000 x .9 = $3,600) or, 100 percent of the previous liability, which is $3,000. Because your obligation is to pay the *lesser* of these two amounts, you will avoid the penalty if current estimated payments equal at least $3,000. The balance of the current liability will then be due at the time the return is filed on or before April 15th.

Experience has revealed two conceivable problems with the penalty under Code §6654. Each is potentially costly; both are easily resolved. Let us examine them.

Problem One. A man I knew worked for a large corporation in 1987. He earned an average income and paid approximately $4,000 in federal taxes. In 1988, he struck out on his own and scored with his business. His income rose substantially, and his tax liability followed. For tax year 1988, he owed federal income taxes in excess of $14,000. During the year, the self-employed man used IRS Form 1040ES to make estimated payments of his 1988 federal income tax liability. He paid around $5,700 to the IRS in four quarterly installments. His return for 1988 was filed timely. With the return he remitted the balance of tax due, approximately $8,300.

Shortly after filing his return, he received a notice from the IRS Service Center that he owed a penalty for underpaying his estimated taxes. The IRS calculated that he was required to make payments equal to 90 percent of his current tax liability, or about $12,600. Using the complicated statutory formula, the IRS demanded approximately $630 as the penalty for underpaying estimated taxes.

Without delay, a letter was written to the Service Center which issued the bill. In the letter, the point was made that Code §6654(d) contains the requirement that the *lesser* of 90 percent of the current tax liability, or 100 percent of the previous tax liability be paid through installments. A copy of the 1987 income tax return was attached to the letter which showed the tax liability for that year of about $4,000. Also attached to the letter were copies of Form 1040ES and cancelled checks for installments made during 1988. The installments totalled about $5,700. With these facts, it was shown that in excess of 100 percent of the 1987 liability was paid through installments, thus complying with the terms of the statute. The final statement in the letter demanded an abatement of the penalty based upon the facts shown. The IRS obliged, abating a penalty in excess of $630.

Problem Two. Earlier I stated that there is a defense contained within the statute which, in some cases, may be broader and hence, more universally applicable than is the defense of "good faith, reasonable cause" explored earlier. The defense is found in section 6654(e)(3) and applies when sufficient installments under either of the above formulas have not been made. The exceptions (there are two of them) to the penalty read as follows:

"(A) No addition to the tax shall be imposed under (§6654) with respect to any underpayment to the extent the Secretary determines that by reason of casualty, disaster, or other unusual circumstances the imposition of such addition to tax would be against equity and good conscience.

"(B) No addition to tax shall be imposed under (§6654) with respect to any underpayment if the Secretary determines that:

"1. The taxpayer (I) retired after having attained the age of 62, or (II) became disabled, in the taxable year for which estimated payments were required to be made or in the taxable year preceding such taxable year, and such underpayment was due to reasonable cause and not willful neglect."

The first of these additional defenses to the penalty we shall call the "good conscience" defense. The second we shall refer to as the "retired/disabled" defense.

The "good conscience" defense is extremely broad. Under this provision of the law, the failure to make estimated payments can be avoided upon showing that some type of disaster, such as fire or flood, or "other unusual circumstances" were present. This could include extensive medical bills, which made payment of installments difficult or impossible. I am encouraged with the "good conscience" defense because unlike the "reasonable cause" defense, in order to prevail in the request for abatemet, I believe we need only show that some disaster, casualty or other unusual circumstance was present. Having done so, we can argue under the language of the statute that the presence of such circumstances renders the imposition of the penalty contrary to "equity," or fundamental fairness, and "good conscience."

We are not required to show that one exercised ordinary business care and prudence, or some other affirmative showing as we discussed regarding the other penalties. Instead, the elements of "fairness" and "justice," and "good conscience" enter the picture. Frankly, as far as I know, this is the one and only location in the entire 10,000 pages of the Internal Revenue Code where the IRS is called upon by law to apply the fundamental principles of fairness and justice when passing upon citizen requests.

Some may argue that the undefined, subjective element of "good conscience" could operate to the disadvantage of the average citizen, since it is questionable whether any level of "good conscience" exists within the IRS. I respond by pointing out that not every person within the IRS is a certified ogre. Certainly every person has *some* standard of justice and operates under *some* form of conscience. The statute's lack of a firm definition of "good conscience" to me, provides broad latitude to argue points and present facts which may go beyond the narrow definitions I offered in earlier discussion of other penalties. Stated another way, I believe that we have a license, given the language of this penalty, to present everything but the kitchen sink (and maybe that too, if it caused a flood) as grounds for abating this penalty based upon the standard of "good conscience."

The "retired/disabled" test is more narrow and clearly defined. If you have reached the age of 62 and retired during the year in question, or become disabled, either in the year in question or in the previous year, you can have the penalty abated. In order to prevail under the "retired/disabled" test, you must also show "reasonable cause" for the failure to make estimated payments. Here we are back to the requirement to show a causal link between the facts asserted as reasonable cause and the failure to make the estimated payments. As already pointed out, the facts and circumstances alleged as reasonable cause must allow the reader to reach the conclusion that despite your effort to comply with the law, events beyond your control made it impossible. Refer to the list of possible defenses in item number 3 above for further discussion.

5. Fraud

The fraud penalty has been altered somewhat by IMPACT. First of all, the fraud penalty applies when "any part of the underpayment of tax required to be shown on a return is due to fraud." Code §6663 (Code §6653(b) applies for returns filed before January 1, 1990). What constitutes fraud in connection with a tax return has been the subject of much debate over the years, but the courts have settled upon a definition which stood the test of time. Before the civil fraud penalty of 75 percent can be imposed, the IRS must prove that the citizen committed an *overt* act in furtherance of an attempt to illegally underpay his income taxes. The *overt* act, as opposed to an act of omission, must hve the effect of deceiving or misleading the IRS with regard to the citizen's income tax liability. When the IRS is able to prove, with "clear and convincing evidence" that the citizen committed such an act, the penalty will be imposed.

The fraud penalty under §6663 applies only to tax returns which are filed. When no return is filed, no fraud penalty under §6663 may be assessed. However, I mentioned earlier that IMPACT altered the civil failure to file penalty (Code §6651), adding subsection (f). This subsection establishes a penalty of up to 75 percent when it is shown that the citizen's failure to file the return was "fraudulent." The penalty is graduated in that the rate is 15 percent per month, for a maximum of 5 months, or 75 percent. In this regard, fraudulent failures to file are treated in the same manner as fraud committed in connection with a return which is filed.

When the fraud penalty is assessed, either under §6663 or 6651 (relating to fraudulent failure to file), the IRS may not impose other civil penalties related to the accuracy of the return. For example, the accuracy penalty under §6662 cannot be stacked with the fraud penalty, thus limiting the punitive effect of the penalty.

The fraud penalty under either statute is substantially different in its operational manner than is any of the other penalties we have discussed. The most important aspect of this penalty is that unlike *any* of the others, you do not have the burden of proof in the matter. In order to sustain the penalty, the IRS must prove with clear and convincing evidence that you committed an overt act (as opposed to an act of omission) the effect of which was to deceive or mislead the IRS in the ascertainment, computation, or assessment of your correct tax liability.

This element of the penalty is critical, and speaks to the axiom that ignorance of the law is no excuse. I hope by now we have established the fact that where federal tax laws are concerned, ignorance of the law is every excuse if the citizen has acted in good faith and did not deliberately avoid his obligations under the law. When a citizen did not act in bad faith, or in the case of the fraud penalty, did not act with a deliberate intent to violate what he knew were his obligations under the law, the fraud penalty does not apply. Moreover, the IRS must prove that the citizen intentionally and deliberately set out to violate a known legal duty in connection with his income tax obligations before the penalty will be enforced.

Bad faith and intent to violate the law refers to your state of mind at the time of the alleged offense.[8] This, as you might imagine, is a difficult element to prove. To do so, the IRS will draw from any statements you may have made, or activities in which you engaged in order to infer your intent from those activities. Examples of the required overt act, or act of *commission*, necessary to sustain the fraud penalty include:

(a) Deliberate understatement of income or overstatement of deductions in your return;

(b) Using two sets of records for the purpose of masking income;

(c) The use of cash only as a means of doing business in order to avoid creating records of income;

(d) Making deliberately false or misleading statements in other tax forms, such as Form W-4, or upon loan applications, for the purpose of misleading the IRS;

(e) Placing assets in the hands of third parties or "nominees" in order to conceal them from the IRS; or

(f) The use of fictitious names or social security numbers on bank accounts to mislead the IRS.

This is just a partial list of items which the IRS will consider to be evidence of fraud if present in your case. I do not intend it be exhaustive, nor do I mean to suggest that *all* must be present in order for the IRS to prevail. The agency need only prove *one* act of commission, or overt act, in order to establish the fraud penalty. As you can see, however, these actions are very serious and certainly are confined to just a very minute minority of citizens who are probably criminals anyway. Persons such as drug dealers, illegal gamblers, etc., are the sort typically involved in these activities, and are those generally hit with the 75 percent fraud penalty.

However, Dale did not fit into any of the molds usually reserved for tax criminals worthy of the fraud penalty. Dale did not file income tax returns for a number of years. When the IRS caught up with him, it not only computed his tax liability based upon available information in the absence of returns, but included the penalty for fraud. Dale was most upset, because the inclusion of the fraud penalty not only implies dubious conduct, but nearly doubles the tax bill *without* regard to interest.

Dale demanded that the IRS drop the fraud penalty. When the agency refused, he requested that it provide a statement or copies of all evidence the agency possessed which supported its claim of fraud. Remember, the IRS must prove the fraud question. The citizen need not prove good faith or any other standard to resist the fraud penalty assessment. As the case developed, it became clear that the IRS had no substantive evidence that Dale committed fraud. Its only support for assessment of the penalty was that Dale failed to file returns for several years. It was the "pattern of conduct," the IRS suggested, which supported its demand for the penalty.

As I endeavored to illustrate above, the mere failure to file a return, an act of *omission,* does not by itself prove fraud. Rather, in addition to the failure to file, the IRS must demonstrate that some other affirmative act, the effect of which is to deceive or mislead the IRS, accompanied the failure to file. In Dale's case, there was no affirmative act. He did not file false documents with the IRS, made no false statements to investigators, did not attempt to conceal assets, or otherwise conduct his affairs in a criminal or inappropriate manner. Dale failed to file his returns—period. That did not make him a criminal subject to the fraud penalty.

This point was emphasized and in the absence of any "clear and convincing evidence" that Dale willfully attempted to defraud the IRS, the fraud penalty was dropped. Dale was not forced to incur the substantial increase in his tax bill, a fate reserved for only deliberate tax cheats.

6. The Social Security Number And Minor Children

With the passage of the Tax Reform Act of 1986, Congress imposed a rule which has incensed most Americans. The rule at the time of passage was that minor children who reached the age of five years and were claimed as dependent exemptions on their parents' income tax return, must have a social security number in order for the claim to stand. In 1988 the rule was altered. Congress *reduced* the age requirement to *two years*. Initially, the penalty for failure to have a social security number for minor children was $5. Since IMPACT, it increased to $50.

The notion of branding children with a national identification number at such a tender age caused something of an uprising among citizens concerned with privacy. Others were simply concerned that subjecting such innocent beings to the microscope of federal scrutiny was contrary to good judgment and the American way. Lastly, but perhaps most significantly, many Christian Americans object on religious grounds to the branding of their minor children with a number that arguably constitutes "the number of their name." Such an act is contrary to their spiritual dictates as expressed in the Bible. See the Book of Revelation, Chapter 13, vs. 13-18.

The dilemma presented to those objecting to the assignment and use of a social security number by minor children is simple. Either obtain the number in violation of moral or religious grounds, or face the prospect of not only the $50 fine, but loss of the $2,500 exemption provided for each dependent. With a family of any size, the loss of this deduction could prove financially troublesome. To these people, I offer three separate alternatives. We shall address them in turn.

The *first* is to recognize that the Code section creating the penalty for failure to disclose a social security number for minor children (§6724) contains a "waiver" clause not unlike those already examined. The law provides that:

"No penalty shall be imposed...if it is shown that such failure is due to reasonable cause and not to willful neglect."

In February of 1980, I wrote a Special Report on the topic of social security numbers, minor children and the religious objection.[9] In that report, I illustrated that the established federal law recognizes and accepts the proposition that certain individuals hold a deep-seated, religious opposition to the use of the social security number. Because of that good faith, deeply held religious belief, the federal courts decreed that such persons may not be required to obtain or use a social security number for either themselves, or their minor children. Furthermore, and perhaps most importantly, the courts observed that in the event a Christian were to exercise his right to refuse to obtain or utilize such a number, he *may not* be deprived of rights or privileges to which he would otherwise be entitled if he disclosed such a number.[10]

When this principal is applied to the income tax laws, we come away with the proposition that when you can otherwise prove you are entitlted to claim a minor as a dependent exemption, i.e., you are able to prove that you are provided at least 51 percent of the support for such child during the year in question, you will not be deprived of the dependent exemption merely because you are religiously opposed to the use of the number. Parenthetically, it should be noted that the courts are adamant that the religious objection to the use of the number will not be extended to those with merely a "casual" or "logistical" opposition. Rather, the objection must be solidly grounded in deeply held religious principle. Anything less will be rejected.

Next, it should be noted that objection to the use of the number as a matter of "privacy" has been expressly rejected by the courts as a "good faith" reason for not using the number. According to contemporary federal law, you have no "right of privacy" with regard to your name, an identifying number, and the desire to prevent any person (in particular, the federal government) from tracing your financial life through that nexus.

While the waiver provision cited above clearly applies to the $50 penalty, religious objectors may be faced with year-to-year challenges to their tax returns if other measures are not pursued. The next two alternatives illustrate the manner in which any long-term effects of a religious objection may be overcome.

The *second* alternative involves Louis. He was a religious objector to the use of a social security number for his daughter Monica. No SSN was provided for Monica on the 1988 federal income tax return. By letter dated June of 1990, the IRS notified Louis that his dependency exemption for Monica was disallowed. With that action, the IRS increased Louis' tax liability and tacked on penalties. Louis responded with a surprisingly simple letter to the IRS which proved successful. In addition to explaining the religious objection to using the number, Louis provided independent proof of the validity of his exemption. He mailed a photocopy of Monica's birth certificate and passport to the IRS. Without ado, the IRS responded to Louis, declaring that "We are pleased to tell you that we were able to clear up the discrepancy from the information you provided." An example of Louis' letter is shown in Exhibit 6-3.

The beauty of Louis' approach to the matter was that his act of providing *independent proof* of the validity of his exemption left the IRS without an argument to his failure to use the number. After all, the sole *stated purpose* behind requiring a number is to prevent exemption fraud. Naturally, when the validity of the exemption is established through alternative means, the question of possible fraud and the need for the number are eliminated with the same sweep.

Certainly one way to short circuit the IRS' audit computer is to attach birth certificates directly to your income tax return when minor children lacking social security numbers are claimed as dependent exemptions. As explained in the previous chapter, this will act to provide the IRS with the needed proof *in the first instance*, thereby eliminating the agency's claim such as was made against Louis.

The *third* and final angle, of which I wrote extensively in my Special Report on this subject, involves the use of an Internal Revenue Service Number. The "IRSN" is a number assigned by the IRS to those who are not "required" to obtain a social security number, but nevertheless, need an identification number for income tax purposes. I submit that persons possessing a religious opposition to the social security number as a universal means of identification fall squarely into this category. First, federal law as expressed in the cases mentioned in the footnote above establish that religious objectors "are not required" to obtain or use an SSN. Yet they may, particularly if they are adults, require a number for tax purposes. I believe that the IRSN fulfills this need without infringing the religious opposition.

When an IRSN is issued by the agency, the *sole and exclusive* use to which that number is put is for tax identification purposes. The IRSN is not, and rightfully *should not* be put to any other use, or provided to any other person or organization as an identification

EXHIBIT 6-3

June 16, 1990

Internal Revenue Service
Service Center
Cincinnati, Ohio 54999

Dear IRS:

This is in response to your letter dated June 8, 1990. In the letter
you stated that my dependent exemption shown for tax year 1988 is
disallowed because I did not have a social security number on the
return for my daughter.

Be advised that I have a religious objection to using a social
security number for my minor daughter. My faith is the foundation of
my beliefs and opinion, including the implication of the SSN for minor
children. Please see the Biblical Book of Revelation, Chapter 13, vs
13-18. Therefore, as a "religious objector" my sincerely held
religious beliefs prevented using the number on the tax return.

Please see Federal Court decision in STEVENS V. BERGER, 428 F.SUPP.
896 (D.C. NY 1977) and CALLAHAN V. WOODS, 658 F.2d 679 (9TH Cir.
1981).

Please accept the enclosed Certificate of Live Birth and US Passport
as substantiation of dependent Monica ⬤ ⬤ for tax years 1988,
1989 and 1990. If these documents are acceptable please reply by mail
to me.

Thank you.

Louis ⬤
⬤ Boston Road
⬤, Ohio ⬤
Phone: 216-⬤ ⬤

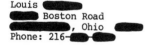

number. When asked for a "social security number" by any person wishing to use it, the answer is simply, "I don't have one." By carefully limiting the number's use in this manner, you will successfully prevent the number from becoming universally and inextricably associated with your name. Hence, the Christian's scriptural admonition to avoid such an act is honored. At the same time, the IRS is provided with what it claims to need in order to achieve its goal of effectively administering the tax laws.

The IRS' Philadelphia Service Center will issue a Taxpayer Identification Number (TIN) upon request. You must explain that you are not required to obtain a social security number, but are in need of a TIN for income tax purposes. Your request should be addressed to: IRS Service Center, Entity Control Section, 11601 Roosevelt Blvd., Philadelphia, PA 19255. Once assigned, use the number *only* for tax purposes. *Do not* use it elsewhere, lest it, too, evolve into an anathema.

7. False Withholding Certificate

Two of the legislative changes made by Congress in an effort to quell the tax protester movement of the late 1970s and early 1980s, was to create procedures for reviewing the Forms W-4, *Withholding Allowance Certificate,* submitted by employees to their employers, and to create a civil penalty for filing a "false Form W-4." The Code section creating the penalty is §6682. The law provides that you are subject to a penalty of $500 if you submit a Form W-4 which (1) "results in a *decrease*" in the amount of tax withheld from your paycheck, and (2) "there was no reasonable basis for such statement" at the time it was made.

Under the procedures presently in effect, your employer is required to mail to the IRS a copy of your Form W-4 if you claim more than 10 withholding allowances, or you claim that you are exempt from federal income tax withholding entirely. When the Form W-4 is submitted to the IRS under this rule, the IRS will review the form to determine whether it is "appropriate" under the circumstances. If the agency is troubled by the claim, it will notify the citizen that the form will be "disallowed" by the IRS (via written notice to your employer) and you will be subjected to the $500 penalty.

There are two approaches to handling this problem. The first addresses the merits of the Form W-4, while the second is dedicated to avoiding the penalty should your Form W-4 be in error.

With regard to the merits of the Form W-4, it is now beyond question that the Form W-4 is perhaps as troublesome as the 1040 itself. I believe it was in 1987 when the IRS released a revised edition of Form W-4 which literally "raised the roof" in this nation. The reason was the form was so complicated that a major segment of the public was forced to seek the advice of an accountant merely to prepare the form! The outrage caused the IRS and Congress to go back to the drawing board. Later, the IRS kindly agreed to forego the assessment of this penalty in connection with those extremely complicated forms. However, the IRS beneficence has long since evaporated. It can be expected to assess penalties in connection with any Form W-4 which it believes to be "false."

The purpose of the Form W-4 is such that the employee may communicate to his employer the extent to which he desires federal income taxes be withheld from his pay. To be sure, all employees are subject to withholding, but it is equally true that each has the right to play a role in determining the extent to which this will occur. For example, a single person with no withholding allowances claimed on his Form W-4 will be subject to the *highest rate* of withholding, while a married person with several allowances claimed will reap the benefits of lesser amounts withheld each week.

The number of withholding allowances to which you are entitled is determined by a number of factors. First, you are entitled to claim one allowance for each dependent exemption to which you are entitled. If you are married with three children, you would be entitled to five allowances (one for yourself, your spouse, and each child). Next, you are entitled to take into consideration all itemized deductions to which you are entitled on Schedule A, any tax credits, and any other deductions such as for the aged or blind, to which you may be entitled.

These allowances are computed in the worksheet attached to Form W-4. Clearly, given the broad definition and application of the term "allowance," the average family with itemized deductions for such things as interest, state taxes and charitable contributions, will be entitled to 10 *or more* withholding allowances. See Code §3402(m).

The law also creates an *exemption* from withholding for certain individuals. These persons may claim "exempt" on Form W-4. Upon making such claim, they will not be subjected to the weekly withholding ritual. A person may claim this exemption if: (1) he incurred *no* income tax liability for the preceding year, and (2) reasonably anticipates that he will incur *no* income tax liability for the present year. See Code §3402(n). On the *current* Form W-4, all rules covering the correct number of withholding allowances you may claim are explained in relatively simple fashion. See Form W-4, Exhibit 6-4.

If you claim an exemption from withholding, or you claim in excess of 10 withholding allowances, you must stand prepared to explain the correctness of your Form W-4. When confronted by the IRS regarding the form, be prepared to explain:

(a) The manner in which you determined your withholding status;

(b) Specific facts and circumstances which justify your claim;

(c) That your claim was made in good faith, based upon the reasonable cause as shown by the facts, and most importantly;

(d) That to your best knowledge and belief, and as shown by the facts, you had a "reasonable basis" for making the claim in the form. You must emphasize that you did not file the form for the purpose of unlawfully reducing your withholding, nor did you do so with the knowledge or belief that you had no reasonable basis for making the claim. See Code §6682.

The letter should be promptly mailed to the IRS at the address shown on its notice to you. You should be careful to identify the letter as one in response to the Form W-4 inquiry and that the letter is written to avoid the penalty under Code §6682. These procedures will apply when your form is in fact correct, but merely questioned by the agency.

When it is shown, however, that your form is *incorrect,* you must take care to quickly explain your actions in order to avoid the $500 penalty. The statute provides a two-pronged test for determining whether the penalty applies. The first is that the W-4 led to a reduction in your withholding, and the second is that "at the time the statement was made," there was no "reasonable basis" for making it. If your withholding statement is incorrect, you may nevertheless avoid the $500 penalty by setting forth, in writing, the specific facts and circumstances which led you to the conclusion that you had a "reasonable basis" for your claim. Not the least of the facts establishing "reasonable basis" is if an accountant or return preparer completed or advised you in the completion of your Form W-4.

Moreover, any and all financial circumstances which affected

EXHIBIT 6-4

19**90** Form W-4

Department of the Treasury
Internal Revenue Service

Purpose. Complete Form W-4 so that your employer can withhold the correct amount of Federal income tax from your pay.

Exemption From Withholding. Read line 6 of the certificate below to see if you can claim exempt status. *If exempt, complete line 6; but do not complete lines 4 and 5.* No Federal income tax will be withheld from your pay. This exemption expires February 15, 1991.

Basic Instructions. Employees who are not exempt should complete the Personal Allowances Worksheet. Additional worksheets are provided on page 2 for employees to adjust their withholding allowances based on itemized deductions, adjustments to income, or two-earner/two-job situations. Complete all worksheets that apply to your situation. The worksheets will help you figure the number of withholding allowances you are

entitled to claim. However, you may claim fewer allowances than this.

Head of Household. Generally, you may claim head of household filing status on your tax return only if you are unmarried and pay more than 50% of the costs of keeping up a home for yourself and your dependent(s) or other qualifying individuals.

Nonwage Income. If you have a large amount of nonwage income, such as interest or dividends, you should consider making estimated tax payments using Form 1040-ES. Otherwise, you may find that you owe additional tax at the end of the year.

Two-Earner/Two-Jobs. If you have a working spouse or more than one job, figure the total number of allowances you are entitled to claim on all jobs using worksheets from only one Form

W-4. This total should be divided among all jobs. Your withholding will usually be most accurate when all allowances are claimed on the W-4 filed for the highest paying job and zero allowances are claimed for the others.

Advance Earned Income Credit. If you are eligible for this credit, you can receive it added to your paycheck throughout the year. For details, obtain Form W-5 from your employer.

Check Your Withholding. After your W-4 takes effect, you can use **Publication 919,** Is My Withholding Correct for 1990?, to see how the dollar amount you are having withheld compares to your estimated total annual tax. Call 1-800-424-3676 (in Hawaii and Alaska, check your local telephone directory) to order this publication. Check your local telephone directory for the IRS assistance number if you need further help.

Personal Allowances Worksheet

A Enter "1" for **yourself** if no one else can claim you as a dependent . . . . **A** ____

B Enter "1" if:
1. You are single and have only one job; or
2. You are married, have only one job, and your spouse does not work; or
3. Your wages from a second job or your spouse's wages (or the total of both) are $2,500 or less.
. . . . **B** ____

C Enter "1" for your **spouse.** But, you may choose to enter "0" if you are married and have either a working spouse or more than one job (this may help you avoid having too little tax withheld) . . . . **C** ____

D Enter number of **dependents** (other than your spouse or yourself) whom you will claim on your tax return . . . **D** ____

E Enter "1" if you will file as a **head of household** on your tax return (see conditions under "Head of Household," above) . . . **E** ____

F Enter "1" if you have at least $1,500 of **child or dependent care expenses** for which you plan to claim a credit . . . **F** ____

G Add lines A through F and enter total here . . . . ► **G** ____

For accuracy, do all worksheets that apply.
- If you plan to **itemize or claim adjustments to income** and want to reduce your withholding, turn to the Deductions and Adjustments Worksheet on page 2.
- If you are **single** and have **more than one job** and your combined earnings from all jobs exceed $25,000 OR if you are **married** and have a **working spouse or more than one job,** and the combined earnings from all jobs exceed $44,000, then turn to the Two-Earner/Two-Job Worksheet on page 2 if you want to avoid having too little tax withheld.
- If **neither** of the above situations applies to you, **stop here** and enter the number from line G on line 4 of Form W-4 below.

--------------------- Cut here and give the certificate to your employer. Keep the top portion for your records. ---------------------

Form **W-4** Department of the Treasury Internal Revenue Service	**Employee's Withholding Allowance Certificate** ► For Privacy Act and Paperwork Reduction Act Notice, see reverse.	OMB No. 1545-0010 19**90**

1 Type or print your first name and middle initial | Last name | **2** Your social security number

Home address (number and street or rural route)

City or town, state, and ZIP code

3 Marital status
☐ Single ☐ Married
☐ Married, but withhold at higher Single rate.
Note: If married, but legally separated, or spouse is a nonresident alien, check the Single box.

4 Total number of allowances you are claiming (from line G above or from the Worksheets on back if they apply) . . . **4** ____

5 Additional amount, if any, you want deducted from each pay . . . . **5** $ ____

6 I claim exemption from withholding and I certify that I meet **ALL** of the following conditions for exemption:
- Last year I had a right to a refund of **ALL** Federal income tax withheld because I had **NO** tax liability; **AND**
- This year I expect a refund of **ALL** Federal income tax withheld because I expect to have **NO** tax liability; **AND**
- This year if my income exceeds $500 and includes nonwage income, another person cannot claim me as a dependent.

If you meet all of the above conditions, enter the year effective and "EXEMPT" here . . . . ► **6** 19__

7 Are you a full-time student? (**Note:** Full-time students are not automatically exempt.) . . . . **7** ☐ Yes ☐ No

Under penalties of perjury, I certify that I am entitled to the number of withholding allowances claimed on this certificate or entitled to claim exempt status.

Employee's signature ► | Date ► , 19__

8 Employer's name and address (**Employer:** Complete 8 an 10 only if sending to IRS) | **9** Office code (optional) | **10** Employer identification number

EXHIBIT 6-4 (continued)

Form W-4 (1990) Page **2**

Deductions and Adjustments Worksheet

Note: *Use this worksheet only if you plan to itemize deductions or claim adjustments to income on your 1990 tax return.*

1   Enter an estimate of your 1990 itemized deductions. These include: qualifying home mortgage interest, 10% of personal interest, charitable contributions, state and local taxes (but not sales taxes), medical expenses in excess of 7.5% of your income, and miscellaneous deductions (most miscellaneous deductions are now deductible only in excess of 2% of your income) . . . .   1 $_____

2   Enter: { $5,450 if married filing jointly or qualifying widow(er)
$4,750 if head of household
$3,250 if single
$2,725 if married filing separately } . . . .   2 $_____

3   **Subtract** line 2 from line 1. If line 2 is greater than line 1, enter zero . . . .   3 $_____
4   Enter an estimate of your 1990 adjustments to income. These include alimony paid and deductible IRA contributions . .   4 $_____
5   **Add** lines 3 and 4 and enter the total . . . .   5 $_____
6   Enter an estimate of your 1990 nonwage income (such as dividends or interest income) . . . .   6 $_____
7   **Subtract** line 6 from line 5. Enter the result, but not less than zero . . . .   7 $_____
8   **Divide** the amount on line 7 by $2,000 and enter the result here. Drop any fraction . . . .   8 _____
9   Enter the number from Personal Allowances Worksheet, line G, on page 1 . . . .   9 _____
10 **Add** lines 8 and 9 and enter the total here. If you plan to use the Two-Earner/Two-Job Worksheet, also enter the total on line 1, below. Otherwise, **stop here** and enter this total on Form W-4, line 4 on page 1 . . . . . 10 _____

Two-Earner/Two-Job Worksheet

Note: *Use this worksheet only if the instructions at line G on page 1 direct you here.*

1   Enter the number from line G on page 1 (or from line 10 above if you used the Deductions and Adjustments Worksheet) .   1 _____
2   Find the number in **Table 1** below that applies to the **LOWEST** paying job and enter it here . . . .   2 _____
3   If line 1 is **GREATER THAN OR EQUAL TO** line 2, subtract line 2 from line 1. Enter the result here (if zero, enter "0") and on Form W-4, line 4, on page 1. **DO NOT** use the rest of this worksheet . . . .   3 _____

Note: *If line 1 is **LESS THAN** line 2, enter "0" on Form W-4, line 4, on page 1. Complete lines 4–9 to calculate the additional dollar withholding necessary to avoid a year-end tax bill.*

4   Enter the number from line 2 of this worksheet . . . .   4 _____
5   Enter the number from line 1 of this worksheet . . . .   5 _____
6   **Subtract** line 5 from line 4 . . . .   6 _____
7   Find the amount in **Table 2** below that applies to the **HIGHEST** paying job and enter it here . . . . . .   7 $_____
8   **Multiply** line 7 by line 6 and enter the result here. This is the additional annual withholding amount needed   8 $_____
9   Divide line 8 by the number of pay periods each year. (For example, divide by 26 if you are paid every other week.) Enter the result here and on Form W-4, line 5, page 1. This is the additional amount to be withheld from each paycheck . . .   9 $_____

Table 1: Two-Earner/Two-Job Worksheet

Married Filing Jointly		All Others	
If wages from **LOWEST** paying job are—	Enter on line 2 above	If wages from **LOWEST** paying job are—	Enter on line 2 above
0 - $4,000	0	0 - $4,000	0
4,001 - 8,000	1	4,001 - 8,000	1
8,001 - 19,000	2	8,001 - 14,000	2
19,001 - 23,000	3	14,001 - 16,000	3
23,001 - 25,000	4	16,001 - 21,000	4
25,001 - 27,000	5	21,001 and over	5
27,001 - 29,000	6		
29,001 - 35,000	7		
35,001 - 41,000	8		
41,001 - 46,000	9		
46,001 and over	10		

Table 2: Two-Earner/Two-Job Worksheet

Married Filing Jointly		All Others	
If wages from **HIGHEST** paying job are—	Enter on line 7 above	If wages from **HIGHEST** paying job are—	Enter on line 7 above
0 - $44,000	$310	0 - $25,000	$310
44,001 - 90,000	570	25,001 - 52,000	570
90,001 and over	680	52,001 and over	680

Privacy Act and Paperwork Reduction Act Notice.—We ask for this information to carry out the Internal Revenue laws of the United States. We may give the information to the Department of Justice for civil or criminal litigation and to cities, states, and the District of Columbia for use in administering their tax laws. You are required to give this information to your employer.

The time needed to complete this form will vary depending on individual circumstances. The estimated average time is: **Recordkeeping** 46 min., **Learning about the law or the form** 10 min., **Preparing the form** 70 min. If you have comments concerning the accuracy of these time estimates or suggestions for making this form more simple, we would be happy to hear from you. You can write to the **Internal Revenue Service**, Washington, DC 20224, Attn: IRS Reports Clearance Officer, T:FP; or the **Office of Management and Budget**, Paperwork Reduction Project (1545-0010), Washington, DC 20503.

★U.S.GPO:1989-0-245-064

your determination must be set forth in the letter. Important language from the statute must be noted. It provides that the facts considered in determining whether there is a "reasonable basis" for the statement are the facts which existed *at the time* the statement was made. I say this because the IRS is likely to examine your Form W-4 several months, perhaps years, after the statement was made. Because of this, the IRS may apply the *current* facts to the form in determining its validity. However, the statute is clear that the facts which apply in answering the "reasonable basis" test are those which existed "at the time" the statement was made. You must take care to recite the facts which existed at the time the statement was made in order to establish your "reasonable basis" for making the claim, thus avoiding the penalty.

Penalties Applicable To Business

At this juncture, we shall examine some of the more common penalties which relate to business. In keeping with the format established, I will explore the extent to which, if at all, IMPACT has altered the procedural or financial aspects of the penalty.

1. Employment Tax Penalties

The lion's share of penalties which most businesses face apply to employment taxes. Employment taxes consist of the *employee's* share of withheld income and social security taxes ("trust fund" taxes). These are the taxes withheld directly from the employee's check and paid to the IRS by the employer. Employment taxes also include the *employer's* share of social security and unemployment taxes ("non-trust fund" taxes). These are the sums for which the employer himself, not the employee, is responsible to pay. Simply stated, trust fund taxes are taken from the pocket of the employee, while the non-trust fund taxes come directly from the employer.

All employers are required to report wages paid to each employee on a quarterly basis. Form 941 is used for this purpose. Form 941 functions as the tax return for all trust fund taxes. Form 940 is filed annually and functions as the tax return for non-trust fund taxes. While the Form 941 is due quarterly, employers must make *deposits* of trust fund taxes on a *monthly* basis if the tax liability exceeds $500 for any one quarter. Within the folds of these extensive requirements, we find three individual penalties which, when assessed against your business, can be most oppressive. We shall address them in turn.

A. **The Failure to Deposit Penalty.** IMPACT has altered the manner in which this penalty is computed. Prior law established that the penalty was a flat 10 percent of the amount required to be deposited, but which was not deposited. For deposits required to be made after January 31, 1989, the law creates a graduated penalty, beginning with just two percent. The graduated scale was implemented in order to provide the citizen with "an incentive to correct any underpayments before the IRS discovers the underpayment and demands payment." House Committee Report on IMPACT.

Code §6656 establishes the following graduated scale:

● Two percent if the failure is not more than five days;

● Five percent if the failure is more than five days, but not more than 15 days;

● Ten percent if the failure is more than 15 days.

In the event the tax is not deposited by the time the IRS begins making demands, the penalty increases to its maximum level, 15 percent.

In all events, the penalty is inapplicable at any level when it is shown that "such failure (to deposit) is due to reasonable cause and not due to willful neglect." Code §6656(a). The "reasonable cause" standard used here is the same as that discussed in earlier portions of this chapter. See e.g., the discussion under the heading, *Late Payment of Tax.* As I have already declared, when demanding an abatement of this penalty or any penalty, you must set forth facts which establish that you acted with reasonable cause and not due to willful neglect of your duties and obligations under the Code. More specifically, you must show that your failure to act was due to circumstances out of your control, and that you acted with ordinary business care and prudence, but were nevertheless unable to comply.

B. **Failure to File Forms 941.** The failure to file penalty which we discussed earlier is also used to penalize those who fail to file employment tax returns. After IMPACT, the civil failure to file penalty is assessed at the rate of five percent per month, for a total of five months. We have already discussed this penalty in detail under the heading, *Late Filing or Failure to File.* Therefore, I will not attempt to reinvent the wheel. I will state, however, that when employment taxes are concerned, the IRS is much more keen as to what constitutes reasonable cause than when the matter involves your personal income taxes.

Bear in mind that Form 941 covers trust fund taxes, those withheld from others. The agency is understandably tough on the subject of failing to file trust fund returns or payment of trust fund taxes. You should take special care to set forth facts which are clear and specific. Included as Exhibit 6-5 is Mike's letter which does set forth clear and specific facts establishing reasonable cause for failure to file Form 941. You will note that it goes into much detail on the causal relationship between events in his business, and his failure to timely file the return. This is the nature of specifity which you must achieve in any demand for abatement of this penalty.

C. **Failure to Pay Employment Taxes.** The penalty for failure to pay employment taxes is assessed in the same manner as the penalty for failure to pay income taxes. This topic, too, has been thoroughly discussed earlier. However, because trust fund taxes are involved, the IRS takes a dim view of failure to pay the tax. Consequently, as with the failure to file penalty, extra care must be taken to ensure that you present specific facts which establish that you did exercise ordinary business care and prudence in providing for your tax liability and were nevertheless unable to pay. Based upon the facts shown in your letter, you must argue that you had "reasonable cause" for failure to pay. When this showing is made, the penalty will be abated.

2. Failure To File Information Returns

I have been reporting for years that in order for the IRS to usher in a paperless return system and hence, gain absolute control over the computation of your income tax liability, it must create a system whereby information regarding every conceivable transaction is reported to the agency. At present, federal law requires that one file an information return, at last count, in approximately 52 different circumstances. Can you name just ten? The most common example of information returns are Forms W-2, which report wages paid to employees, and Form 1099, which reports payment of non-employee compensation such as dividends or interest. When one

EXHIBIT 6-5

Michael
████████ Inc.
████████ Avenue ████
St. Paul, Minnesota ████

December 11, 1989

Internal Revenue Service
Regional Service Center
Kansas City, MO 64999

RE: Notice of Tax, Interest and Penalty Due --
     Dated September 25, 1989
     EIN: ████████

Dear Sir:

On or about September 30, 1989, I received Form 8937, Notice of Tax Due in the
amount of $10,113.94 (copy enclosed). The bill reflects an assessment of
employment taxes due for the above corporation on account of Form 941,
Employer's Quarterly Federal Tax Return for the fourth quarter of 1986 (1286).
Included in the assessment of taxes are penalties in the amount of $2,618.17.
This letter is a written request for abatement of penalties pursuant to
Internal Revenue Code §6404. That provision of law permits the IRS to abate
any assessment of penalties when it appears from all the facts and
circumstances that such assessment is erroneous or excessive. Based upon the
facts as shown below, it is clear that such assessment of penalties is
excessive and is due to be abated.

The return in question is Form 941, Employer's Quarterly Federal Tax Return.
The return, which covers the fourth quarter of 1986, was due to be filed on or
before January 31, 1987, 30 days after the close of the calendar quarter.
However, the return was not filed until the summer of 1989, approximately two
years late. The amount of $2,618.17 assessed as penalties reflect the failure
to timely file penalty, and the failure to pay tax penalty, both of which are
due to be abated.

In mid-December of 1986, the corporation changed bookkeepers. The first
bookkeeper, ████████, was self-employed working for a number of small businesses
in the area. ████████ was not only performing bookkeeping services for several
small businesses, but was caring for her ailing husband as well. In the fall
of 1986, ████████ husband suffered a serious heart attack, the effects of
which disabled him. Thereafter, he required constant care from ████████. What
I did not realize at the time, however, was that ████████ was not attending to
her bookkeeping dutes. Her time and concerns were occupied by her husband and
his grave illness.

By early January, 1987, it became apparent that ████████ could not adequately
discharge her duties in connection with the corporate books. She quit and was
replaced by ████████ in mid-January. ████████ immediately began the task of
straightening out the mess left behind by ████████. The books were in a
condition of complete disaray. The first order of business was to attend to
the check book. We learned from ████████ that the checking account had not been
reconcilied for the past four months. In a retail jewelry business, the
Christmas buying season presents the busiest time of the year. Nearly 80
percent of all sales occur in the few weeks that follow Thanksgiving. As a
result of this intense business period, the company experiences an extremely

EXHIBIT 6-5 (continued)

high volume of sales and purchase activity. The need to reconcile the bank account statements covering this volitile period time was paramount.

During the same period, the company experienced a massive turnover of employees. For a number of reasons, 60 percent of the employees working during 1986 left the business in the first month of 1987. The turnover necessitated an immediate hunt for, and training of new personnel competent to continue business operations. This task was most time consuming and occupied nearly all of my personal attention and time during the early months of 1987. Meanwhile, the bank account activity, business books of account and other matters of a bookkeeping nature were attended by our new bookkeeper. This included the task of preparing and mailing Forms W-2 as required by law.

After having conquered the dual crisis created by ▮▮▮▮ ill husband and the mass exodus of qualified employees, we settled in to business as usual during the summer of 1987. At that time, we had no idea that the Form 941 for the fourth quarter of 1986 was yet unfiled. Given the circumstances of my being occupied with seeking and training new help, and ▮▮▮▮'s intensive involvement with bringing the books up to date, we simply lost sight of the Form 941 for that period.

The failure to file this return was not as the result of negligence on the part of any person within this company. Rather, the failure to file was occasioned directly by the failure of ▮▮▮▮, a self-employed bookkeeper, to attend to her business. ▮▮▮▮, precipitated by the illness of her husband which eventually led to her abandoning her occupation to attend to her disabled husband on a full time basis, was prevented due to this personal crisis, from lending her full time and attention to her business affairs.

Picking up the pieces left by ▮▮▮▮ was also a full time occupation during the first few months of 1987. The crisis caused by ▮▮▮▮'s crisis and the departing employees demanded our full, undivided attention. At all times, we exercised ordinary business care and prudence in these matters, but nevertheless were unable to submit the return in a timely manner or pay the tax in a timely manner. Once we were notified that the return was delinquent, we immediatley prepared and submitted the return. There was no delay whatsoever in this regard. At no time did we undertake to deliberately or intentionally attempt to avoid the IRS' rules and regulations.

The penalty assessment includes a penalty for delinquency and failure to pay the tax. Based upon all of the facts and circumstances of this case as shown above, it is clear that the assessment of penalties is inappropriate and should be abated. Therefore, I request that the penalties shown in the enclosed statement be abated in full.

Under penalty of perjury, I declare that all of the facts stated in this letter are true and correct in all respects.

Sincerely,

Michael

▮▮▮▮ Inc.

encl.

fails to file a required information return, or files an erroneous information return, Code §§6721 and 6722 create a penalty.

Under prior law, the penalty for failure to file an information return, or filing an incorrect information return, was $50 per return. IMPACT established a three-tier penalty in cases of failure to file. The purpose is to encourage persons to file corrected information returns so that the data can be transmitted into the IRS' Information Retrns Program (IRP). That massive computer program compares data reflected within information returns, to that shown on individual tax retrns. When a variance is detected, the IRS' computer spits out the billing notices and demands which were the subject of Chapters Two and Three. The IRS is extremely possessive of its information returns because absent the data shown in these documents, it cannot operate its IRP program. The penalty applies when one either fails to file an information return, or files an information return which fails to accurately report all information required on the form.

The three-tier penalty operates in this fashion.

(a) If any error or omission is corrected within 30 days after the return's filing date, the amount of the penalty is $15 per return, with a yearly maximum of $75,000 ($25,000 for small businesses) In most cases, this penalty amount applies if the corrected returns are filed by March 30, as many information returns are due on or before February 28.

(b) If any error or omission is corrected between the period of 31 days after the filing due date for the return, and August 1, the amount of the penalty is $30 per return, with a yearly maximum of $150,000 ($50,000 for small businesses).

(c) If the error or omission is corrected after August 1, the penalty is $50 per return, with a yearly maximum of $250,000 ($100,000 for small businesses).

As you can see, the IRS is most serious, for the reasons stated above, when it comes to the submission of timely and accurate information returns. As a matter of fact, so serious is this matter in the eyes of the agency, that when it is shown that the failure to file timely or accurate information returns is "due to intentional disregard," the penalty per return jumps to $100, and there is no benefit of the graduated system mentioned. See Code §6721(e).

It remains true, however, as with each and every penalty in the Code, the penalty does not apply when the failure is due to "reasonable cause" and not "willful neglect." See Code §6724.The standards and elements of reasonable cause addressed at length earlier in this chapter apply here as well.

You no doubt noticed a limitation on the penalty when assessed against "small businesses." A small business is one defined as having fewer than $5,000,000 in average annual gross receipts for the "most recent three taxable years" prior to the year for which the penalty is assessed.

Section 6721 provides a further ground upon which one may obtain statutory absolution where information returns are concerned. It is worth noting here. When an errant information return (as opposed to a failure to file the information return) is corrected before August 1, the return is considered to have been correctly filed, and hence, not subject to the penalty. Such forgiveness applies only to the greater of ten information returns, or one-half of one percent of the total number of information returns required to be filed during the year in question. See Code §6721(c).

In any case, whether asserting good faith, reasonable cause as a defense to the penalty, or maintaining the application of one or more of the described statutory limitations, the demand for abatement must be made in writing as explored in great detail in this chapter.

3. Filing Information Returns On Magnetic Media

In the face of my repeated claims that the IRS is steadily moving toward achieving its goal of eliminating the paper income tax return and ushering in the total electronic information tax system, certain segments of the public continue to question how the agency can accomplish such an aggressive goal. We have already examined many of the ways in which this will be accomplished, but certainly a major facet of the IRS' plan is found in Code §6011(e). That provision of law permits the IRS to create regulations, the first of which appeared in early 1986, about two years after the 1984 *Strategic Plan* was approved, which require that businesses submit large volumes of information returns on "magnetic media or in other machine-readable form." That is to say, the IRS has placed upon private businesses not only the requirement to do its bookkeeping, reporting and collection of taxes, but now has shouldered it with the obligation to do the government's electronic data processing as well. In answer to certain challenges to the effect that the IRS cannot possibly audit everyone or administer a paperless return system, I might be inclined to agree. However, the IRS does not have to when it places the burden on the private sector to do all the work! Naturally, you must bear the cost of this endeavor, and when you fail, penalties apply.

Prior to IMPACT, "high-volume" filers of information returns were required to use magnetic media when filing their documents. However, with the broad range of information returns in use, we saw different levels of filing volume at which the requirement to use magnetic media became effective. For example, a business filing in excess of 250 Forms 1099 or W-2 were required to use magnetic media, while those filing just 50 interest or dividend information returns were required to use magnetic media.

IMPACT amended Code §6011(e) to provide that the use of magnetic media is required only when a business submits "at least 250 returns during the calendar year." Consequently, the new law has made the application of the magnetic media requirement more uniform. Moreover, in the past, the IRS required the magnetic media used, i.e., the computer disk or tape, to meet a particular format. In the Committee Report on IMPACT, Congress declared that:

> "***The committee also intends that the IRS permit payors to file in as many formats as is feasible, and that IRS requirements keep pace with technological advances." House Committee Report on H.R. 3299.

In addition, Congress provided in IMPACT that the penalty for not filing on magnetic media would apply *only* to the returns *in excess* of 250, as opposed to the entire number filed by the citizen. The penalty for not using magnetic media is assessed under precisely the same scheme as discussed under the heading *Failure to File Information Returns*. Thus, the penalty is graduated up to $50 per return in excess of 250 not filed on magnetic media. See Code §6724(c).

In addition to the general, uniformly applicable "good faith, reasonable cause" standard, Code §6011(e) now contains a Congressional directive which instructs the IRS that in drafting its regulations, it "shall take into account (among other relevant factors) the ability of the taxpayer to comply at reasonable cost with the requirements of such regulations." In explaining this provision, Congress declared:

> "***The committee intends that the IRS take into consideration

other instances of undue hardship, such as temporary equipment breakdowns or destruction of magnetic media equipment, in granting one-year or multi-year exemption from this requirement." House Committee Report on H.R. 3299.

Another exemption to the magnetic media requirement is found in IRS regulations. The regulation expresses the "low-volume" exception. Simply stated, the regulation holds that if you filed fewer than 250 information returns in the previous calendar year, and "reasonably expect to file fewer than 250 returns" for the current calendar year, you are considered a "low-volume" filer and "may make such returns on the prescribed paper form." See Rev. Reg. §301.6011-2(c).

From this information we learn that there are several grounds upon which a business may obtain relief from the penalty for failure to submit information returns on magnetic media. Let us list them:

(a) The returns filed did not exceed 250, or if they did, the penalty is applicable only to the number *in excess* of 250;

(b) You filed fewer than 250 information returns last year, and reasonably expected to file fewer than 250 in the current year;

(c) You are entitled to a hardship single- or multi-year extension by reason of excessive cost or equipment failures or deficiencies; and

(d) The failure to file was due to reasonable cause and not willful neglect.

Included here as Exhibit 6-6 is a letter requesting abatement which incorporates most of the above arguments. The letter was used by a property company which was assessed a penalty of $23,250 for failure to file information returns on magnetic media. The letter was written *prior* to the passage of IMPACT, so the argument expressed in paragraph (a) above was not yet available. Had it been, it would have been even simpler to gain an abatement of the penalty. As it stands, however, the letter is a fine example of the manner in which the good faith, reasonble cause, and other arguments are presented to the IRS.

4. The 100 Percent Penalty

The 100 percent penalty sounds ominous and it can be. It applies only to corporations and is the vehicle by which the IRS assesses and collects employment tax deficiencies from delinquent corporations. The penalty is assessed under Code §6672. This is how it works:

EXHIBIT 6-6

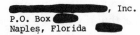, Inc.
P.O. Box ████
Naples, Florida ███

January 26, 1989

Internal Revenue Service
Regional Service Center
Atlanta, Georgia 39901

Re: Claim for Abatement of Penalties
     EIN: ████████

Dear Sir:

This letter is in response to your Notice 8850, dated December 26,
1988 (copy attached). By letter dated January 6, 1989, we informed
you that we would be submitting a request for abatement of all
penalties. This letter is a request for abatement of the penalty
demanded in your notice 8850, for reasons set forth below. This
Request for Abatement is made under the authority of 26 USC §6724(a).

Section 6724(a) of the Internal Revenue Code provides that the penalty
assessed by your Notice 8850 may be abated if it is shown that the
failure to file the information returns in question was "due to
reasonable cause and not willful neglect." On the basis of all of the
facts and circumstances shown in this letter, we submit that
"reasonable cause" exists in this case, and we further submit that the
penalty assessment of $23,250 should be, in all things, abated.

The penalty in question here was assessed under the authority of Rev.
Reg. §301.6011-2(b)(2). That regulation requires that information
returns such as forms 1099-MISC be filed with the IRS on
machine-readable magnetic media, rather than in the traditional
paper-form method. The regulation provides that any failure to comply
with such requirement will be considered by the IRS as a "failure to
file the form," even if submitted in paper form. Such a presumptive
failure will then lead to the assessment of the penalty provided for
under Code §6721.

The taxpayer in question here was assessed the $50 penalty for failure
to file 465 forms 1099-MISC for tax period 1987. In addition to the
"reasonable cause" asserted herein, the taxpayer maintains that as a
"low-volume filer" of information returns, Forms 1099-MISC, it was
exempt from the requirement to file such forms on magnetic media
during 1987. Consequently, taxpayer asserts that it is not
responsible for the penalty assessed against it for failure to file on
magnetic media.

Rev. Reg. 301.6011-2(c)(1)(B) provides as follows:

"(B) In the case of a calendar year or annual period beginning on or
after January 1, 1987-

"(1) On the first day of such calendar year or annual period the
person reasonably expects to file fewer than 250 returns on such form
for the calendar year or annual period; and

EXHIBIT 6-6 (continued)

"(2) The person was not required to file 250 or more returns on such
form for the preceding calendar year or annual period." (Emphasis
added.)

The period in question here is 1987. During calendar year 1986, the
"preceding period," the taxpayer was required to, and did file, just
thirty (30) forms 1099-MISC. As of the first day of the calendar year
in question, January 1, 1987, the taxpayer reasonably expected to be
required to file substantially fewer than 250 forms 1099-MISC. This
expectation was based upon the number of forms filed for calendar year
1986. Because of the insignificant number of information returns
filed by the taxpayer during 1986, the taxpayer had no reason to
believe that it would be required to file many more than that during
1987. In any event, the taxpayer certainly had no reasonable
expectation that it would be required to file more than 250 such
forms, as such would be an increase of in excess of eight times as
many Forms 1099-MISC from one year to the next. Such an enormous
increase was never anticipated by the taxpayer.

On the basis of these facts, the taxpayer is considered a "low-volume
filer" for 1987 and should not be held responsible for the penalty
assessment demanded by Notice 8850.

In addition to being a "low-volume filer" for 1987, the taxpayer
should be relieved of the penalty by reason of the existence of "good
faith, reasonable cause." The taxpayer has never taken any steps to
deliberately or intentionally violate or ignore the rules and
regulations of the Internal Revenue Service. With respect to the
requirement that information returns be submitted on magnetic tape,
the taxpayer did not become aware of this requirement until the fall
of 1988, long after all such returns for 1987 were in fact submitted.
Taxpayer became aware of the requirement only after its corporate
officer, the undersigned Robert ████████ read an article on the
subject in a trade journal. Attached to this letter and made a part
of this good faith showing is a true and correct copy of the article
in question. The date on the article demonstrates the time of its
publication, after which it was read by Mr. ████████.

Upon becoming aware of the requirement to submit such forms on
magnetic media, the taxpayer took immediate steps to comply with this
requirement for tax year 1988. The taxpayer has just recently
received approval from the Internal Revenue Service to file its forms
in the future on magnetic media, and has been assigned a Transaction
Control Number. That number is 30981, and was assigned by letter
dated January 13th, 1989. Attached to this letter made a part of this
good faith showing is a true and correct copy of the IRS' letter of
January 13th, 1989. This letter fully evidences the fact that the
taxpayer is in full compliance with the requirements of law for the
year 1988. Such compliance demonstrates that taxpayer never intended
to violate or ignore the requirements of the law, but rather was
ignorant of any requirement to submit the forms on magnetic tape.

In addition to the above showing the the taxpayer was a "low-volume
filer" for 1987 and that good faith, reasonable cause exists in this
case, the taxpayer asserts the existence of undue hardship as
described in Rev. Reg. §301.6011-2(c)(4). That regulation provides

EXHIBIT 6-6 (continued)

that "undue hardship" is determined by considering the amount, "if
any, by which the cost of filing return in accordance with this
section exceeds the cost of filing the return on other media."

The 465 forms which are at issue here were prepared by the taxpayers'
secretaries. These forms were prepared in the ordinary course of the
required duties of such secretaries. Taxpayer estimates that the cost
of such preparation amounted to 4-6 hours of secretarial time, at $10
per hour. Since the paper forms were provided by the Internal Revenue
Service, there was no added materials cost involved with compliance.
The total cost was thereafter, at most, $60.

On the other hand, the taxpayer will incur significant costs in
submitting the forms on magnetic media. Attached to this letter are
two estimates demonstrating the anticipated cost of submitting the
forms on magnetic tape. One estimate places the cost at $2 per
return, while the second fixes the cost at $1.10 per return, plus a
flat rate of $500. In either event, outside charges will be in excess
of $900, and as much as $1,000. These estimates are based upon 465
forms being submitted. Moreover, these outside charges do not include
the cost of reprogramming the taxpayer's computer to correctly
assimilate the needed data. These charges are anticipated by the
taxpayer to range from $600 to $700. The total cost of compliance is
therefore anywhere from $1,500 to $1,700.

These charges will exceed the cost of submitting the forms on paper by
as many as 28 times. Still, in an effort to be in full compliance for
1988, the taxpayer has elected to absorb these costs.

In summary, the taxpayer requests an abatement of all penalties shown
in Notice 8850 for the following reasons:

a. The taxpayer was a "low-volume filer" as defined in Rev.
Rev. §301.6011-2(c)(1)(B). This is because taxpayer submitted just 30
forms 1099-MISC in 1986, and did not reasonably anticipate submitting
more than that for the year 1987.

b. The taxpayer did not act with "willful neglect" in
connection with the requirement to submit the forms on magnetic media.
Rather, the taxpayer has taken full steps, including incurring
substantial costs, to come into compliance with the magnetic media
requirement. Taxpayer has been assigned a Transaction Control Number
by the IRS and will be submitting all forms 1099-MISC in
machine-readable front from this time on. For this reason, Code
§6724(a) provides for the abatement of the penalty at issue here.

c. The cost of complying with the requirement to submit the
forms in machine-readable format in 1987 was substantial. This is
demonstrated by the attached estimates which depict the probable costs
to be incurred by the taxpayer for 1988 forms. Such cost creates
"undue hardship" would should be considered as bearing upon the good
faith, reasonable cause asserted by the taxpayer. Such good faith
provides ample cause to abate the penalty under Code §6724(a).

The taxpayer did not at any time take any steps, knowingly or
otherwise, to ignore the requirements of the regulations. The
taxpayer has at all times made every reasonable effort to comply with

EXHIBIT 6-6 (continued)

the law. The fact that taxpayer has taken all steps necessary to
comply for 1988 is evidence of that. Because the taxpayer was a
"low-volume filer" for 1986, and because good faith, reasonable cause
does indeed exist in this case, the taxpayer submits, under the
authority of Code §6724(a), that the penalty should be, in all
things, abated.

Under the penalties of perjury, we the undersigned officers of the
taxpayer corporation declare that all of the facts stated in this
letter are true and correct to our best knowledge and belief, and that
all the attached documents are true and correct in all respects to our
best knowledge and belief.

Based upon the above showing of reasonable cause and good faith, we
demand that that the penalty shown in Notice 8850 be abated in its
entirety.

Sincerely,

Donald ██████████   Robert ██████████
President   Vice-President
████████████████, Inc.   ████████████████, Inc.

When a corporation, large or small, becomes deficient in its trust fund taxes, the IRS' Collection Division immediately becomes involved. First, all efforts to collect the tax from the corporation's assets is made. If that fails, the IRS will make an assessment of the penalty against the "responsible officers" of the corporation who were required to withhold, truthfully account for, and pay over the trust fund taxes, but who "willfully failed" to do so. See Code §6672.

In this manner, the law permits the IRS to transform a corporate liability into the personal liability of certain officers or employees of the delinquent corporation. Once assessed, the penalty is collected from the personal assets of the individuals.

The law is clear that two factors must be present before the tax may be assessed against any individual. First, the person against whom the tax is assessed must be the "responsible person." That term is defined as the one who exercised control over the corporation's income and assets, and made the decision not to pay the taxes at a time when they were due. A person lacking sufficient control over the corporation's assets and income such as will enable him to make final decisions over these matters cannot be held responsible under the law.

Next, and most importantly, the person against whom the tax is assessed must have acted "willfully." That is, he must have made a conscious and knowing decision to favor other creditors at a time when he knew that the trust fund taxes were delinquent. Absent a showing of willfullness, even the responsible person cannot be subjected to the penalty assessment.

Any proposal for the 100 percent penalty will come from the Collection Division. A person faced with such an assessment must immediately write a letter setting forth facts in detail which will enable the IRS to conclude that he was either, not the responsible person, or he did not act willfully in connection with the corporation's failure to pay taxes. All facts and circumstances in your control which will help to establish these facts, including your own affidavit regarding your powers and duties, must be brought to bear on this question.

Because the IRS is so serious about collecting trust fund taxes, it often takes a shotgun approach to this penalty, assessing it against as many corporate officers and employees as is possible. It will then let the individuals fight it out, pursuing only the losers. For this reason, one facing the penalty must be prepared to not only demand the abatement as discussed above, but he must be cognizant of all rights of appeal.

First, as we shall examine shortly, all penalty assessments are subject to appeal. Thus, if you fail in your attempt to abate any of the penalties discussed in this chapter, you enjoy a right of appeal. With regard to the 100 percent penalty, however, you may well be forced to "go the distance" before you win an abatement. In Chapter Six of the *Taxpayers' Ultimate Defense Manual,* I explain the step-by-step procedures to follow should you fail with the letter of abatement or appeal discussed here.

A Standard Cover Form

In Chapter Two, I mentioned that whenever a claim is made against the agency, it is good practice to use a standard cover form. That form is Form 843, *Claim.* Please see Chapter Two, Exhibit 2-6. By using the Form 843, you ensure that the thoughtful employees of the IRS Service Centers will immediately recognize that you have made a claim against the agency. With hope, the claim will be routed to the proper personnel for review and disposition. By merely sending your letter with the Form 843 attached, you run the risk that intake personnel will not read or understand enough of your letter to recognize it as a claim.

When using Form 843 as a cover to demand a penalty abatement, you should add some language to the form. In the margin above the word "Claim," type the words, "Demand for Abatement of Penalty." Complete the balance of the form with the information requested, and on Line 11 where it asks for your reason why the claim should be granted, state, "see attached letter." To the form you will then attach the letter demanding abatement which sets forth detailed facts as outlined above. You must then copy the submission and mail the original to the IRS via certified mail.

When The Answer Is "NO"

How many times have I declared that decisions of IRS examiners are *never final?* One hundred? One thousand? The point is, this rule applies to requests for penalty abatements *as well as* the decisions of tax auditors. Should the IRS, in response to any request for abatement of penalty (or any other demand for abatement discussed in this book), deny your request, you will be informed in writing. Also, the IRS should explain (but often fails) that you enjoy the right to appeal the decision denying your request for abatement. In this regard, IRS Publication 1, *Your Rights as a Taxpayer,* does not even mention the right to appeal the denial of a demand for abatement of penalties. Please see Publication 1, page 4, under the heading, *Cancellation of Penalties* (in Chapter 4). I believe the IRS' failure to explain the nature of this right accounts for the fact that very few persons ever appeal an adverse decision regarding a request for abatement of penalties.

The appeal of which I speak is perfected by drafting a written protest letter within 30 days of the date of the IRS' letter denying your demand for abatement. The protest letter should be addressed to the Service Center which denied your claim. It must clearly state that you wish to appeal the adverse decision. Exhibit 6-7 is an example of a written protest letter appealing the denial of a request for penalty abatement. Please see Exhibit 6-7.

You will note from Exhibit 6-7 that we have restated facts which will allow the reader to come to the conclusion that we are entitled to the relief we are seeking. I recommend that in all cases, you not only restate the key facts of your case in the appeal letter, but you attach a copy of your initial request for abatement to the protest letter as an exhibit. This helps to complete the record. Make certain that all your letters are specific and clearly set forth the facts of your case.

The submission of a written protest in a timely fashion will entitle you to an Appeals Conference. This generally (but not always) involves an appearance before an Appeals Officer of the IRS. At that time, you may present any evidence which you believe supports your position and justifies your demands. The details of the conduct of such a conference are discussed at length in each of my previous three books. Please see *The Naked Truth,* Chapter Two; *How Anyone Can Negotiate With the IRS—And WIN!,* Chapter One; and the *Taxpayers' Ultimate Defense Manual,* Chapter Four.

There is *no reason* for you to fall victim to the IRS' "penalty parade." Though the IRS' penalty assessments mean big bucks for the agency, precious few citizens ever exercise their right to demand an abatement. Even more scarce are those who appeal an adverse decision regarding a request for abatement! Remember, you have the power! Take back the power!

EXHIBIT 6-7

Michael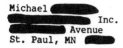
█████████ Inc.
█████████ Avenue
St. Paul, MN ██████

February 7, 1990

Internal Revenue Service
Penalty Appeals Coordinator
Regional Service Center
Kansas City, MO 64999

Re: Demand for Appeal of Penalty Assessment
    EIN: ██████████

Dear Sir:

On December 11, 1989, I submitted a written request for the abatement
of civil penalties related to employment tax liabilities of the
above-mentioned corporation. By letter dated January 9, 1990, the IRS
informed me that me request for abatement has been denied (copy of the
denial is attached). Therefore,

PLEASE TAKE NOTICE, that it is my desire to <u>appeal</u> the decision
denying my request for abatement, and that I wish to have a <u>hearing</u>
before an Appeals Officer in <u>St. Paul, Minnesota</u>, relative to my
request for abatement.

The name and address of the appellant is:

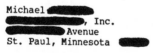

          Michael ██████████
          █████████████, Inc.
          █████████████ Avenue
          St. Paul, Minnesota ██████

A statement of the facts supporting my position is expressed in the
attached request for abatement, dated December 11, 1989. The letter
is attached hereto and made a part hereof, as through fully set out
here. Such letter sets out facts which demonstrate that I executed
<u>reasonable business care and prudence</u>, as well as <u>due diligence</u> in
connection with this issue. Despite my own efforts, and due to
factors beyond my control (as shown in the attached letter), I was
unable to timely pay employment tax liablities, resulting in the
assessment of penalties.

EXHIBIT 6-7 (continued)

A statement of the law supporting my position is based upon Code
§§6651, 6654, and 6655. Each provision of law stipulates that the
penalty (as assessd here) does not apply when it is shown that the
failure was due to "reasonable cause and not willful neglect." The
Code does not define what constitutes "reasonable cause" but it is
settled that reasonable cause exists when it is shown that a person

did "what a reasonable and ordinarily prudent person would do under
the circumstances." See Marcello v. Commissioner, 380 F.2d 509 (5th
Cir. 1967). Such a showing has been made in this case.

The facts of this case, as shown in the attached letter of December
11, 1989, plainly indicate that Michael███████ exercised such
reasonable care and ordinary business prudence as to justify the full
and complete abatement of all civil penalties. Under the
circumstances, it is appropriate that the penalties at issue here be
abated.

Under penalties of perjury, I declare that above facts, as well as
those contained in the letter of December 11, 1989, attached hereto
and made a part hereof as though fully set out herein, are true and
correct in all respect.

WHEREFORE, an appeals conference is requested as soon as possible.

Sincerely,

Michael███████
President
██████████ Inc.

encl.

Notes To Chapter 6

1. See the chart on page 83, *Taxpayers' Ultimate Defense Manual.*

2. 1989 IRS *Highlights,* chart 14.

3. Public Law 101-239, Dec. 19, 1989.

4. Definitions of items one through five are provided in Code §6662(d), (e), (f) and (g).

5. It should be noted that in 1988, the second aspect of the negligence penalty was repealed by Public Law 100-647, of which the *Taxpayers' Bill of Rights Act* was a portion. Thus, the 50-percent of the interest paid aspect of the penalty applies only to returns filed before January 1, 1989.

6. IRM, Audit—§4562.2 (2-25-87).

7. Please see *How Anyone Can Negotiate,* pages 176-180 for details on "undue hardship."

8. For a more exhaustive discussion of this concept, see *The Naked Truth,* pages 147-153.

9. WINNING Publications, $19.95.

10. Please see the federal court decisions of *Stevens v. Berger,* 428 F.Supp. 896 (D.C. New York, 1977); *Callahan v. Woods,* 658 F.2d 679 (9th Cir. 1981).

— CHAPTER 7 —

Letters That
Abate Interest Assessments

The double-barreled approach used by the IRS to punish citizens comes in the form of penalties *and* interest. The manner in which the IRS assesses interest on unpaid tax liabilities can be particularly troublesome. The reason is that the IRS will assess interest from the time the tax was *due to be paid*, rather than from the time the tax was *determined* to be owed. In no other area of the law do we find a creditor given the ability to assess interest retroactively from the date of the determination of the debt. Yet where the IRS is concerned, it is not uncommon for lawmakers to afford special privileges to tax collectors. Therefore, it should come as no surprise that the IRS is presented with such an advantage.

What does come as a surprise, however, is that assessments of interest, which can be crushing, may be *abated*. The right to abate assessments of interest was created with the passage of the Taxpayers' Bill of Rights Act. Specifically, the law holds that assessments of interest can be abated under two conditions. We will explore those conditions, as well as others, in this Chapter. Before we reach the meat of the discussion, however, permit me to take another shot at IRS Publication 1. The document purporting to be a statement of your rights as a taxpayer is *silent* on the right to abate interest assessments. As a matter of fact, the publication is daringly misleading with respect to this right. On page four of the document, under the heading, *Cancellation of Penalties,* the IRS declares:

"You have the right to ask that certain penalties *(but not interest)* be cancelled..." Publication 1, page 4 (emphasis added).

Now I ask you, how can it possibly be an oversight that something so basic as the right to abate interest, an issue hotly debated in hearings on the Taxpayers' Bill of Rights Act before Congress, is ignored by the IRS? If the document were *devoid* of any remarks on the subject, I might buy that explanation. However, the document openly boasts information which is *false and misleading* regarding this critical right. As is my incliniation, I will be happy to set the record straight on the question. The following discussion addresses itself to simple letters which can abate interest assessments.

Interest on Penalties

The status of the law of interest has, for some time, provided that interest will be assessed on penalties and will be computed from the time the return was due to be filed. In making its many changes to the penalty provisions of the Code, Congress deliberately did not alter this rule. In the Committee Reports on IMPACT, Congress observed that:

"The bill retains the general rule of present law that interest on these penalties commences with the date the return was required to be filed. The committee believes this rule is appropriate because the behavior being penalized is reflected on the tax return, so that imposition of interest from this date will reduce the incentive of taxpayers and their advisors to 'play the audit lottery'." House Committee Report on H.R. 3299, IMPACT.

While it is true that assessed penalties will bear interest from the time the return was due to be filed, it is also true that when a penalty is abated under the conditions discussed in Chapter Six, any corresponding interest assessments must also fall. If the penalty upon which the interest is based has been cancelled, no lawful authority remains for the assessment or collection of the interest accumulated pursuant to that penalty. Consequently, whenever an application for a penalty abatement is made, one would do well to add a simple paragraph to the written demand for abatement. That paragraph could read as follows:

"In addition to the abatement of the penalties mentioned in this

letter, I also request that any and all interest assessed in connection
with, and which accrued as a direct result of such penalties, also be
fully abated."

This language is simple and does not require the submission of a
separate demand for abatement. Merely include it with your initial
request for abatement of penalties.

Interest on the "Tax Motivated Transaction"

In 1984, as a part of the legislative assault on tax shelters,
Congress added a myriad of new penalties to the Code. One of these
penalties comes under Code §6621(c), and is called the "tax
motivated transaction penalty." The penalty provided that when the
IRS determined that an underpayment of taxes occurred as a result
of a transaction motivated purely for the purposes of reducing one's
income tax liability, the rate of interest on the tax deficiency is 120
percent of that normally charged. In other words, if the standard
rate of interest on unpaid taxes is 12 percent, the penalty under Code
§6621(c) would operate to hike the rate to 14.4 percent.

The interst penalty for tax motivated transactions applies only to
tax returns filed *prior* to January 1, 1990. One aspect of the reform
brought about by IMPACT is that Code §6621(c) is *repealed*
effective for returns filed after December 31, 1989. Thus, while the
interest penalty will not operate for any return filed beginning in
1990 and beyond, prior returns remain at risk.

As noted, the IRS may assess the interest penalty only when the
understatement is due to a tax motivated transaction. Generally
speaking, a tax motivated transaction is one which is not engaged in
for profit. Rather, the transaction is consumated solely for the
purposes of reducing one's income tax liability. The question of
whether or not one engaged in a particular transaction for profit, is
purely a question of fact which can only be answered by a careful
examination of all the circumstances. A controlling factor in
answering the question is, of course, your *intent* at the time of the
transaction. If your *intent* was to earn income, a profit motive exists
and the penalty is inappropriate. On the other hand, if you lacked a
profit motive, but were merely looking for "tax deductions and
credits," the transaction could well be tax motivated and hence, the
interest and penalty would apply.

The interest penalty is defeated as are each of the numerous other penalties we have already examined. This done by demonstrating good faith, reasonable cause as previously illustrated. However, good faith in connection with the interest penalty can only be fully established by proving that your *intent* in connection with the transaction was to earn a profit. Should the profit motive be lacking, your attempt to abate the interest penalty will not succeed.

IRS Error and IRS Delay

In the June, 1990, issue of *Money* Magazine, the story was told of a terrible tragedy visited upon one family by the IRS. In an article entitled "Horribly Out of Control," *Money* related the story of Kay Council, whose husband, on June 9, 1988, committed suicide as a result of a debilitating battle with the IRS that dragged on year after costly year. Facing an unjust tax bill of nearly $300,000 and no way to pay for lawyers to continue the battle, Alex Council's decision to take his own life was made as purely a "business decision." It allowed his wife to continue the fight with the only resource the family had remaining—Alex's life insurance death benefit.

The lion's share of the nearly $300,000 bill which accumulated over the years was, as you can probably guess, interest and penalties. After all was said and done, Kay Council was successful in proving that the IRS' own errors were responsible for the bill. But while she was successful in finally vindicating herself and her husband, the victory was a hollow one. She lost her husband in the process.

This is not the only occasion on which abusive and bungling IRS policies and employees have claimed the very life of a citizen. I have no intention of creating a laundry list of casualties, but believe me when I say that I have personal knowledge of such occurances. The *Money* article states that:

> "Kay Council wants you to believe that the IRS could destroy your family just as it crushed her, her husband of 14 years, and their four children."

I was interviewed on several occasions after the Council story broke nationally. In each interview, I was asked how such a thing could happen, and how we might prevent such a thing from happening in the future. My heart goes out to Kay Council and her family. What the IRS did was terrible and indefensible. Such an act should never have been permitted to occur in a nation which brags that its system of justice is the best in the world. The truth be told, however, it *does not* have to happen to you.

As I explained in those numerous interviews, the Taxpayers' Bill of Rights Act provides a vehicle by which, contrary to IRS' claims, a citizen can win the abatement of interest assessments. The provision is found within the folds of Code §6404(e). There we find two express circumstances under which a citizen may win an abatement of interest. The grounds for abating interest are, when it is shown that the interest is due:

"...in whole or in part to any error or delay by an officer or employee of the Internal Revenue Service..."

When it can be shown that the interest on your tax bill has accumulated, in whole or in part, as a result of the IRS' own mistakes or delays in connection with your case, you are entitled to an abatement of that interest.

In requesting an abatement of interest under this rule, you must demonstrate the existence of *three* factors. First, that "no significant aspect" of the error or delay can be attributed to the citizen. That is to say, you were not responsible for dragging your feet or otherwise hindering the IRS in its disposition of the matter.

Next, you must show that the error or delay occurred after the IRS contacted you "in writing with respect to such deficiency or payment." This means simply that until you are contacted in writing by the IRS, interest is not subject to abatement. The interest may be abated only after the case is opened. This is accomplished through written notice to you.

Last, you must show that the error or delay occurred in connection with the performace of "a ministerial act" by the officer or employee of the IRS. Regulations define a "ministerial act" as a procedural or mechanical act that does not involve the exercise of judgment or discretion. It occurs during the processing of a taxpayers' case *after* all prerequisites to the act, such as conferences and review by supervisors, have taken place. See Rev. Reg. §301.6404-2T. Further guidance on the question of what constitutes a "ministerial act" is found in the Committee Report on the Taxpayers' Bill of Rights Act. The Senate Committee report states:

"***Thus, a ministerial act is a procedural action, not a decision in a substantive area of tax law. For example, a delay in the issuance of a statutory notice of deficiency after the IRS and the taxpayer have completed efforts to resolve the matter could be grounds for abatement of interest.★★★"

It is not unusual for a tax dispute to take years to run its full cycle to complete resolution. All the while, the interest clock is ticking and if three or four—or more—years lapse, you, like the Council's, can be faced with a crushing bill, the least portion of which represents tax. No longer is there any reason to labor under the weight of such a yoke when the law provides that an abatement is possible when the IRS is responsible for the delay, or the error giving rise to the interest.

Carol was the victim of a late-blooming IRS audit. Her 1979 income tax return was audited by the IRS in 1984. But it was not until 1987 that a notice of deficiency was issued and Carol was able to petition the Tax Court. A court decision was not reached until August of 1989. When Carol received her bill from the Service Center, $2,871 was for tax, but $6,139 was for interest! Carol demanded an abatement of the interest under the authority of Code §6404(e). Exhibit 7-1 is Carol's letter demanding abatement of interest. You will notice that care is taken to illustrate the progression of the case. This is done so it can be established that the delay in Carol's case was attributable not to her, but to the IRS.

The statute under which interest abatements are pursued is new. There are no court decisions which guide us in determining the precise circumstances under which the IRS will be required to abate interest. However, this should not deter anyone from aggressively pursuing a demand for abatement of interest. My standard rule of thumb is, when in doubt, make a demand for abatement. This rule is certainly applicable to interest assessments. One fact is certain: The IRS will not *offer* to abate any interest!

The Erroneous Refund Check

I have spoken with dozens of persons who, through a mix up at the Service Center, received a refund of taxes to which they were not entitled. While on radio, I spoke with a man in Ohio who received a refund check from the IRS in the amount of several thousand dollars. He returned the check to the IRS, uncashed, with a note indicating that he was not entitled to the funds. Like a stray cat, the refund check found its way into the man's mailbox a second time. This time, the IRS went to the effort of explaining that he was

EXHIBIT 7-1

Carol A.
 Lane NE
, MN 55434

January 5, 1990

Internal Revenue Service
Kansas City, MO 64131

RE: Statement of Tax Due -- Dated October 13, 1989

Dear Sir:

I am in receipt of your statement of tax due dated October 13, 1989. The bill is
for income taxes, penalty and interest for the year 1979. The amounts demanded
in the bill are as follows:

Taxes =	$2,871.00
Penalty =	717.50
Interest =	6,139.97
Total Demanded =	$9,728.47

Enclosed you will find a cashier's check in the amount of $3,588.50. This amount
represents payment in full of the income tax and penalty assessments. It should
be applied as such. I hereby request an abatement of the interest assessment for
good cause shown below.

My request for abatement of interest is based upon Internal Revenue Code
§6404(e). In general, that provision of law requires the IRS to abate" all or
part of" any interest assessments when the deficiency is "attributable in whole
or in part to any error or delay by an officer or employee of the Internal
Revenue Service." See §6404(e)(1)(A). As more fully set out here, the facts
demonstrate that the delay in this case is due in large measure to the IRS
Examination Division.

My Tax return for the year 1979 was filed late. It was filed to an officer of
the IRS Collection Division in Brooklyn Center, Minnesota, on July 22, 1981. At
that time, all tax shown due on the return was paid. Later, in the fall of 1984,
I received notice from the Examination Division that my 1979 tax return was not
filed and that the IRS intended to conduct an examination to determine whether
one was required to be filed. At that time, I wrote the revenue agent and
explained that my return was in fact filed, and that it was filed to the Revenue
Officer in 1981. The file copy of the tax return Form 1040 I have in my
possession for 1979 bears the "received" stamp of the IRS and is dated July 22,
1981.

On October 15, 1984, I received a response from the revenue agent which indicated
that he had no record of receiving my Form 1040 for 1979. He mentioned that he
questioned the revenue officer regarding my claim that it was filed to him, and
found that no such return was filed. Still, my file copy bears the "received"
stamp of the IRS dated July 22, 1981, at Brooklyn Center, Minnesota. My copy was
stamped by the revenue officer, who, according to the revenue agent in 1984, did
not recall receiving the document. I was told by the revenue agent that he would
proceed with the examination as though no return was filed. He stated in his
October 15, 1984 letter that an appointment was set for October 29, 1984.

At that time I contacted a representative who, after discussing the matter with

EXHIBIT 7-1 (continued)

me, requested that I locate my file copy of the 1979 income tax return bearing the IRS "received" stamp dated July 21, 1981. This took some time as the same had been misplaced. In the meantime, my representative cancelled the conference set for October 29, 1984.

After locating my file copy of the 1979 income tax return bearing the IRS "received" stamp dated July 21, 1981, it was mailed to the revenue agent. This occurred at about the end of 1984. After a copy of the return was mailed to the agent, I heard absolutely nothing from the IRS for over two years.

The next notification I received was dated April 24, 1987. It was a request by the revenue agent for me to sign IRS form 872, consent to extend time to assess tax for 1979. Because I was under the impression that the three year period of assessment for 1979 had already expired by that time, I did not sign the form per the advice of my representative. In May of 1987, I received another request from the revenue agent to sign a Form 872 extending the statute of limitation for 1979. Again, under the belief that the statutory period had already expired, and per the advice of counsel, I did not sign the form.

The next word I received from the IRS came on June 18, 1987, when the IRS mailed a notice of deficiency for the year 1979. A prompt petition was filed with the U.S. Tax Court. This was done on or about September 14, 1987. It was not until November of 1988 that I was contacted by the Appeals Division of the IRS in St. Paul, Minnesota and informed of the opportunity to negotiate with Appeals to settle the case.

I took full advantage of the opportunity to settle the case through the Appeals process. I and my representative negotiated with the Appeals Officer in good faith, and on August 7, 1989, I was notified that the agreement we reached with the Appeals Office was approved. Decision documents were signed on August 16, 1989, and were immediately transmitted to the IRS. Two months later, I received a bill for the tax and penalty we agreed to, but that bill included an assessment of interest well in excess of the tax we agreed on in the negotiation process.

As shown from the facts set forth in this letter, the greatest period of delay in this case is directly attributed to the IRS Examination Division. First, they apparently lost my tax return and were therefore under the impression that it was not filed. They attempted to conduct an examination solely for the purpose of preparing a retun which was already filed. When they discovered that the return was in fact filed, they delayed well over two years before requesting that I sign a Form 872. However, the period of limitation had already expired to the best of my belief.

When a notice of deficiency was issued and a Tax Court petition was filed, it was again a matter of well over a year before the case was assigned to the Appeals Office for settlement discussion. At that time, I immediately and without delay undertook negotiations with Appeals and reached a settlement with little delay.

Because the interest assessment is based "in whole or in part" upon delay which is directly attributed to the IRS, that interest should be abated in accordance with Code §6404(e).

Under penalty of perjury, I declare that the facts stated in this letter are true and correct in all respects.

Sincerely,

Carol A. ▬▬▬

indeed entitled to the refund and that he should deposit the check. So he did.

About nine months later, the IRS again notified the man, but this time the agency was not in a giving mood. It demanded that the money, now recognized as an erroneous refund, be returned to the IRS. That part was not so bad. The man knew he was not entitled to the funds in the first place. The bad part was that the agency demanded interest on the money from the time of the date it *initially* issued the refund. Not only was this man incensed at the notion that the IRS would demand any interest at all, but was particularly disturbed that it would demand that interest be paid during a time when he did not even possess the money.

Like interest associated with IRS error and delay, Congress made it possible to abate all interest assessed in connection with "any erroneous refund" issued by the IRS. When the demand is made on the strength of Code §6404(e)(2), all interest must be abated "until the date a demand for repayment is made." In other words, the only interest which may be charged by the IRS is that which accrues *after* the agency demanded repayment of the funds. In addition, in order to win the abatement, the citizen must show that he "or a related party has in (no) way caused such erroneous refund" to be issued.

Thus, a letter demanding abatement of interest assessed as a result of an erroneous refund must address two elements. First, it must show the date the refund was received by the citizen, and the date of the IRS' notice demanding repayment. All interest accrued prior to the date of the IRS' demand for repayment must be abated. Second, the letter must show with an affirmative declaration that you or a related party "in no way caused the refund." When this showing is made, all interest is due to be abated.[1]

Erroneous IRS Advice

It has been proven over and over again that advice given to citizens by the IRS is erroneous much of the time. Recent GAO studies have shown the error rate to be in excess of 37 percent. When you are the victim of erroneous IRS advice, not only can you win an abatement of the penalty attributable to the error, but under current law, the interest must also be cancelled. The provision of law which I speak of (not mentioned in Publication 1) is found in Code §6404(f).

Section 6404(f) is broad in its declarations regarding abatements. The statute provides that "any penalty or addition to tax" is due to be abated when the additions are attributable to erroneous advice provided by the IRS. Thus, not only will the interest be cancelled, but all penalties must also be cancelled when it is shown that the IRS' advice led to the incorrect computation of your income tax liability.

There are some simple limitations. These must be considered and accounted for in your demand for abatement. First, the advice must be provided by the IRS to you *in writing,* and in response to a specific written request made by you. Second, you must have reasonably relied upon the written advice. That is to say, this advice must be followed by you in the preparation of your income tax return. Third, you must provide adequate and accurate information to the IRS in connection with your request for written advice. Information may be considered adequate if it is sufficient to apprise the IRS of all the facts and circumstances of the case, and is correct and complete.

Your letter demanding abatement of "all additions" to the tax based upon erroneous IRS advice must set forth facts which establish the existence of the above elements. You must also include a copy of your written request for advice, the IRS' written response upon which you relied, and the report of adjustments to your return which includes the computation of penalties and interest.

A Standard Cover Form

For the same reasons expressed in Chapter Six, Form 843 should be used as a cover form when demanding abatement of interest assessments. In the top margin, above the word "Claim," you should type the phrase, "Demand for Abatement of Interest." You should also include reference to either Code §6404(e), if the demand is based upon IRS error or delay in processing your case, or Code §6404(f), if the demand is based upon erroneous advice furnished in writing by the IRS. You should attach your written demand to the form together with any documentary evidence needed to support your claim. Mail the form via certified mail and retain a copy for your records.

When The Answer Is "NO"

Demands for abatement of interest under the terms and conditions explored above are subject to review just as demands for abatement of penalties. When the answer is "no," you have the right to execute an appeal by submitting a written protest letter within 30 days of the date the IRS denies your request. A written protest letter regarding interest is essentially the same as that regarding penalties. Please see Exhibit 6-7 (Chapter Six). Naturally, the language of the protest letter must be altered to reflect the fact that you are appealing the denial of your interest abatement request. Your appeal will be considered by the IRS' Appeals Division, and you have the right to present any additional evidence to the agency which is necessary to support your claim.

The right to demand an abatement of interest assessments is very important. In light of this important protection, we do not have to fear that the IRS' collection freight train will crash through your financial house as it so often does to others. You will stand ready to protect yourself with the demands for abatement as shown here. When you exercise this right, you assure yourself that you will never pay interest which you do not owe.

Notes To Chapter 7

1. The only exception to this rule is when the erroneous refund is in excess of $50,000. When this occurs, there appears to be no statutory provision permitting an abatement. It is my opinion that such a limitation is improper and will likely be challenged in the future. Certainly the interest on sizeable erroneous refunds, such as one in excess of $50,000 have greater potential to cause financial hardship than does interest on refunds of much lesser amounts.

— CHAPTER 8 —

Secrets To Buying Time

Have you ever felt the crush of time closing in upon you as a tax return filing deadline approaches? How many times have you stayed up past midnight, spent an entire weekend or otherwise missed out on planned events in order to file a return by its due date? Even worse, how many times have you filed the return late in order to complete it accurately, only to be penalized later? In times past, it was true that with the onset of spring it was said that "love is in the air." Now, with the complexity of our tax laws choking all of us, we can say that with the onset of spring, "insanity is in the air." As we wrestle with the task of completing form after puzzling form, our patience is taxed at a level which exceeds even that of our income.

The overwhelming feeling of paper anxiety is even more oppressive when you are the owner or operator of a small business. Not only must your personal income tax return be filed, but you must file on behalf of the company (if it is incorporated) and you must prepare and submit all information returns reflecting payments made to others during the course of the year. The time and expense incurred in fulfilling this myriad of reporting obligations usually brings on a headache just thinking about them.

But like every area of income tax law, relief from spring insanity is just an application away. Among the many forms which we must prepare and submit each spring, the IRS is not likely to fully explain each of the forms I am about to discuss. The forms in this final chapter, some well-known and others little-known, can bring relief to anyone suffering from spring insanity. Read this chapter carefully. The peace-of-mind it can bring may be your own!

Individual Income Tax Returns

We all know that individual income tax returns are due on April 15th. In the event the 15th of the month falls upon either a Saturday, Sunday or legal holiday, we are given a brief filing reprieve. When this occurs, the return is not due until the following business day. Most citizens are well-aware that an extension for filing the return is available if the appropriate application is submitted on or before the returns' due date. That extension is automatic, and provides four additional months, up to and including August 15th, in which to submit the return. The application is submitted on Form 4868, and a copy of the application should be included with your return when it is eventually filed.

In addition to the automatic four-month extension available through Form 4868, one can win a *second* extension of time in which to file his return. The second extension will increase your filing deadline by two additional months. This allows you to file your return as late as *October 15th*. The second extension of time in which to file your individual income tax return is made on Form 2688. Please see Exhibit 8-1.

The extension of time granted pursuant to Form 2688 is *not automatic*. In order to win an extension of two additional months, you must show "good cause." This is not a difficult matter to demonstrate. The application will generally be accepted when you need additional time to obtain records necessary to complete the return accurately. Other grounds are when, due to circumstances out of your control or the control of your preparer, you are unable to complete the return on time. Examples could be sickness, death of a family member, an unexpected move or job change, or any other reason which indicates that matters were out of your control. Please note the language of the instructions which indicate that an extension will not be granted "just for the convenience of your tax return preparer."

The Form 2688 must be filed on or before the expiration of the

EXHIBIT 8-1

Form **2688**	**Application for Additional Extension of Time To File**	OMB No. 1545-0066
Department of the Treasury Internal Revenue Service	**U.S. Individual Income Tax Return** **(See back for filing instructions. Be sure to complete all items.)**	**1989** Attachment Sequence No. **59**

Please type or print. **File the original and one copy by the due date for filing your return.**	Your first name and initial (if joint return, also give spouse's name and initial) JOSEPH P	Last name	Your social security number ▮▮▮▮
	Present home address (number, street, and apt. no. or rural route). (If you have a P.O. box, see the instructions.) Ave		Spouse's social security number
	City, town or post office, state, and ZIP code mn		

1 I request an extension of time until __October, 15__ 19 __90__ , to file Form 1040A or Form 1040 for the calendar year 1989, or other tax year ending __December 31__ 19 __89__ .

2 Have you previously requested an extension of time to file for this tax year? . . . . ☑ Yes ☐ No

3 Explain why you need an extension __Additional time is needed to obtain__
__Records necessary to file an Accurate__
__Schedule C. Without the records, an__
__accurate schedule C cannot Be filed.__
__I Do not wish to file an inaccurate Schedules.__
__Therefore, please grant the extension to__
__October 15, 1990__

Complete line 4 only if you expect to owe gift or generation-skipping transfer (GST) tax.

4 If you or your spouse expect to file a gift tax return (Form 709 or 709-A) for 1989, generally due by April 16, 1990, see the instructions and check here . . . . } Yourself . . ▶ ☐   Spouse . . ▶ ☐

Signature and Verification

Under penalties of perjury, I declare that I have examined this form, including accompanying schedules and statements, and to the best of my knowledge and belief, it is true, correct, and complete; and, if prepared by someone other than the taxpayer, that I am authorized to prepare this form.

Signature of taxpayer ▶ _Joseph Q_____ Date ▶ _8-15-90_

Signature of spouse ▶ _____ Date ▶ _____
(If filing jointly, BOTH must sign even if only one had income)

Signature of preparer
other than taxpayer ▶ _____ Date ▶ _____

File original and one copy. IRS will show below whether or not your application is approved and will return the copy.

Notice to Applicant—To Be Completed by IRS

☑ We **HAVE** approved your application. (Please attach this form to your return.)

☐ We **HAVE NOT** approved your application. (Please attach this form to your return.)
However, because of your reasons stated above, we have granted a 10-day grace period from the date shown below or due date of your return, whichever is later. This grace period is considered to be a valid extension of time for elections otherwise required to be made on returns filed on time.

☐ We **HAVE NOT** approved your application. After considering your reasons stated above, we cannot grant your request for an extension of time to file. (We are not granting the 10-day grace period.)

☐ We cannot consider your application because it was filed after the due date of your return.

☐ We **HAVE NOT** approved your application. The maximum extension of time allowed by law is 6 months.

☐ Other _____

AUG 2 _____ _____   Director (617)
Date   By: _____

For Paperwork Reduction Act Notice, see back of form.   Form **2688** (1989)

EXHIBIT 8-1 (continued)

Form 2688 (1989)   Page **2**

If the copy of this form is to be returned to you at an address other than that shown on page 1 or to an agent acting for you, please enter the name of the agent and/or the address where the copy should be sent.

Please Type or Print

Name

Number and street (or P.O. box number if mail is not delivered to street address)

City, town or post office, state, and ZIP code

General Instructions

Paperwork Reduction Act Notice.—We ask for this information to carry out the Internal Revenue laws of the United States. We need it to ensure that taxpayers are complying with these laws and to allow us to figure and collect the right amount of tax. You are required to give us this information.

The time needed to complete and file this form will vary depending on individual circumstances. The estimated average time is:

Learning about the
law or the form . . . . 7 min.

Preparing the form . . . . . 10 min.

Copying, assembling, and
sending the form to IRS . . . 20 min.

If you have comments concerning the accuracy of these time estimates or suggestions for making this form more simple, we would be happy to hear from you. You can write to the **Internal Revenue Service,** Washington, DC 20224, Attention: IRS Reports Clearance Officer, T:FP; or the **Office of Management and Budget,** Paperwork Reduction Project (1545-0066), Washington, DC 20503.

Purpose

Use Form 2688 to ask for more time to file **Form 1040A** or **Form 1040.** Use it only if you already asked for more time on **Form 4868,** and that time was not enough. (Form 4868 is the "automatic" extension form.)

To get the extra time you MUST:

1. File Form 2688 on time, AND

2. Have a good reason why the first 4 months were not enough. Explain the reason on line 3.

Generally, we will not give you more time to file just for the convenience of your tax return preparer. However, if the reasons for being late are beyond his or her control, or if despite a good effort you cannot get professional help in time to file, we will usually give you the extra time.

We usually do not approve Form 2688 unless Form 4868 is filed first. We will make an exception to this rule only for undue hardship. You must clearly explain this reason on line 3.

You cannot have IRS figure your tax if you file after the regular due date of your return.

Note: *An extension to file a 1989 calendar year income tax return also extends the time to file a gift tax return for 1989.*

If you live abroad.—U.S. citizens or resident aliens living abroad may qualify for special tax treatment if they meet the required residence or presence tests. If you do not expect to meet either of those tests by the due date of your return, request an extension to a date after you expect to qualify. See **Form 2350,** Application for Extension of Time To File U.S. Income Tax Return. See Pub. 54, Tax Guide for U.S. Citizens and Resident Aliens Abroad.

Total Time Allowed

We cannot extend the due date of your return for more than 6 months. This includes the 4 extra months allowed by Form 4868. (There may be an exception if you live abroad. See previous discussion.)

When To File Form 2688

File Form 2688 by the due date of your return (April 16, 1990, for a calendar year return), or extended due date if you filed Form 4868. For most taxpayers, this is by August 15, 1990.

Be sure to file Form 2688 early, so that if your request is not approved, you can still file your return on time.

Out of the country.—You may have been allowed 2 extra months to file if you were a U.S. citizen or resident out of the country on the due date of your return. For this purpose, "out of the country" means you met one of the following conditions: (1) You live outside the U.S. and Puerto Rico, AND your main place of business is outside the U.S. and Puerto Rico; or (2) You are in military or naval service outside the U.S. and Puerto Rico.

Where To File

Make an extra copy of Form 2688. *Mail both the original and the copy* to the IRS address where you send your return.

Filing Your Tax Return

You may file Form 1040A or Form 1040 any time before your extension of time is up. But remember, Form 2688 does not extend the time to pay these taxes. If you do not pay the amount due by the regular due date, you will owe interest. If you do not make a reasonable estimate of taxes due, you may also be charged penalties.

Interest.—You will owe interest on tax not paid by the regular due date of your return. The interest runs until you pay the tax. Even if you had a good reason not to pay on time, you will still owe interest.

Late payment penalty.—Generally, the penalty is ½ of 1% of any tax (other than estimated tax) not paid by the regular due date. It is charged for each month, or part of a month, that the tax is unpaid. The most you have to pay is 25%. You might not owe this penalty if you have a good reason for not paying on time. Attach a statement to your return explaining the reason.

Late filing penalty.—A penalty is usually charged if your return is filed after the due date (including extensions). It is 5% of the tax not paid by the regular due date for each month, or part of a month, that your return is late. The most you have to pay is 25%. If your return is more than 60 days late, the penalty will not be less than $100 or the balance of tax due on your return, whichever is smaller. You might not owe the penalty if you have a good reason for filing late. Attach a full explanation to your return if you file late.

How to claim credit for payment made with this form.—When you file your return, show the amount of any payment sent with Form

2688. Form 1040A filers should include the payment on line 26 and write "Form 2688" in the space to the left. Form 1040 filers should enter it on line 59.

If you and your spouse each filed a separate Form 2688, but later file a joint return for 1989, then enter the total paid with the two Forms 2688 on the correct line of your joint return.

If you and your spouse jointly filed Form 2688, but later file separate returns for 1989, you may enter the total amount paid with Form 2688 on either of your separate returns. Or, you and your spouse may divide the payment in any agreed amounts. Be sure each separate return has the social security numbers of both spouses.

Specific Instructions

Name, address, and social security numbers.—Enter your name, address, social security number, and spouse's social security number if filing a joint return. If you and your spouse have different last names, please separate the names with an "and." For example: "John Brown and Mary Smith." If the post office does not bring mail to your street address and you have a P.O. box, enter your P.O. box number instead of your street address.

Line 3.—Clearly describe the reasons that will delay your return. We cannot accept incomplete reasons, such as "illness" or "practitioner too busy," without adequate explanations. If it is clear that you have no important reason, but only want more time, we will deny your request. The 10-day grace period will also be denied.

If because of undue hardship you are filing Form 2688 without filing Form 4868 first, clearly explain why on line 3. Attach any information you have that helps explain the hardship.

Caution: *If we give you more time to file and later find that the statements made on this form are false or misleading, the extension is null and void. You will owe the late filing penalty, explained above.*

Line 4.—If you or your spouse expect to file Form 709 or 709-A for 1989, check whichever box applies. However, if your spouse files a separate Form 2688, do not check the box for your spouse.

Your signature.—This form must be signed. If you plan to file a joint return, both of you should sign. If there is a good reason why one of you cannot, then the other spouse may sign for both. Attach an explanation why the other spouse cannot sign.

Others who can sign for you.—Anyone with a power of attorney can sign, but the following can sign for you without a power of attorney:

• Attorneys, CPAs, and other persons qualified to practice before the IRS, or

• A person in close personal or business relationship to you who is signing because you cannot. There must be a good reason why you cannot sign (such as illness or absence). Attach an explanation to the form.

first extended due date of the return, which is August 15th. Under ordinary circumstances, you *cannot* obtain an extension with Form 2688 *unless* you first filed Form 4868. Therefore, you should take care to file Form 4868 whenever you are in doubt as to your ability to submit your return in a timely manner. If your application is denied, you are entitled to a 10-day grace period for filing the return.

When sufficient cause is shown, you will win the extension, giving you a combined total of six additional months in which to file your income tax return. At the very least, the 10-day grace period often provides all the cushion one needs to get him over the preparation hump. While it is true that the grace period itself is not guaranteed, it will be denied only when Form 2688 is patently frivolous. Nearly any showing of need will eliminate such a finding.

Business tax returns

If your business is a sole-proprietorship, your business income tax return consists of Schedule C, *Gain or Loss from Business,* which is attached to the Form 1040. When your business is incorporated, either as a subchapter "s" corporation, or a regular corporation, the business tax return is due to be filed by the 15th day of the *third* month following the close of the year. When your business operates on the basis of a calendar year, the return is due to be filed by March 15th. An extension of time for filing a business tax return is available on a separate form. The form used to win a tax return filing extension is Form 7004.

Form 7004, when filed on or before the due date of the business income tax return, *automatically* wins an additional six months in which to file the return. Please note that the six-month extension available through Form 7004 is the *one and only* return filing extension available to a business. The return is due at the end of the extension period.

In the case of both Form 4868 (personal extension) and the Form 7004 (business extension), the applicant will win *only* an extension of time in which to file the return. *No* extension of time to *pay* the income tax is available through the use of these forms. This, of course, is no secret. Later we shall discuss, under the heading, *Payment of Taxes Due,* the extension available when additional time is needed to pay your taxes.

Information Returns

Until January of 1989, there was no provision for an extension of time in which to file information returns. Yet it is true that the most burdensome of all tax returns can well be information returns, particularly when you are faced with the duty to file hundreds of them. In January of 1989, the IRS quietly released a new tax form created especially for those struggling to comply with information reporting requirements. The new form is Form 8809, *Request for Extension of Time to File Information Return.*

Generally speaking, most of the numerous information returns covering payments made to others during the course of the year are due to be filed by February 28th. When these returns are not filed in a timely manner, extensive penalties can be heaped upon the individual responsible. (The subject of these penalties is discussed in Chapter Six). An extension of time of 30 days in which to submit information returns can be obtained by filing Form 8809 on or before the return's filing deadline. See Exhibit 8-2.

Like Form 2688, the 30-day filing extension available through the use of Form 8809 is *not automatic.* The IRS will rule upon your application and inform you whether the extension has been allowed. In order to win the extension, your application must contain "a full recital of the reasons" why the extension is sought. The instructions for Form 8809 (see Exhibit 8-2) do not provide any information as to what constitutes cause for granting the extension. I submit that the reasons applicable to other requests for extension are equally dispositive regarding Form 8809. When you are able to demonstrate that additional time is needed to comply with the law and that through no fault of your own (due to circumstances beyond your control) you cannot meet the filing deadline, the application will be granted.

The instructions for Form 8809 indicate that a *second* extension of time is available for the submission of information returns. The instructions read:

> "If you need additional time to file, you may request an additional 30 days by submitting a letter and attaching a copy of the first approval letter you received from IRS before the end of the initial extension period."

It is clear that *two* 30-day extensions are available concerning information returns. The first is obtained by showing cause on Form

EXHIBIT 8-2

Form **8809** (December 1988) Department of the Treasury Internal Revenue Service	**Request for Extension of Time To File Information Returns** (Forms W-2, W-2P, 1098, 1099, 5498, and W-2G)	OMB No. 1545-1081 Expires 11-30-91

Extension Request for Tax Year 19___ (Enter only 1 tax year)	1 Filer or transmitter name and mailing address (number and street or post office box, city, state, and ZIP code)	2 Federal identification number (must be a 9-digit number)
	3 Transmitter control code (IRS magnetic media filers only) 4 Person IRS can contact about this request	5 Telephone number ( )

6 Check the boxes that apply. You need not enter the number of returns.

Type of Return	Paper Returns (✓)	Magnetic Media (✓)	Type of Return	Paper Returns (✓)	Magnetic Media (✓)	Type of Return	Paper Returns (✓)	Magnetic Media (✓)
W-2			1099-DIV			1099-PATR		
W-2P			1099-G			1099-R		
1098			1099-INT			1099-S		
1099-A			1099-MISC			5498		
1099-B			1099-OID			W-2G		

7 State in detail why you need an extension. If you need more space, attach additional sheets.

8 Will you provide, or have you provided, a copy of the information return or the required statement to the recipient on time? (See instructions.)   Yes ☐   No ☐

Under penalties of perjury, I declare that I have examined this form, including any accompanying statements, and, to the best of my knowledge and belief, it is true, correct, and complete.

Signature   **Title**   **Date**

For Paperwork Reduction Act Notice, see back of form.   Form **8809** (12-88)

309

EXHIBIT 8-2 (continued)

Paperwork Reduction Act Notice.—We ask for this information to carry out the Internal Revenue laws of the United States. We need it to ensure that taxpayers are complying with these laws and to allow us to figure and collect the right amount of tax. You are required to give us this information.

The time needed to complete and file this form will vary depending on individual circumstances. The estimated average time is:

Recordkeeping	44 min.
Learning about the law or the form	14 min.
Preparing the form	50 min.
Copying, assembling, and sending the form to IRS	26 min.

If you have comments concerning the accuracy of these time estimates or suggestions for making this form more simple, we would be happy to hear from you. You can write to the **Internal Revenue Service,** Washington, DC 20224, Attention: IRS Reports Clearance Officer, TR:FP; or the **Office of Management and Budget,** Paperwork Reduction Project, Washington, DC 20503.

General Instructions

Purpose of Form.—Use this form to request an extension of time to file Forms W-2, W-2P, 1098, 1099, 5498, or W-2G. **Do NOT use this form to request an extension of time to furnish the statement to the recipient.**

Who May File.—Filers of paper forms or magnetic media may request an extension of time to file. A transmitter for multiple filers may file this form but must attach a list of the names, addresses, and employer identification numbers of those for whom they will be filing.

When To File.—Your request for an extension of time to file must be filed by the due date of the returns. For example, a request for an extension of time to file Form 1099-INT, Statement for Recipients of Interest Income, must be filed (postmarked) by February 28. If you are requesting an extension of time to file several types of forms, you may use one Form 8809, but you must file Form 8809 by the earliest due date. For example, if you are requesting an extension of time to file both Forms 1099-INT and Forms 5498, Individual Retirement Arrangement Information, you must file Form 8809 by February 28. You may complete more than one Form 8809 to avoid this problem. You can request an extension for only one tax year on this form.

Filing Due Dates

Form Number	Due Date
W-2	February 28
W-2P	February 28
1098	February 28
1099	February 28
5498	May 31
W-2G	February 28

Where To File.—Send Form 8809 to Internal Revenue Service, Martinsburg Computing Center, P.O. Box 1359, Martinsburg, WV 25401-1359, or Internal Revenue Service, Martinsburg Computing Center, Route 9 and Needy Road, Martinsburg, WV 25401.

Extension Period.—If your extension request is approved, you will be granted an extension for 30 days from the original due date.

Additional extension.—If you need additional time to file, you may request an additional 30 days by submitting a letter and attaching a copy of the first approval letter you received from IRS before the end of the initial extension period.

Approval or Denial of Request.— Requests for extensions of time to file information returns are NOT automatically granted. Approval or denial is based on administrative criteria and guidelines. IRS will send you a letter of explanation approving or denying your request. If the request is approved, a copy of the letter of approval must be sent with the returns that you file after February 28 (May 31 for Forms 5498).

Penalty.—If you file required information returns late and you have not applied for and received an approved extension of time to file, you may be subject to a late filing penalty of $50 per return.

Specific Instructions

Item 1.—Enter the name and complete mailing address of the filer requesting the extension of time. If you act as transmitter for a group of filers, enter the transmitter name and address here, and attach a list of filer names, addresses, and employer identification numbers (EINs).

Note: Approval or denial notification will be sent only to the person who requested the extension (filer or transmitter).

Item 2.—Enter your nine-digit Federal employer identification number or social security number if you are not required to have an employer identification number. Do not enter hyphens. A transmitter should enter the transmitter's

Federal EIN in this box. Failure to provide this number, or list of numbers if you are acting as a transmitter as explained under Item 1, will result in an automatic denial of the extension request.

Item 3.—For magnetic media filers only, enter your Transmitter Control Code (TCC). This will apply only if you have filed **Form 4419,** Application for Filing Information Returns on Magnetic Media, to file Forms 1098, 1099, 5498, and/or W-2G, with IRS on magnetic media. The IRS Martinsburg Computing Center assigns a five-character TCC on approval of the Form 4419. See Form 4419 for more information. Leave this item blank if your extension request is for paper forms, Forms W-2 or W-2P, or if you have not yet been assigned a TCC.

Item 4.—Enter the name of someone who is familiar with this request that IRS can contact if additional information is required.

Item 5.—Enter the telephone number, including area code, of the person shown in item 4.

Item 6.—Indicate the type(s) of information returns for which you are requesting an extension of time to file and how they will be filed by checking the appropriate box(es). For example, if you are requesting an extension of time to file Forms 1099-INT on magnetic media, check the box titled "Magnetic Media" beside the block for 1099-INT. **Note:** You may be required to file your information returns on magnetic media if you file more than a certain number of returns. See the **Instructions for Forms 1099, 1098, 5498, 1096, and W-2G,** and the **Instructions for Forms W-2 and W-2P,** for information about who is required to file on magnetic media.

Item 7.—Explain why you need an extension of time to file your information returns.

Item 8.—Check the appropriate box to indicate whether you will provide, or have provided, a copy of the information return or the required statement to the recipients on time. **Note:** If this extension request is approved, it will only extend the due date for filing the returns. It will not extend the due date for furnishing the required copies or statements to recipients.

Signature.—The extension request must be signed by you or a person who is duly authorized to sign a return, statement, or other document.

Note: Failure to properly complete and sign this form may cause delay in processing or result in denial of your request.

8809, and filing the same before the due date of the return. The second is obtained by drafting a simple letter setting forth cause, and mailing the same to the IRS with a copy of the letter of approval obtained pursuant to Form 8809. The letter must be mailed *prior* to the expiration of the 30-day extension period granted pursuant to Form 8809.

Information returns are the primary cause of the paperwork blizzard we face each and every tax filing season. Now, Form 8809 provides a means to lighten the load when it comes to complying with your reporting obligations.

Payment Of Taxes Due

As I stated previously, Form 4868, *Extension of Time to File Return,* does not provide an extension of time in which to pay your income taxes. Even when the extension of four months is granted in accordance with Form 4868, full payment of your income tax liability is due on or before April 15th. Form 4868 itself requires that you make a declaration of your estimated income tax liability on the face of the form. You must then *include* payment of that liability with your Form 4868 if sufficient installments were not made during the year. If you fail to estimate your liability and make payment, Form 4868 is considered invalid.

How, then, does one obtain an extension of time in which to pay? Many of the "experts," including the IRS' hierarchy, will explain that an extension of time in which to pay taxes cannot be obtained. In Chapter Three, under the heading, *The Form 1127,* I described an experience I had with former acting IRS Commissioner Michael J. Murphy, in April of 1989. I explained that Murphy declared on national television the morning of April 15th that it was not possible to obtain an extension of time in which to pay your income taxes. I went on in Chapter Three to prove that Murphy and the other experts who propogate this nonsense are either terribly ignorant or deliberately lying.

Form 1127, included as Exhibit 8-3 in this chapter, will, if accepted, grant an additional six months in which to pay your taxes. The six-month extension is *not automatic.* In order to win the extension, you must show that "undue hardship" exists, rendering impossible full payment of the tax at the time it is due. Undue

EXHIBIT 8-3

Form **1127** (Rev. October 1988) **Department of the Treasury** **Internal Revenue Service**	APPLICATION FOR EXTENSION OF TIME FOR PAYMENT OF TAX *(Please read conditions on back before completing this form)*

District Director of Internal Revenue at _____

(Enter City and State where IRS Office is located)

I request an extension of time from _____, 19 ____, to _____, 19 ____

(Enter Due Date of Return)

in which to pay tax of $ _____ for the year ended. _____, 19 ____

This extension is necessary because *(If more space is needed, please attach a separate sheet):* _____

_____

_____

I am unable to borrow money to pay the tax because: _____

_____

As evidence of the need for the extension, I am attaching: (1) a statement of assets and liabilities as of the last day of the preceding month (showing book and market values of assets and whether any securities are listed or unlisted); and (2) an itemized list of receipts and disbursements for the 3 months before the date the tax is due.

I propose to secure the liability covered by this extension as follows:

_____

Under penalties of perjury, I declare that I have examined this application, including any accompanying schedules and statements, and to the best of my knowledge and belief it is true, correct, and complete.

_____   _____
(SIGNATURE OF APPLICANT)   (DATE)

_____   _____
(ADDRESS OF APPLICANT)   (EMPLOYER IDENTIFICATION OR
                                           SOCIAL SECURITY NUMBER)

The District Director will let you know whether the extension is granted or denied and will give you the form of bond, if necessary. However, he or she cannot consider an application if it is filed after the due date of the return. A list of approved surety companies will be sent to you upon request.

(The following will be filled in by the IRS.)

This application is   ☐ approved   for the following reasons:
                        ☐ disapproved

_____

_____

Interest _____   Date of assessment _____   Identifying no. _____

Penalty _____   _____   _____
                                    (SIGNATURE)   (DATE)

                                    (over)   Form **1127** (Rev. 10-88)

EXHIBIT 8-3 (continued)

CONDITIONS UNDER WHICH EXTENSIONS OF TIME FOR PAYMENTS MAY BE GRANTED UNDER SECTION 6161 OF THE INTERNAL REVENUE CODE

The District Director may grant an extension of time for payment of your tax if you can show that it will cause you undue hardship to pay it on the date it is due. To receive consideration, your application must be filed with the District Director on or before the date prescribed for payment of the tax.

1. **Undue hardship.**—This means more than mere inconvenience. You must show that you will have substantial financial loss if you pay your tax on the date it is due. (Such a loss could be caused by having to sell property at a sacrifice price.) You must show that you do not have enough cash, above necessary working capital, to pay the tax. In determining cash available, include anything you can convert into cash, and use current market prices. Also show that you are unable to borrow money to pay the tax, except under terms that will cause you severe loss and hardship.

2. **Limitations.**—As a general rule, an extension of time to pay any part of income or gift tax shown on a return is limited to 6 months from the date fixed for payment. An extension may be granted for more than 6 months if you are abroad.

An extension of time to pay any part of a deficiency (an amount determined to be due after an examination of your return) in income or gift tax is limited to 18 months from the date fixed for payment and, in exceptional cases, for an additional period of not more than 12 months.

No extension is granted to pay a deficiency that is due to negligence, intentional disregard of rules and regulations, or fraud with intent to evade tax.

3. **Interest.**—Interest is charged at the underpayment rate established under Code section 6621(a)(2).

4. **Security.**—Security satisfactory to the District Director is required as a condition for granting an extension. This is to assure that the risk of loss to the Government will be no greater at the end of the extension period than it was at the beginning. The determination of the kind of security, such as bond, filing of notice of lien, mortgage, pledge, deed of trust of specific property or general assets, personal surety, or other, will depend on the circumstances in each case. Ordinarily, when you receive notice of approval of your application, you should deposit with the District Director any collateral that was agreed upon for security purposes. No collateral is required if you have no assets.

5. **Due date of payment for which extension is granted.**—On or before the end of the extension period, pay the tax for which the extension is granted (without notice and demand from the District Director).

6. **Filing requirements.**—If you need an extension of time to pay tax, submit an application with supporting documents on or before the date the tax is due. File the application with the District Director where you maintain your legal residence or principal place of business. If, however, the tax is to be paid to the Director, Foreign Operations District, file the application with that office. If you need an extension to pay estate tax, file Form 4768, Application for Extension of Time to File U.S. Estate Tax Return and/or Pay Estate Tax.

Form 1127 (Rev. 10-88)

☆ U.S.G.P.O.: 1989- 526-067/85038

hardship means more than just "inconvenience." As explained in
the instructions to Form 1127 (see Exhibit 8-3):

> "You must show that you will have substantial financial loss if you
> pay your tax on the date it is due. (Such loss could be caused by
> having to sell property at a sacrifice price.) You must show that
> you do not have enough cash, above necessary working capital, to
> pay the tax.***" Also see *How Anyone Can Negotiate,* page 180.

Beyond what is stated above, no definition of "undue hardship" is
provided us by the IRS. We know, however, that you must provide
records which indicate your financial condition. You must also
"show that you are unable to borrow money to pay the tax, except
under conditions that will cause you severe loss and hardship."
Form 1127, Instructions.

Form 1127, with supporting documents, must be filed on or
before the due date of the tax. With respect to your Form 1040, the
due date of the tax is April 15th. This date *is not* extended by filing
Form 4868. Therefore, if you cannot pay the tax by April 15th, a
Form 4868 will not help. If you intend to file a Form 4868 in order to
win additional time to *prepare* the return, be careful *also to file* Form
1127 if you cannot pay by April 15th. When the application for
extension of time to pay is granted, you are afforded up to six
additional months to pay *without* penalties. Because the failure to
pay the tax penalty (see Chapter Six) is assessed at the rate of one
percent per month, your savings are substantial.

This form may be one of the most important documents for the
average citizen. But like so many of these "helpful" tax forms, the
IRS does not publicize their availability. For example, *not one word*
regarding Form 1127 is found in the IRS' lengthy publication
describing the tax return preparation, filing and tax payment
process. See IRS Publication 17, *Your Federal Income Tax.* At page
12 of the publication, the IRS declares:

> "If you owe additional tax (at the time of filing) you should pay it
> with your return... **If you do not pay your tax by the due date,**
> you may have to pay a failure-to-pay penalty. See *Penalties,* later."
> IRS Publication 17 (emphasis in original).

Later in this publication, at page 13, the failure-to-pay penalty is
described in general terms. However, the IRS is completely silent on
the right of citizens to entirely avoid the penalty by submitting a
properly drafted Form 1127 on or before the due date of the tax.

In addition to the failure to describe these rights in Publication 17,
IRS' Publication 1, *Your Rights as a Taxpayer,* also fails to address

Form 1127 in any particular. Yet the extension of time to pay taxes is a very important right. One of the most common problems citizens face when dealing with the IRS is those who, like Chris (discussed in Chapter Six) incur the failure to pay penalty after filing a return without paying the tax. You will recall that Chris and her husband fell upon hard times because of being laid off. You will also recall that in order to survive, Chris and her husband were forced to live on their small savings, which was quickly depleted, and then borrowed money. Still, in the face of such financial adversity, the IRS demanded full payment of their income tax liability, with *penalties* because of failure to pay in a timely manner.

All of the additional penalties Chris faced could have been entirely avoided if a timely and adequate application for extension, Form 1127, was submitted to the IRS prior to the due date of the tax. With this step executed, not only are the penalties avoided, but one is spared the time and effort needed to draft a demand for abatement. Perhaps most significantly, one is spared the stress and imposition of repeated IRS demands for payment at a time when one is wholly unable to pay. Form 1127, will, when granted, turn off the switch on the IRS' collection computer, freeing you to concentrate on business and solving the problems at hand.

Conclusion

This book is not about large-scale IRS problems. But then, the vast majority of citizens will never face large-scale IRS problems. At the same time, virtually every tax return filer will be subjected to the "invisible audit" and the potential for the notices and demands which they spawn. Millions will be subjected to assessments of penalties and interest. Millions will be potential victims of IRS negligence and blundering. And *100 percent* of all individual return filers will face the confusing, frustrating mass of complicated IRS forms and instructions. Even if you use a professional, the obligation to file a correct tax return rests entirely with you. What is more, you and you alone must gather the required data and organize it into a form acceptable to your preparer. Yes, Virginia, you are hip-deep in the IRS mess whether you like it or not.

Fortunately, this fact does not have to be cause for sleepless nights. The purpose of this book is to communicate the fact that small IRS problems are attended with small solutions. Simple errors are cured with simple letters and forms. This book, more so than any only I have written in the past, constitues a message of hope. It is intended to communicate the proposition that the IRS can never get out of hand if you read and understand the signposts which appear during the progression of a given case. This book is intended to communicate to the average person a reality. When you recognize and attack an IRS problem in its infant stages, or anticipate the problem *before* it even exists, you will, for yourself and all Americans, begin to proliferate justice within a system that has all but abandoned the concept.

As Victor Hugo once stated, "There is one thing stronger than all the armies in the world, and that is an idea whose time has come." Now is the time for middle class Americans to cast aside the chains of fear which bind them to the whim of the IRS. Now is the time to once again declare our independence from the unjust oppressions of an overzealous government. Now is the time to once again proclaim the blessings of liberty which are rightfully ours to enjoy.

Take back the power!!

Other Writings by Daniel J. Pilla

Taxpayers' Ultimate Defense Manual

How Anyone Can Negotiate With The IRS—And WIN!

The Naked Truth

Pilla Talks Taxes—A Monthly Newsletter

Special Report:
The Taxpayers' Bill of Rights Act

Special Report:
Social Security Numbers and Your Minor Children

Special Report:
Save Our Home Mortgage Interest Deduction